RIVER KINGS

RIVER KINGS

A New History of the Vikings
from Scandinavia to the Silk Roads

Cat Jarman

PEGASUS BOOKS
NEW YORK LONDON

RIVER KINGS

Pegasus Books, Ltd.
148 West 37th Street, 13th Floor
New York, NY 10018

First Pegasus Books paperback edition February 2023
First Pegasus Books cloth edition February 2022

Hardcover ISBN: 978-1-64313-869-5
Paperback ISBN: 978-1-63936-542-5

10 9 8 7 6 5 4 3

Printed in the United States of America
Distributed by Simon & Schuster
www.pegasusbooks.com

Til Mormor

CONTENTS

PART TWO: HOMELANDS

PART THREE: EAST

LIST OF ILLUSTRATIONS

PROLOGUE

CARNELIAN

In 1982, during the summer that I was born, archaeologists excavating a Viking winter camp in the sleepy Derbyshire village of Repton found a small orange bead among the jumbled-up bones of nearly three hundred people buried there in a mass grave. For the next thirty-five years, the bead's existence was all but forgotten. Tucked away in a plastic box, it waited to be deposited in the depths of a museum archive or displayed in a brightly lit cabinet: to be marvelled at by curious children and hassled parents on a rainy Sunday afternoon. In 2017, that bead found its way into my temporary possession. At that point the task of disentangling the stories of the Repton dead had become a significant part of my life: I had spent over half a decade forensically examining their bones, piecing together fragmented information from pathology reports and chemical analyses, attempting to understand who they were and where they came from. I didn't know it at the time, but this bead would take my search for the Vikings in a whole new direction and radically change my understanding of the Viking Age.

I found it in a large Tupperware tub, nestled among hundreds of bags, boxes and envelopes in the Repton artefact archives. A colleague had lugged all of this to my house the evening before, and on that morning I was gradually working my way through the boxes to get an overview of the work to be done. Four decades' worth of specialist reports, illustrations, and the records of more than nine thousand objects uncovered during excavations in the 1970s and 1980s had been passed over to me so that I could help to bring the archives to publication. Along with them were a large number of artefacts that had yet to be fully analysed, drawn and photographed before being sent to Derby Museum. The excavations in Repton covered more than 1300 years of history, representing a real-life journey through time: from the site's prehistoric and Roman origins, and its Anglo-Saxon monastery desecrated by the Vikings, stopping briefly at its Norman castle and Augustinian priory, to its present vicarage, church and well-known public school. The objects in those boxes stemmed from each and every one of these periods: there were Roman enamel brooches lying next to fragments of decorated medieval window glass, and a nineteenth-century bone toothbrush alongside an Anglo-Saxon comb. I felt like a child let loose in a toy shop after hours.

The bead itself was carefully wrapped in tissue paper within a clear polythene bag. Its orange colour bordered on brown; it was approximately a centimetre long and half a centimetre wide, with neatly cut, faceted corners and a polished and shiny surface. Apart from a few scars on one side, and some dirt still stuck in the hole bored through it, the bead was in perfect condition. Nothing about its appearance revealed its age: you'd be forgiven for thinking it a piece of twentieth-century costume jewellery. I couldn't tell how old it was just by looking at it. I took out its cardboard tag from the bag, which included a series of numbers, words and letters decipherable only to the initiated. On an archaeological excavation, every single object is meticulously recorded, its context documented with military precision so that its final circumstances can be reconstructed decades or even centuries later.

29.8.82, Tr8. 3710, 703 [circled], very dark black

Translating these codes into plain English told me that the bead had been found in the late summer of 1982, in the same trench as the mass grave: the grave that I had dedicated six years of my life to analysing. The circled number 703 referred to the specific context or layer in which it was discovered; the description to the colour of the soil – a very dark colour indicated a high organic content or, in other words, an area rich in human activity. I turned to the eight-volume list of finds from the excavations to check if the bead had been found alongside the Victorians, the Vikings or the Romans. The same layer had yielded a variety of finds, including a fragment of Anglo-Saxon window glass, a finely lattice-carved piece of bone that had probably come from a Saxon book cover, metalworking waste, and nondescript fragments of iron, but nothing dating to more recently than the ninth century. In other words, the bead had been found within the detritus of a Viking terror attack, alongside the remains of the 264 people I believe were some of the Viking Great Army war dead. Why had I never heard of this bead before?

Looking more closely, I could see the word 'carnelian' written faintly in pen across the top of the bag. My knowledge of this material was a little sketchy, but the word alone seemed exotic and enticing. Searching online, I learned that carnelian is a mineral commonly used as a semiprecious gemstone, a variety of the silica mineral chalcedony. It had been fashionable among Vikings in the late ninth and early tenth centuries but would originally have come from India or the areas that are now Iran and Iraq. As such, beads like this provide evidence of contact with the Islamic caliphate and the trading routes that formed part of the Silk Roads, the ancient trading networks that stretched like spidery veins across large parts of Asia and central Europe. This was a world I knew little of but one that felt deeply alluring. While Viking expansion through eastern Europe and along trading routes bringing goods back to Scandinavia is well known, the Vikings who arrived in England have typically been considered a distinct movement. In history books, maps illustrate this spread with bold arrows: eastwards from Sweden, westwards from Denmark and Norway. Repton was no different – the accepted interpretation of the bones that I'd been working on seemed to fit neatly into the traditional Viking Age narrative: that of the Norsemen and Danes who travelled west* in the late eighth century, launching a savage attack on unsuspecting monks at Lindisfarne in 793 and kick-starting the Viking Age in the process; and that of the hit-and-run raids of the succeeding decades that eventually, in the ninth century, led to ambitions of political conquest and settlement. This, it had been agreed, is what brought a certain *Great Army* – a military force active in England between 865 and the late 870s – to conquer Repton and the Anglo-Saxon kingdom of Mercia in 873. A neat story, but this small piece of carnelian was beginning to make me wonder if it painted the entire picture. The general consensus has been that the eastern trade routes played little part in the western Viking tale. So what was a Middle Eastern or Asian carnelian bead doing in rural Derbyshire in the ninth century?

My part in this story had begun five years earlier on a crisp, wintry morning in January 2012, when I travelled to Oxford in a borrowed Land Rover Defender built for far more adventurous journeys than a trip down the motorway. I had come to meet two renowned men. The first was one of the UK's most eminent professors of

---

* Throughout this book, the term 'west' will be used to loosely represent north-western Europe and parts of the North Atlantic, while 'east' represents areas from the eastern shores of the Baltic Sea, through the river systems of eastern Europe and to the Middle East.

archaeology, whose accolades include a CBE for services to British archaeology, and whose record of excavations reads like a gazetteer of the greatest archaeological sites. The other was one of the most infamous Viking warriors in England.

I was coming to the end of my Master's degree at the University of Oslo, where I had been studying the diet and migration patterns of Norwegian Vikings by analysing their skeletons (concluding that they (a) often ate a lot of fish and (b) were pretty mobile, neither of which was particularly surprising). A few months before, while I was looking for a suitable PhD research topic, one of my old undergraduate professors had introduced me to Professor Martin Biddle and to the Repton Viking camp. Maybe, he suggested, I could apply my newly learnt forensic skills to the unresolved questions surrounding the Repton dead that Martin and his late wife, Birthe Kjølbye-Biddle, had excavated in the 1970s and 1980s. Martin, in his Oxford office, was everything I, as a child in Norway, had imagined England to be (although disappointingly it was not in a Hogwarts-style wood-panelled college but a 1970s concrete block in Summertown). Fast forward five years and my PhD was coming to an end, with the analyses of the Repton dead nearly complete, when the carnelian bead came into my possession.

To me, there was something compelling about that tiny bead. The smooth, almost translucent material; the sharply cut corners; the faceted shape with angles that looked so perfect and so modern. I couldn't help but obsess over all the hands, all the lives, that it had intersected with over more than a millennium including, now, my own. Who had it belonged to? Was it dropped accidentally, or placed in the mass grave deliberately? How did it end up in Repton and were there other links to the east there that we had not previously considered – could this be a major new discovery? Certain parts of my research into the bones from Repton didn't quite fit into the traditional picture. And in the past few years our knowledge of the Vikings in England had started to increase radically, especially through the discoveries made by metal detectorists painstakingly searching muddy fields at the weekends; finds like ninth-century Islamic coins turning up in the middle of nowhere. Along with such discoveries, could this tiny bead demonstrate a greater connection between the eastern and the western worlds in the Viking Age than we previously thought? But this was, after all, only a single bead. Surely an object like this did not have the power to retell a major narrative? It is unlikely (albeit not impossible) that the bead travelled with one person all the way from Asia to Repton. So what was the connection, the common thread that had brought it to England?

In this book I retrace the journey I believe the carnelian bead travelled to get to its final resting place in Derbyshire, going back to its likely origin in Gujarat, India. Following the trail of the bead deliberately misses out parts of the Viking phenomenon, such as the Vikings' exploration of the North Atlantic towards North America, and the elaborate political dynamics of Viking Age Britain, Ireland and France. Those stories have been told extensively before, but the stepwise movement eastwards, searching for specific connections between east and west, enables a different perspective on the Vikings. My approach here is that of an archaeologist, first and foremost working from the objects and remains left behind, focusing especially on the new, scientific methods that are revolutionising our knowledge. From these, the stories uncovered can be woven into the rich narratives we have from other forms of evidence, to search for traces of the people who migrated in and out of Scandinavia more than a millennium ago in search of riches, power, adventure, or simply a new life; some willingly and some who had no choice. It was this line of thinking that led me to the world of the River Kings. Along the way, a series of objects act as stepping stones, with each representing a particular aspect of the narrative. For every object, I start with a scenario of someone whose life might have interacted with it: some real, some imagined. I will leave it to the reader to decide which is which.

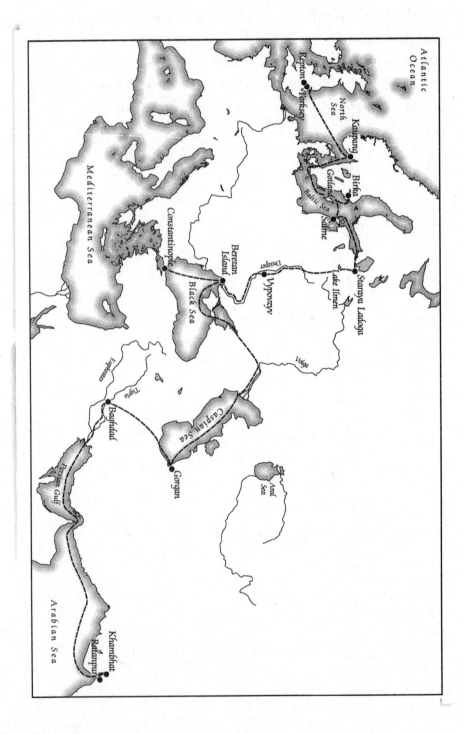

PART ONE

WEST

Trent

Repton

Foremark

Heath Wood

Dumbarton
Rock

Lindisfarne

North

Sea

Tyne

York

Humber

Irish Sea

Dublin

Torksey

Lincoln

Derby

Trent

See Above

Offa's Dyke

M E R C I A

Bury
St Edmunds

Severn

Cirencester

Thames

London

Atlantic

Ocean

Winchester

Southampton

Isle of Portland

English Channel

I.

HAMMER OF THOR: BONES

REPTON, C.874 AND 1986

*F*or five days he had held onto it, safely tucked away in the leather purse hanging from his waist. With the necklace in his hand, he traced the outline of the hammer and turned over the beads that were threaded alongside it a couple of times, before tying the leather thong around the man's neck. His skin was cold and pallid, covered in an oily sheen from the liquids anointed onto it to prepare the body for transport. Kneeling on the pebbly surface at the side of the grave, he pushed the hammer into place, so it nestled just below the man's collarbone – just as he'd worn it in life. One by one, the other objects were placed around the body, each presented as an offering carrying meaning about both who he had been and who he was about to become.

Eleven hundred years later, the necklace saw daylight once again. The stony and loamy soil covering its surface was gingerly brushed away by a volunteer excavator who mistook it for an anchor. You could understand her error: its upside-down T-shape, with a pointed lower edge, is certainly reminiscent of something you would have used to moor a ship. Yet the pendant is small and delicate, with neat, straight lines. You could even describe its design as understated, especially when you know what it represents: a portrayal of Mjölnir, the hammer of Thor forged in a smouldering furnace by the dwarves of Svartálfaheimr.

THE VIKING WARRIOR

According to the traditional narrative, the Viking Age began when a band of Vikings attacked the wealthy monastery at Lindisfarne in Northumbria on 8 June 793. The attack, technically not the first accounted Viking raid on English soil, was described in a letter to Ethelred, king of Northumbria, by Alcuin of York, a scholar living in what is now Germany: 'Never before has such terror appeared in Britain as we have now suffered from a pagan race, nor is it thought that such an inroad from the sea could be made.'

The Viking attacks are typically thought to have been brought about by a combination of pulls and pushes: the lure of undefended Saxon monastic riches coupled with the pressures of Scandinavian population growth, poor agricultural land in Norway, political disputes and perhaps even a lack of marriageable women back home.[1] As a result, a new era emerged. Records like the *Anglo-Saxon Chronicle** describe the toils of the Angles and Saxons over the next centuries, focusing largely on the royal families and the ongoing battles for control of the numerous kingdoms making up what was to become modern-day England. The narrative presented in the *Chronicle* fits well within the established tale of the Vikings who turned from their Norwegian and Danish homelands and travelled west to raid, pillage and conquer throughout Britain and

---

* This historical source is a compilation of accounts surviving in a number of versions, which detail the history of England from 60 BC until the twelfth century. The majority of the text was compiled in the ninth century in monasteries in the southern Anglo-Saxon kingdom of Wessex.

Ireland, wreaking havoc both there and elsewhere on the continent of Europe. By the end of the Viking Age, in the mid-eleventh century, the Scandinavians' impact on Britain would be profound, affecting everything from the development of towns to the currency, culture, language and art.

By the time we get to Repton and the Great Army in 873, the Vikings were old news. In the 850s, Viking raiders had begun overwintering in England rather than travelling back home to Scandinavia at the end of the raiding season. According to the narrative in the *Chronicle*, the Great Army first appeared on English soil in the winter of 865. That year this large force landed in East Anglia, where they were provided with horses by the king in return for peace, overwintering in Thetford. Over the next thirteen years, the army would move across the country, capturing York in 866 and East Anglia in 868. The campaign was a step up for the Vikings, with smaller, hit-and-run raids having been replaced by a thirst for something entirely different, namely long-term political conquest. By the 870s, the pattern of seasonal raiding had become an established military strategy and one that seemed to be successful.

The Viking camp at Repton has remained one of the most significant Viking sites in England for more than forty years. The excavations carried out by Martin and Birthe initially focused on the village's Anglo-Saxon church, St Wystan's[2] – one of the best surviving examples of early medieval architecture in England. In the 1970s, little was known about the Great Army's presence in Repton beyond an entry in the *Anglo-Saxon Chronicle* for the year 873 stating that 'here the raiding army went from Lindsey to Repton and took winter-quarters there, and drove the King Burghred across the sea twenty-two years after he had the kingdom, and conquered all that land'. This overwintering was to become a turning point in the story of the Vikings in England.

While excavating the cemeteries around the church, the team came across a large ditch, cutting through earlier graves and abutting the church wall. Nearby, they found several distinctly Scandinavian-style burials, as well as the broken pieces of a finely carved Anglo-Saxon cross head and a buried sculpture of a mounted Mercian warrior. The ditch was interpreted to be part of a defensive enclosure, showing that with little doubt here was the historically attested winter camp of the Great Army.

Prior to these excavations, nobody had looked for the Viking winter camp at Repton. Nor, for that matter, had anyone known what it would look like or how to find it. At the time this was quite a common story: despite a wide range of written sources relating to Viking Age England, surprisingly little physical evidence of the Vikings' presence remained and for the most part this is still the case. Historical records like the *Anglo-Saxon Chronicle* give detailed, blow-by-blow accounts of battles against the invaders, detailing casualties and lamenting the threat the heathens imposed on the natives. It can be argued that the development of major towns and the unification of England as a country happened in response to Viking incursions, but because there has been a relative dearth of archaeological evidence, the written records have often been used as our primary source of knowledge.

The archaeological discoveries around St Wystan's fitted well within this familiar picture of the Vikings. The defensive ditch was thought to represent a D-shaped enclosure similar to examples in Scandinavia, incorporating the desecrated church as a gatehouse, allowing the marauding army time to regroup safely over winter and plan their next attack. The church itself had formed part of a wealthy monastery and was the most sacred burial place of the Mercian royal family. Several noteworthy kings had been buried there and its crypt had become a site of pilgrimage to visit the bones of the sainted Wigstan, a ninth-century Mercian king later known as Wystan. This reveals that the Viking takeover was not only a way to grab the wealth and supplies that would have been found in a monastery, but also a statement of political power. Thanks to the attack, the Mercian king Burghred had been driven into exile in Paris with his wife, never to return. In his place was installed Ceolwulf, described by the *Chronicle* as 'a foolish king's thegn' – a puppet king. Ceolwulf apparently promised allegiance to the Vikings, guaranteeing to make himself and the kingdom of Mercia available to them whenever they needed it.

After that winter of 873–4, the Great Army split, with one part moving north into Northumbria, and the other south to fight against Alfred the Great, the king of Wessex. At Repton, the graves with Scandinavian artefacts were placed in prominent positions around the church, perhaps with the aim of legitimising the rule of those leaders who had 'conquered all that land', and to claim a more long-term presence. The association with a former ruling elite was a common tactic of the Vikings to emphasise their political and territorial claims.

When I first visited Oxford that day in 2012, Martin Biddle introduced me to the so-called Repton warrior, also known as Grave 511. His remains had been carefully placed in three beige cardboard boxes, stacked neatly in a corner of the office: a smaller box for his skull, and two larger, rectangular ones for his remaining bones. I have seen thousands of boxes identical to this, each containing an excavated skeleton that has been removed from the ground for storage in a museum collection. I'd read all the reports I could find about G511 and knew all there was to know about his injuries. Often the evidence that remains of traumatic injury is subtle: by the time a blade has cut through skin, flesh and muscle, its momentum has been lost and the energy remaining has only been sufficient to make a small scratch on the surface of the bone. So as horrific and lethal as an injury might have been to a victim, the bones frequently escape relatively unscathed, leaving us unaware of the cause of death. But in this case the injuries were almost impossible to miss. As I lifted his well-preserved left femur out of the box, I could see the deep cut where the axe had sliced through his hip, the angle of the blade clearly defined, leaving no doubt as to its gruesome impact.

This man had been thought of as a stereotypical Viking with a capital 'V': tall, strong, blond-haired and blue-eyed (although those particular details would not be revealed until several years later). He had been buried with a sword of a Scandinavian type by his side and he wore a silver Thor's hammer pendant around his neck; artefacts that made his affiliation with the Viking world immediately apparent to his excavators, the hammer being considered by many the ultimate symbol of a traditional Viking warrior. Whoever buried him had placed several other items around him, presumably for use in the afterlife: a key, two iron knives and several buckles and fasteners for clothes. Either side of the Thor's hammer was a brightly coloured glass bead. Between his legs, a rectangular patch of softer soil may have been all that remained of a wooden box; inside it, a bone from a jackdaw, perhaps symbolic of the god Odin's two ravens Hugin and Munin. Near his pelvis lay a boar's tusk.

Later, when the bones had been taken out of the ground and cleaned, it was discovered that G511 had received a number of gruesome and fatal injuries. He had wounds to his skull, with scars suggesting he may have been wearing a helmet when he died, and a cut into his eye socket. On his vertebrae were cut marks that are consistent with evisceration, i.e. the removal of his guts or internal organs. The most severe injury was the deep, diagonal cut into his left thigh, caused by an axe slicing downwards through the hip joint and thigh bone. Somewhere along the line, it has been suggested that this would have cut through his penis, rendering him emasculated. The boar's tusk found between his legs, therefore, may have been put there as a replacement to ensure he was complete upon arrival in Valhalla, Odin's hall where fallen warriors could feast at night, and where a penis would surely be needed.

Perhaps this is a little creative but, in any case, the grave bears all the hallmarks of that of a warrior,[3] and G511's grave is significant because his is the only such Viking warrior grave in the whole of England that has been properly excavated. There are no comparative graves with the bones intact, despite historical records informing us that such warriors died here in the hundreds or even thousands. Much about the grave suggests that he was a man of high status, perhaps even one of the leaders of the Great Army. His burial, right next to what was once the mausoleum of a whole dynasty of Mercian kings, demonstrates that those who buried him wanted to assert his (and, by extension, their) power and legitimacy over this territory.

For my PhD research, I was re-investigating the Vikings at Repton and a key part of this new research on G511 and the Repton dead was to take samples from several of the skeletons in order to use one of the latest forensic techniques – isotope analysis – to learn as much as I could about who they were and where they came from. In archaeology, isotope analysis has become one of the primary methods used to retrace a person's geographical origins and background. Traditionally, this would have been done by identifying the origins of grave goods – objects buried with a body – if present. That method has some obvious flaws. For one thing, burying the dead with artefacts was not always common practice, leaving us with very little to attempt to reconstruct a past life. And even when grave goods do exist, the objects a person has been buried with – like a Viking sword or a carnelian bead – could have been traded or exchanged, arriving at the burial destination separately from their final owners. The graves we find are multifaceted: we have no way of knowing whether those items even belonged to the deceased or whether they were gifts placed there by the mourners. They may not even reflect much about the person's life. As one archaeologist noted: 'The dead do not bury themselves.'

Isotope analysis, on the other hand, allows us to study the skeletons directly, in an attempt to discover aspects of their individual life histories. Although DNA has the potential to do this too, it largely provides information about someone's inherited markers, not their unique circumstances. If I am buried in the south-west of England when I die, a DNA analysis of my bones would reveal Scandinavian ancestry, which might give you a clue to my immigration history. But you would find the same genes in the bones of my children, who were born and raised in the UK. In other words, DNA analysis cannot discriminate between first and subsequent generation immigrants. Even so, DNA can give us the bigger picture: how we have spread across the globe, how our ancestors have migrated over thousands of years. It can also tell us about family relationships, or help you find long-lost cousins and reveal markers of illness and disease. In the case of the Repton graves, I was interested in whether, like we thought, we could prove that they were immigrant Vikings from Scandinavia.

We are, quite literally, what we eat. While you are reading this, your body is digesting your latest meal and is taking all the building blocks it can from it to create new cells, new blood and new skin. Since you started the book, that process of change has been taking place throughout your body so that by now even your bones have begun to change subtly: new bone gets laid down to replace fragments of the old, to maintain strength and structure. This is true for practically everything in your body, with one exception: the enamel in your teeth. Once it has formed during childhood, enamel remains unaltered and it's even strong enough to stay intact in very poor conditions in the ground for thousands of years. For this reason, teeth are the bioarchaeologist's best friend.

Because all tissues, while they are forming, are constantly taking up nutrients from your diet, they also absorb traces of substances that can tell us something about what you ate and, crucially, for my purposes: *where* you ate it. When, as a child, your teeth form, the food and water you have consumed are their building blocks. That food and drink, again, carries with it markers, or chemical variations, that are particular to the environment in which it was produced. Plants, for instance, get most of their nutrients from the soils in which they grow. These soils get their characteristics from the underlying geology. So, in other words, a loaf of bread made from wheat grown in Derbyshire will have subtly different chemical characteristics from a loaf made from wheat grown in Denmark.

A way to detect this is through an element called strontium that occurs naturally in pretty much everything. Strontium has several isotopes, which are different forms of the same element. The ratio of one of these in relation to another is what varies in different types of geology and therefore in different soils. And that ratio remains the same as the strontium passes up the food chain: from soil to wheat to bread to Viking. And when the strontium ratio becomes a part of the newly formed enamel in a child's tooth, it is locked in for the rest of his or her life – and beyond. Returning to the Repton warrior, then, it should be possible to discover whether he really *was* an invading Viking, or if, instead, he had grown up locally.

I should add here that the issue of *identity* is a complex one and despite all the incredible promise of these methods, it's not one that science alone can answer. Even if the isotope data strongly suggest that someone grew up in Scandinavia, that doesn't make them a 'Viking'; in fact, there is no such defined identity that scientific methods can conclusively reveal. Equally, seemingly local origins wouldn't automatically make someone an 'Anglo-Saxon'.* Our identities are multifaceted, and we change and manipulate them throughout our lives. I am an archaeologist, scientist, writer, mother and immigrant, but apart from my migration history, none of these identities would be apparent in my bones. So however we interpret the scientific results, we must do so with caution, and always in the context of as many different sources of evidence as possible. Nevertheless, these new techniques have provided us with opportunities to study past lives that we could only dream of a few decades ago.

While the methods sound straightforward, it takes months of lab work to get all the necessary data, followed by even more months of wrangling said data into spreadsheets, databases, charts and comparative maps. But the strontium results from G511 were relatively easy to interpret: he definitely could not have grown up in or near Repton. The values from his teeth were consistent with an origin in southern Scandinavia, most likely Denmark, which fitted perfectly with the archaeological interpretation. Yet there was another result from the isotope analysis that was notable too: that of the man he was buried next to. G511 had not been buried alone, but right next to another, younger man, G295. While the actual bodies had been interred separately – the younger man's body was put in the ground very shortly after G511's – their graves

---

* Both the terms 'Viking' and 'Anglo-Saxon' can arguably be seen as purely modern inventions: they are unlikely to have made sense to someone living in the ninth century. Here, the term 'Viking' is used to describe in a very broad sense the people and cultural traits that emerged and spread from Scandinavia during the Viking Age. The term 'Anglo-Saxon', while subject to a long history of misuse by racists and extremists, remains a widely understood frame of reference for the communities and kingdoms of England between the fifth and early eleventh centuries. Neither this nor Viking is used to imply ethnicity; they are, simply, the most useful, if inaccurate, terms we have available today.

had been covered by a joint, rectangular stone setting – including a broken-up, finely carved Anglo-Saxon sculpture – which made it clear that they were associated with each other. Double graves like this are common in Viking Age Scandinavia: sometimes couples were buried together and other times two people of the same sex, almost always men. In the latter case, nobody has been able to determine what the relationship was between the two.

What the isotope results could add was that the younger man had grown up in a location that was almost identical to that of the warrior, isotopically speaking. He too had sustained violent injuries, and may well have been killed in battle, but he had none of the wealthy grave goods of G511 – only a single knife. It seemed likely that these two men came from the same place, quite possibly Denmark. New radiocarbon dates provided a narrow window for their deaths, between the years 873 and 886. This made their association with the Great Army even more likely. It has been suggested that this was the grave of a leader and his weapon-bearer, and even that the younger man was deliberately murdered to accompany his master. Several years later, the reason they were buried together was revealed.

In a collaboration with geneticist Dr Lars Fehren-Schmitz at the University of California Santa Cruz, we wanted to try to extract ancient DNA from the Repton samples. The aim was to find more proof that these men really were of Scandinavian descent, but also to investigate any possible family relationships, especially to look for a link between the warrior and his companion. Over a decade earlier, other geneticists had tried to do the same, but they had been unsuccessful. Using the methods available at the time, it had not been possible to separate the original DNA in the bones from external contamination by the DNA of all those people who had excavated, cleaned and examined the bones previously. By 2016, technology had moved on so far that not only was it possible to access the uncontaminated DNA, it was also possible to investigate both maternal and paternal ancestry (mtDNA and Y-DNA respectively), as well as autosomal DNA, which is the unique combination of chromosomes that someone inherits from their parents. Lars and his colleagues discovered that there was a direct, first-degree family relationship between the two men on the paternal side, meaning that they could be either half-brothers or father and son. With the age difference in mind, the latter is more likely. In addition, they had discovered that G511's eye colour was most likely blue and his hair most likely blond. So, G511 really did live up to the stereotypical image of the tall blond Viking. Perhaps with one exception; the genetic data also told us that he was most likely bald.

Knowing the family relationship between G511 and his son is important – and exciting – for several reasons, especially that of understanding the dynamics of the Viking world on a broader scale. Historical records and saga literature – prose stories about the Vikings written down largely in Iceland in the twelfth and thirteenth centuries – often deal with specific characters: people who were the actors and antagonists in the stories that make up much of our knowledge of the Vikings. But these sources must be used with some caution. Not only is there a bias in what has been preserved and what hasn't, but the writer's motivations also need to be taken into account. The sagas are especially tempting to use as evidence for historical events in the Viking Age. The story of the semi-legendary Ragnar Lothbrok, for example, has enjoyed a popular legacy in England.[4] According to the sagas, Ragnar fought here himself, while his fierce warrior sons are credited as having been significant Viking leaders, even some of those who led the Great Army. However, Ragnar's story has been patched together from numerous sources, many of which are not even contemporary, and there is no proof that he was the father of the Vikings who captured Repton in 873.

Knowledge gained from other sources, like objects and bones, can provide a different kind of information (albeit one that is not necessarily more objective), which may serve to verify the historical records. In the case of G511 and his son, the new bioarchaeological evidence verified the sources that describe the significance of patri-archal connections and male descent in Viking society. It also showed that this was a vital element in the movements outside Scandinavia and the taking of new territories. Finally, it demon-strated that these customs were often ultimately expressed through burial rites, as here; a son was brought to Repton to be buried alongside his father, with a monument placed on top of them to show not only their status but also their connection to each other.

The question of Scandinavian ancestry is more complex; as was the question of whether we could further narrow down their identities. A big problem is that we still haven't found a way to conclusively separate Viking Age migrants from Scandinavia from those who came across from north-western, continental Europe (Angles, Saxons and Jutes) just a few centuries earlier. It is for this reason that we haven't yet been able to use DNA analysis to accu-rately estimate the size of the Scandinavian settlement in England. A few years ago, a large-scale survey of modern DNA from Britain analysed genetic clusters in order to identify past migration events. The researchers concluded that they couldn't find any clear genetic evidence of a Danish Viking occupation of large parts of England. This, they said, meant that Viking migrants had left very little of a genetic legacy, and could therefore have arrived only in very small numbers.

This presented a problem: the result was at odds with so much other evidence, like the impact of the Vikings on Britain's language, place names and much of the archaeology: these sources all suggested that the Vikings had had a considerable influence that could only have come from a sizeable migration. The issue was that the researchers hadn't adequately taken into account the fact that many of those they defined as Danish Vikings came from exactly the same region as those they defined as Anglo-Saxons migrating before them, and the statistical modelling had not been able to separate the two. When other researchers took the overlap into account with the same dataset, they were able to estimate a much more realistic total settlement of 20,000–35,000 people, which was consistent with other forms of evidence.[5]

The size of the Great Army has been debated too, with estimates ranging from it being comparatively tiny to many thousands strong. Part of this relates to terminology. In the *Anglo-Saxon Chronicle*, the words used to describe it are the *micel here* – where *micel* means 'great' and *here* is translated as 'army'. This may be a bit imprecise because, according to a seventh-century law code, technically the word *here* was used to mean any group bigger than thirty-five men that was involved in some kind of violent raid or robbery. It's possible that this word was used deliberately by the chroniclers as a way to belittle the invading forces, making them sound more like violent thugs than organised military units. Getting a sense of the scale of the Great Army is important because soon after Repton raiding turned to settlement: from the late 870s those who had formed part of the marauding armies divided out land and started farming for themselves. It's very possible that some of them settled near Repton itself. Only a few miles away, there is a large-scale cemetery at a site called Heath Wood. Here almost sixty burial mounds sit on top of a hill, each containing one or more cremation burials. Many of them included Viking type grave goods and animal offerings; it is possibly the cemetery of a nearby Scandinavian settlement.

In the case of Grave 511 and his companion the DNA evidence could not help directly. There are no known, living relatives to compare them to, and with more than eleven hundred years having passed since their deaths, if they have descendants at all, these would count in the tens of thousands if not more.[6] At present the only way to narrow down the alternatives is to look for individuals named in the historical records who might be a good fit.

In the *Anglo-Saxon Chronicle*, four leaders are named as having been at Repton: Halfdan, Guthrum, Anund and Oscatel. We know that Halfdan and Guthrum survived that winter and for many years beyond, so they are unlikely candidates. Anund and Oscatel disappeared from the records and are not heard of anywhere else, meaning that they could be a fit. Yet there are other intriguing possibilities. Searching through all the named Vikings in historical documents for fathers and sons who fit the timeframe *and* the ages at death, leaves us with a good match. The *Annals of Ulster* describe a man named Amlaib (usually identified as Olaf) as one of the foreign, Viking kings active in Ireland and Britain from 853 onwards. He is described as 'the son of the King of Lochlann' (a location that hasn't been pinned down, thought to be either Norway or somewhere in Scotland or the Northern Isles) and became a dominant person in Irish affairs during the 850s and 860s, essentially establishing himself as the Viking ruler of Dublin. This Olaf frequently raided alongside Ivar (sometimes identified as the semi-legendary Ivar the Boneless, son of Ragnar Lothbrok). The two may have been brothers.

In 874, Olaf was killed in what is now Scotland by Constantin, King of the Picts. There is no evidence for what happened to his body, but the timeline fits with the Repton burial. Having first arrived in Ireland in 853, he was likely in his forties or a little older by the time he died. This matches the forensic analysis of G511. But what makes the identification more compelling is that Olaf had a son named Eysteinn, about whom the *Annals of Ulster* state, for the year 875: 'Eysteinn son of Óláfr, king of the Northmen, was deceitfully killed by Hálfdann.' This Halfdan is believed to be none other than the Halfdan who was at Repton in 873 and, incidentally, Eysteinn's own uncle.

These sources, then, give us a father–son pair of the right age, dating to precisely the right time. The overwintering at Repton would have lasted until 874 and the archaeology shows that the younger man was buried slightly later than the father, which could conceivably have been the year after. While neither Olaf nor Eysteinn can be linked directly to Repton, other than by the presence of Halfdan, it is very possible that Olaf's body was moved there after his death in Scotland. In 874, Repton lay in Scandinavian hands and would have been a fitting location for a former Viking ruler. The forensic evidence might support this, as the osteological analysis carried out by forensic pathologist Dr Bob Stoddart showed that G511 had been disembowelled around the time of his death. This was something that was often carried out in the early medieval period in order to move a corpse, because it would stop the body from decomposing so rapidly. For example, Charles the Bald, emperor of the Carolingian Empire who died in the Alps in 877, had his entrails removed and buried on the spot to stop his body from rotting before it was moved to Paris for burial. This possible identification – while unprovable – is potentially a really exciting discovery as it provides a link between the Great Army and the early Viking rulers of the Irish Sea region.

A HOUSE FOR THE DEAD

Important as he was, G511 didn't represent the most remarkable discovery in Repton. Next to the church, in the vicarage garden, a shallow mound had perplexed the locals for centuries. In an account from the seventeenth century, antiquarian Simon Degg described a workman digging into a 'hillock' somewhere near St Wystan's church, finding inside it a large stone coffin containing the 'skeleton of a humane body nine foot long'. Around the body lay 'one hundred humane skeletons, with their feet pointing to the stone coffin'. After removing the skull of the central figure, the workman swiftly covered the grave over at the instruction of the lady of the manor, who was clearly shocked at the horrors that had been found at the bottom of her garden and stated that she could not bear to have this charnel exposed. Later, in the nineteenth century, others had dug into it again, discovering not only bones but also ancient weapons, yet apparently leaving most of the deposit in place.

It was Martin and Birthe's excavations in the 1980s that were the first to suggest a link to the Vikings. Excavating the mound, they found a partially destroyed two-roomed Anglo-Saxon building underneath that likely dated to the time of the Anglo-Saxon monastery. Inside one of the rooms, they found exactly what those antiquarians had uncovered centuries before: a large mass of jumbled up human remains. At first, there was no way of knowing how old the bones were. But among them, they found artefacts: numerous corroded fragments of metal, some of which they immediately recognised as weapons, including several knives and, crucially, an axe head. The latter could be identified as being of a specific Viking type. But it was the discovery of five silver pennies found together that provided the conclusive evidence. The coins were taken away to be identified by a numismatist, who placed their date between 872 and 875 – precisely the time when the Great Army had camped in Repton. The whole context of the burial fitted with this Viking association and slowly the pieces fell into place. Who else would tear down and desecrate what was likely a high-status, religious Anglo-Saxon building and convert it into a mortuary chamber, covered by an elaborately formed mound?

It seemed that there had been two phases to the use of the building. First, it had been ravaged and used as part of the Viking camp: there were fragments of decorative plaster, broken window glass, traces of metalworking waste and the remains of butchered animals, the likely leftovers of someone's lunch. At the time, the excavators referred to this as the 'squatters' deposit'. It was mostly discovered in the first room you came into, which had steps going down to it from the outside. In a second stage, the second room had been turned into a burial chamber. Here the squatters' detritus had been swept away and a layer of clean, red sand laid down as a surface on which the bones were placed. This suggests that they were put there at a single point in time, in a deliberate, ceremonial act. Somewhere among all this, one of the excavators, whose identity is now as lost as those to whom the bones belong, discovered my tiny orange bead, though it would not come into my possession for almost four decades.

During that summer of 1982, when the Repton charnel deposit was discovered, considerable work was carried out on analysing the bones to try to understand whose bodies they belonged to. Each bone was taken out and cleaned in a large tent set up on the vicarage lawn. There, volunteers washed every fragment carefully and laid out thousands of remains to dry on egg cartons. Local doctors and dentists joined the team to count and understand the remains. In the end it was determined that the room had contained no fewer than 264 individuals, based on a count of adult left femurs (as we each have only one left thigh) and a smaller number of juvenile arm bones. There were seventy-two skulls and, when it was possible to determine age, it was clear that there were practically no children, very few old people, and the majority had been aged between eighteen and forty-five. They were also, remarkably, very tall, with most bones being of a considerably larger size than those excavated from Anglo-Saxon graves in the cemetery nearby. With the context taken into account, then, everything pointed to this being a burial site associated with the Viking Great Army. The bones were presumably those of the war dead: warriors who had died in battle and been given a communal grave.

But the ongoing analysis of the bones was to throw up one more surprise. Where the specialists were able to determine an individual's sex (something that is typically only possible if you have a skull or a relatively complete pelvis, as that is where sex-based differences can be seen on a skeleton), it was clear that not all the individuals were male. In fact, around 20 per cent of those buried in this grave were women. This was wholly unexpected for the team at the time as the Viking warriors, by definition, *should* all have been male.

Publishing the results, Martin and Birthe suggested that the women could have been local wives of the male Vikings. This was supported by the bone analyses indicating that unlike the men, who were *taller* than the average Anglo-Saxon, the women were *shorter* than contemporary Scandinavian women were expected to be. This fitted with general assumptions at the time that the Viking invasions consisted primarily, if not wholly, of all-male raiding parties.

While the interpretation of the bone deposit as that of a Viking army was well received, one issue led to considerable confusion. In the early 1990s, the material was radiocarbon dated at a lab in Utrecht, in full expectation of dates in the late ninth century to fit with the context of the grave and its interpretation. Yet it turned out that many of the bones dated to much earlier: in fact some two hundred years earlier, meaning that they could not possibly all have belonged to the Great Army. For a long time this cast doubt over the whole interpretation of Repton – surely it couldn't really be a Viking war grave if it contained the bones of people who had died centuries before? A number of explanations were suggested, both by Birthe and Martin and later by others, to explain the anomaly. Could the older bones be those of the Vikings' ancestors, whom they had carried with them to a new homeland? This wasn't unheard of from the Icelandic sagas: examples of ancestor veneration exist, in which skeletal remains were either kept on display or buried in or near the home. Alternatively, and more commonly accepted, was the suggestion that the older bones could be the disinterred remains of the Anglo-Saxon monks who had been buried in Repton before the Vikings arrived. In digging their vast defensive ditch, it was suggested, the Great Army may also have stopped to gather the contents of graves they had disturbed, collecting these and transferring them to a new mortuary chamber.

The problem was that none of these explanations was particularly satisfactory. And as long as the riddle of the bones remained, so did the doubt over Repton as a final resting place for members of the Great Army. This, in turn, cast doubt on the carnelian bead and its origins: if the mass grave couldn't be securely associated with the Vikings, neither could the bead.

Martin and Birthe suspected that there was another likely explanation for the radiocarbon date anomaly, but in the 1990s the science behind this was not well enough understood to find out exactly what that might be. It turned out that resolving the Repton radiocarbon dates all came down to a matter of fish. After radiocarbon dating was invented in the 1950s, it quickly became one of the most significant contributions to twentieth-century archaeology. The method made it possible to fairly accurately get a scientific date out of pretty much any object with an organic origin, from a log or a burnt seed to an antler comb or a human bone. Every living organism absorbs carbon while alive. This happens either directly from the atmosphere, as in plants photo-synthesising CO_2, or indirectly, as in animals and people consuming carbon-rich plants and other foods through their diets. The process takes place constantly as we eat and breathe and therefore the supply of carbon in our bodies – our bones, skin and hair – is maintained.

Just as with other elements like strontium, carbon has several isotopes, with a radioactive isotope, ^{14}C, being one of them. When we die, we stop accumulating new carbon while the carbon already in our bodies begins slowly and subtly to decay. So when we die, the clock starts ticking. Crucially, we know how fast it ticks; the rate at which this process takes place. Radioactive decay is measured in something called a half-life, which is the time it takes for the original amount of the element to decay by half; for radiocarbon, that is 5700±30 years. In other words, it will take more than five millennia for the ^{14}C in your body to be reduced to half of the original amount. This means that we can measure the radiocarbon remaining in a sample and work back to find out how long it has been since that organism died. While this is a pretty reliable method, the problem with the Repton remains was that nobody had ever taken into account the *source* of the carbon in those bones. And the fact that some people may have been eating rather a lot of fish.

In recent decades a number of sites have yielded similarly incon-sistent dates to those from Repton, whereby the ^{14}C dates clearly haven't matched the remaining archaeology. The reason for this relates to diet and physiology. As the radiocarbon in human bodies comes largely from the food that we eat, we need to follow the carbon trail back through the food chain. If you eat only land-based foods – either meat or a vegetarian diet – then the carbon in your body will come from plants that fix carbon into their tissues directly from the atmosphere. However, if you eat fish or other seafood, some of that carbon will come from marine or freshwater sources, and that's where it becomes a little more complicated. The carbon in our oceans is different: most of it comes from the atmosphere but when it reaches the water, it stays there and circulates in the ocean for several hundred years. This means that when a fish eats plankton, it is consuming carbon that is considerably older than the carbon a sheep consumes by eating grass. On average, this age difference is around four hundred years, which means that if a Viking were to kill a fish and a sheep on the same day and bury them in the ground for you to find a millennium later, it would look to you like the fish died four centuries *before* the sheep. This difference is passed on up the food chain, meaning that someone eating a substantial amount of fish will also be consuming a lot of older carbon.

While scientists have known about this principle for a long time, the full impact it has on dating archaeological samples wasn't fully realised until very recently. This is especially pertinent for relatively modern material (and considering the full history of humankind, the Vikings are very much modern), when even an extra fifty years can make a huge difference to the interpretation.

The next step in resolving the Repton riddle was to estimate how much seafood each individual was likely to have eaten while their bones were being formed. We can do this now with some confidence: other isotopes can tell us about how much of a person's diet comes from marine or terrestrial sources. Non-radioactive or stable carbon isotope (^{13}C) ratios that we also find in organic materials vary in different environments. This means that a value measured from a sample can be matched against the expected result from a fish consumer or a terrestrial food consumer. On a fundamental level, it's quite a straightforward idea: if you have a mixed diet, we can work out the relative percentage of each type of food that you've eaten. It's a bit like estimating how much white and red paint you used to obtain a particular shade of pink. This, in turn, allows us to work out how much of that four-hundred-year marine offset needs to be taken into account.

In the end, the results lined up beautifully. In each case the individuals whose dates were too early for the Viking Age were people who had consumed a relatively large amount of fish. This meant that the individual graves and the mass grave bones that were tested *all* fitted with a date in the late ninth century.[7]

The new radiocarbon dates brought the Vikings back to Repton and with that, finally the certainty that the objects and artefacts buried with them, like the carnelian bead, must also be linked to their presence. But of course, the dates on their own couldn't prove that the mass grave contained a group of *Vikings* – could it not just as well hold their victims? We may never know the answer to this for certain, but some of the other scientific data can help. Carrying out the same oxygen and strontium analyses as on the warrior and his son showed that the people in the mass grave were of mixed origins – only a few could have grown up in the local area. For the most part, they were found to be largely consistent with a group from Scandinavia, even if for many of them, north-western European or British origins couldn't be ruled out either.

Crucially, though, the results demonstrated that the people in the mass grave hadn't come from a single origin, like a raiding party hailing solely from Norway or Denmark. Evidence emerging from other Viking Age sites has shown similar results, suggesting that Viking groups were composite forces under joint leadership that could pick up and lose members along the way.[8] At Trelleborg, the tenth-century fortress of the Danish king Harald Bluetooth, who is credited with Christianising and consolidating Denmark, a similar pattern has emerged. In the cemeteries thought to contain Harald's warriors, strontium isotope analyses revealed that while many could have been recruited from the local area, a large number came from far away, perhaps seeking employment as mercenaries.[9]

What was especially peculiar about Repton was that a few individuals had oxygen isotope values suggesting they came from a *warmer* climate than that of central England: a completely unexpected result. Possible locations could include the Iberian Peninsula and the Mediterranean.[10] If this really was the Great Army, could it mean that it contained people from places we had not previously considered? An important point is that those who were buried underneath the Repton mound were what are called secondary burials, meaning that they had been buried somewhere else first. After their bodies had turned to skeletons, they were moved – we know this because the excavations showed that in places the bones were neatly stacked, with thigh bones placed together in one corner of the room. This means that the bones had been collected from temporary burial places elsewhere, meaning that they might not all have died in or near Repton.

THE JUVENILES

There was one more discovery from the Repton excavations that needed explaining. Just outside the mass burial site, the team found another unusual grave. It seemed to have been marked by a kind of post, but all that remained of this were some large stones at the base. Its location near the entrance to the mass grave building meant that anyone going towards the charnel would have walked straight past it. What was so special about this grave was that it contained four children who had been buried together. This was uncommon not only in Repton, where most of the cemeteries contained graves of adults: a single grave with four children together is extremely unusual in this period altogether.

It was clear that the four had been buried at the same time, and that their bodies had been very carefully and deliberately arranged. One of the dead lay on his or her back, with two of the other juveniles crouched on their sides up against him or her. The fourth child was facing the other way, back to back with one of the others. It is impossible to tell from their bones whether the children were male or female: the differences in a skeleton that relate to sex are not apparent until after puberty. While initially there was no clear evidence pointing to how the children had died, a more recent analysis by forensic pathologist Bob Stoddart revealed that at least two, probably three, of the children's skeletons showed evidence of violent trauma: in other words, they were most likely murdered.

At the foot end of the grave, the excavators found a sheep's jaw, which would be a very unusual find in a Christian cemetery from this time. However, it is not unusual to find animal offerings in Viking graves. Could this jaw, then, suggest that the grave was also associated with the Vikings? Its proximity to the charnel, and the way that it had been marked, would certainly indicate this could be the case. New radiocarbon dates I obtained from the grave showed that it dated to almost exactly the same time as the warrior and his son, namely to between 873 and 885. In their original interpretation of the discovery, Martin and Birthe suggested that these four, who they thought may have been local children, could have been the victims of sacrifice, buried as a part of a ritual related to the closing of the mass grave mound.

It is almost impossible to prove conclusively that someone, in the distant past, was sacrificed. You can find evidence on someone's body, even when it's been reduced to a skeleton, that they died violently, suffering a traumatic death; but unless you have another form of proof, it is practically impossible to prove the *intention* behind their death. How do you differentiate between somebody who died in a battle situation and someone whose death was caused deliberately for a ritual or religious purpose? But because of the cut marks on their skeletons, it is clear that at least two of these four young people hadn't died of illness or other natural causes; it would seem unlikely, but not impossible, that they had been caught up and killed in a battle.

Human sacrifice *may* have been part of Viking ritual practices; there are written accounts that suggest this was the case. Writing in 1072, the German monk Adam of Bremen told of the horrors he observed on a visit to the temple devoted to Thor, Odin and Frey in Gamla Uppsala in Sweden: every nine years, he wrote, nine males of all living creatures – including humans – were sacrificed there to appease the gods. Similarly, German bishop Thietmar of Merseburg described how at Lejre in Denmark, the Vikings would meet every nine years 'and offer to the gods ninety-nine people and just as many horses, dogs and hens or hawks, for these should serve them in the kingdom of the dead and atone for their evil deeds'.

Both these accounts could, of course, have been Christian propaganda. To uncover the full story of what happened in Viking Repton, though, it seemed important to try to understand what befell these children. There is a case where something similar might have happened: at Trelleborg, in the settlement near the fortress, several wells were found to contain a mix of human remains and animal bones.[11] Most strikingly, two of the wells each contained two very young children's bodies, right at the bottom. In both cases, near complete skeletons of either a goat or a dog had been thrown in too. A likely reason for these tragic burials seems to have been human sacrifice.

The first thing that was certain was that the four Repton children were not all local. One of them could have been: the youngest child, who was crouched in the opposite direction to the others. The other three were more surprising: they came from very different places – not just different from Repton but from each other. One had the most extreme strontium isotope value of all the individuals in the whole project. Put simply, this meant he or she came from an area with considerably older geology. The oxygen isotope values, which can tell us something about the climate they grew up in, indicated that at least two of them could have had origins somewhere milder than Britain. Finally, dietary information from their bones suggested that they had grown up eating different types of food from everyone else buried at the site.

These results were confusing. Clearly, the four had died at the same time, as shown by their simultaneous burial. But because they were so young, they must have arrived in Repton very recently, otherwise their isotope values would be much more similar. It therefore seemed very likely that they had reached Repton with the Vikings. This wouldn't have been unusual: we know some Viking armies travelled with children. When King Alfred attacked a Viking fortification in 894, the *Anglo-Saxon Chronicle* explains that he seized money, women and children, taking the Viking leader's wife and sons as hostages. In Repton, as the isotope results showed it was unlikely that all these children came from Scandinavia, it seemed unlikely that they had migrated with their parents, accidentally getting caught up and killed in a battle. Instead, another possible, if sinister, interpretation was that the four had been brought to Repton as slaves.

So this was the situation when the carnelian bead resurfaced that year. Repton had been reaffirmed as part of the Viking camp of 873, and all the evidence pointed to the mass grave being that of a group of marauding Vikings, perhaps led by a blue-eyed, balding warrior and his son, and maybe even accompanied by a group of women. But there were still several loose threads. Why were the mass grave dead from such different origins, and could some of them really have been from places not typically thought of as part of the Viking world? Had those children been sacrificed and if so, where had they come from? And was the evidence from Repton really the Viking camp in its entirety, or were there other traces of these people hidden in the wider landscape? Most importantly, how did the carnelian bead and its links further east fit into this picture?

The next discovery lay just a few miles downriver.

2.

DIRHAM: SILVER FOR A SLAVE

FOREMARK, C.873

*I*t's surprisingly light. The metal has been hammered thin and cut into a neat, large circle, fragile and impractical. The designs on either side protrude from the surface in intricate patterns and your eye is drawn towards them: curves and lines that contort in unfamiliar ways, like snakes that bend backwards and fold in on themselves. The coin belongs to another world. You've been told the designs are writing, that they contain names and messages in a language you don't understand.

You watch as the sharp iron knife is pressed against its edge, making a tiny peck into its side where, almost impossibly, the material shines even more brightly. As mesmerised by its design as you are though, it is its value you crave; its brightness proving its worth. Later it will be halved, then quartered, weighed out and traded for something even more precious to you.

EXCHANGE

It has long been known that the Vikings played a crucial role in the slave trade. Across Europe the Vikings traded in human lives on a grand scale. So how likely was it that the Great Army in Repton was involved in this too, capturing and selling people alongside their raiding activities? Could some of those buried in the charnel and, importantly, the children outside the mound actually have been slaves?

Nothing in the written sources directly links the Great Army to slave raids, but we do have references indicating that some of those who may have been present there were involved. In the *Annals of Ulster*, one record in particular stands out: in the year 869, Olaf and Ivar attacked Armagh in Northern Ireland. In actions that one would typically expect of the Vikings, they not only killed and raped the locals but also subjected 'ten hundred' of them to slavery. Later, they escaped across the sea, heading for the River Clyde and the Brittonic kingdom of Alt Clut ('Rock of the Clyde'). Together the two of them captured and besieged the Britons' island fortress at Dumbarton Rock in 870. After a gruelling four months their water supplies ran out and the fortress fell, forcing the Britons to admit defeat. According to the annals, in 871 Olaf and Ivar returned to Ireland with two hundred ships filled with enslaved Angles, Britons and Picts – people from different kingdoms in what is now England and Scotland.

While we can't prove that Olaf and Ivar were ever in Repton, it doesn't take too big a leap of faith to suggest that in this sort of environment, captives and slaves would have been a common sight there too, only two years later. An absence of anything written about slaves in the *Anglo-Saxon Chronicle*'s entries relating to the Great Army doesn't mean they weren't there; it could simply be that the chroniclers had little knowledge of or reason to write about them. In this scenario, considering the highly unusual isotope data and the injuries to their skeletons, it seems very possible that the four juveniles in Repton could have arrived there as captives.

Finding definite evidence for the existence and extent of the Viking slave trade is exceptionally hard: the archaeological record is, understandably, almost silent. How do you prove that someone was held in captivity, that they were unfree and perhaps had been taken by force from a home country far away and forced to migrate? Even in more modern times, most of our evidence for past slavery comes from written sources. Similarly, several historical sources give us clues about the Vikings' involvement in the slave trade but unfortunately none of them is very detailed. The Vikings certainly weren't the only ones taking slaves in early medieval times. As early as the 580s, Pope Gregory the Great apparently came across fair-haired slave children from what later became England in an Italian marketplace, and gave his famous response to the description of them being Angles (people from Anglia) that they were 'Not Angles, but angels'. Nonetheless, it does seem – at least from the written descriptions – that the Vikings were among the most prolific slave traders.

One place to start the search is to look at what we know about slaves in the Scandinavian homelands. Much of our knowledge about the Viking Age class system, and the existence of slaves in Scandinavian society, comes from the poem *Rigstula*, or the List of Rig, which is thought to have been written down in the tenth or eleventh century. In the poem, Rig, a pagan god, describes the mythological origins of three distinct social classes, namely slaves, freemen and nobles. From both this and the Icelandic saga literature it is clear that enslaved people were an integral part of Viking society, in which these people were referred to as a *trell* or *thrall* (the root of the modern word 'enthral'). Trells were essentially unfree, owned by somebody else and had no legal rights. They were unable to own property and were not protected from violence or abuse, although if somebody injured or killed another person's slave, they would be liable to pay compensation to the owner. It was possible to be freed from slavery, either through an act of generosity or practicality; otherwise this freedom could be bought. Yet most of the evidence we have from the written sources in Scandinavia seems to relate to how the slaves fitted *into* society, rather than how they were obtained in the first place. Little is known about how the buying and selling of slaves took place, or about the slave raiders themselves.

One thing that's clear is that many of the victims of slave raids were women and children, because this is often spelt out explicitly in historical records. One of the earliest of these relates to Ireland, where the *Annals of Ulster* have an entry for the year 821 of a Viking raid near Dublin in which, among other things, 'a great booty of women was carried away'. In a similar way, the *Royal Frankish Annals* also mention raids by the Vikings in the 830s, including one that specifies the captives included '*multas feminas*': many women. References like these have been hugely influential in creating the popular image of burly Viking raiders selectively picking out women for capture.

Perhaps that was true. An especially striking reference can be found in a thirteenth-century Icelandic account, the *Laxdæla saga*: this is the story of Melkorka, an Irish princess, whose fate reads much like a modern-day fairy tale. Here one of the protagonists, the Icelander Hǫskuldr, travels to a market somewhere in Scandinavia on the pretext of buying building materials for his farm. While there, he meets a man called Gilli, a particularly wealthy merchant known to have traded with the kings of the Rus', who has now turned to the business of selling slaves. Hǫskuldr decides he is not content with just his wife, who is looking after the farm at home while he is away, and wants to acquire a concubine. He proceeds to buy the most expensive of the slave girls that Gilli has for sale. After sleeping with her, he takes her home, not minding the fact that she appears to be mute. It is only after the girl has given birth to a son that she is first heard speaking – in Irish – at which point she proclaims herself to be an Irish princess named Melkorka. Hǫskuldr's long-suffering wife is, understandably, not too pleased with the appearance of Melkorka and her son, so the erstwhile princess is given her own farm to run. Her son ends up leading a very successful life and a relatively happy ending is ensured. Despite the clearly romanticised elements to the story, parts of it are particularly informative: the trader from the east selling slaves at a Scandinavian marketplace, the purchase of a woman to be a concubine, and the appearance of a slave with Irish origins.

It's likely that in a new territory such as Iceland, which was first settled by Scandinavians in the 870s, slaves would have been needed for a number of reasons, not least to provide labour in a fledgling settlement. Between the early ninth and eleventh centuries the Irish annals record scores of large-scale raids in which the Vikings took prisoners, presumably captured for the purpose of enslavement. A question to consider is to what extent this whole venture was planned: was slavery the product of well-organised, professional slave merchants or of more haphazard, small-scale opportunists? Some sources suggest Dalkey Island, just off the coast of Dublin, was a holding point for captured slaves before they were led to their final destiny, which indicates a degree of organisation and forward planning. One source from the tenth or eleventh century, the *Life of St Fintan*, indicates something similar in telling the story of a slave in the ninth century who was sold from one ship to another until finally ending up travelling to Norway or the Orkneys. In many cases, those who were taken never actually ended up in slavery at all: their capture would best be described as kidnapping, with the raiders determined to blackmail the victims' families rather than take them away. This type of ransom-taking appears to have been prolific and a lucrative way of generating income without the responsibility of keeping slaves alive, something that could be both expensive and demanding logistically.

The story of Melkorka isn't the only reference to an Irish woman ending up in a Viking settlement like Iceland and, intriguingly, modern scientific evidence may well back this up too. In 2005,[1] a DNA study looked at ancestry among men and women in Iceland and the northern isles of Britain, using modern DNA samples obtained from the existing populations. The study investigated two different types of ancestry: the male lineage via Y-DNA, and the female via mtDNA, which traces female ancestry as specific markers are only passed down from mother to child. The results showed that while the majority of Icelandic men (75 per cent of those analysed) had Scandinavian ancestry, a majority of women (62 per cent) appeared to have originated in the British Isles – including Scotland and Ireland. This was very different from what the researchers found on other, smaller islands in the North Atlantic, such as Shetland and Orkney, where Scandinavian ancestry was more equal among men and women. In other words, the study suggested that in Iceland in particular, women of Celtic origin had ended up interbreeding with Scandinavian men. However, while this scientific evidence seems compelling, especially as it appears to back up the historical sources so well, this certainly isn't proof that those women arrived there as slaves. We have no way of knowing whether or not they travelled voluntarily. Still, to unravel the questions of enslavement, the observed gender difference is important; as is a consideration of how genetic material is passed on. To be able to leave a genetic legacy, those who were forcefully taken would have had to reproduce to pass on their DNA. Isn't it more likely that enslaved women ended up as concubines or wives, and therefore had children, than enslaved men becoming husbands or lovers to do the same? In other words, even if equal numbers of men and women had been taken as slaves originally, the genetics would only show this if both sexes had reproduced at an equal rate.

Yet this is precisely what a new study of ancient DNA appears to show. Here the researchers analysed DNA from Icelandic archaeological skeletons dating to the Viking Age to see whether the individuals had Scandinavian or Celtic (Irish or Scottish) ancestry. They found examples of both origins, but they didn't find the same differences in the sexes as had appeared in the study of modern DNA, meaning that there was no evidence that more women had moved from the British Isles than men, in contrast to what the modern DNA study suggested. What is particularly intriguing, though, is that by comparing genetic data from the ancient and modern populations, they were able to show statistically that those with Scandinavian ancestry did, in fact, seem to have been more successful in passing on their DNA than those with Celtic ancestry. Even though this might not prove that those who arrived from Scotland and Ireland were slaves, it does quite convincingly show that many of them belonged to a different level of society from that of their fellow migrants who had come from Scandinavia.

In any case, it is clear that there was a demand that the Vikings were able to supply. We know that the trade in human lives was extensive in other parts of the Viking world, so the question is to what degree these same operations were carried out on a large scale in western territories like Britain and Ireland too – and especially in England. And what was the incentive; what did the Vikings get in return? This is where there is a strong link to the Islamic world, and it turned out that for our understanding of how this related to the Great Army a vital clue lay only a few miles from Repton.

RIPPLES FROM THE EAST

One January I had come to a pub in Derbyshire not far from Repton to meet a local metal detectorist, after a chance comment made on Twitter. A few weeks earlier I had been tipped off about a local enthusiast who believed he had found evidence of a brand-new Viking camp. This was exciting for two reasons. First, because I had never heard of Viking artefacts turning up nearby, despite long-held suspicions that there was another Viking site in the area, and second, because I had struggled to make contact with the local metal-detecting community.

Metal detecting is legal in England if you have the landowner's permission and it is a hugely popular pastime, which most carry out responsibly. The relationship between detectorists and archae-ologists, though, is complex and at times fraught. Without a licensing or training system in place, in principle anyone can pick up a detector and dig artefacts out of the ground, and even sell them on without ever sharing what has been discovered and where. This could, of course, mean a huge loss to historic knowledge. However, certain types of objects are classified as 'treasure', meaning that they need to be reported to the government: this includes hoards of coins, objects of silver and gold that are more than three hundred years old, and certain prehistoric artefacts. There is currently no requirement, other than with those treasure items, to report your discoveries to archaeologists or museums, which, for a very long time, meant that a vast amount of knowledge was lost to anyone other than the finders.

This has been particularly problematic for the study of the Viking Age because of the dearth of physical evidence for the Vikings' presence in England. Apart from Repton and other major sites like York, where archaeological excavations back up the written sources' evidence for Viking conquest and settlement, staggeringly few sites can be securely connected to the Vikings. We have no excavated Viking settlements, no farmsteads, no houses, and only a handful of Viking graves across the country. There are place-names that suggest where speakers of Scandinavian languages settled, but on the ground there is hardly a trace of them.

However, a recent systematic way of recording stray metal-detected finds has pretty much revolutionised what we know about Viking Age England. In order to combat the loss of information from those individual objects found by detectorists, a voluntary recording system called the Portable Antiquities Scheme (PAS) was established in 1997. Anyone who finds an archaeological artefact can take it to a local 'finds liaison officer' to add to a central database. As of 2020 more than 1.4 million objects have been recorded and the results have been extraordinary, revealing not only stunning artefacts but also hitherto unknown patterns of occupation and sites that have escaped the written records, from Roman villas to deserted medieval villages.

Still, as the scheme is voluntary, a lot has slipped through the net. I have spent hours trawling the database for Viking artefacts discovered around Repton, without success. Along with many of my colleagues, I had been wondering for some time if the discoveries from the excavations in the 1970s and 1980s really could be it: could a large force like the Great Army truly have descended on Repton and left no other artefacts nearby, and not a single trace of their presence in the wider landscape? Or was it simply that things had been found but not reported? Does an absence of evidence equate to evidence of absence? Surely, with the number of active metal detectorists around Derbyshire, somebody must know *something*. Despite working in the area for half a decade, I had absolutely no idea – nor did anybody else – what might have been found and not recorded. Until that day in January.

When I met him, Rob, who had spent endless weekends trawling the Derbyshire fields, picking up a wealth of local knowledge in the process, had brought along several of the finds he had discovered nearby. The first object he showed me was a fairly obvious one: a Thor's hammer. A partially broken pendant made of silver, it was a near match to that in G511's grave.

Although the hammer suggested a Viking presence, on its own it was not enough to prove this was a Viking camp or settlement. Other items found in the same location included Viking-style brooches and Anglo-Saxon jewellery, some of it having been deliberately cut into pieces at some point in the past, a practice common in the Viking world. Taken together, these finds did point to a substantial Viking presence in the area. However, the last objects that Rob showed me were the most important: several fragmented Islamic dirham coins. These were precisely what I had been hoping for as they represented one of the missing pieces of the puzzle.

Dirhams as single finds are relatively rare in England and to date in 2020, the PAS database lists only fifty-six such entries. Others have been found in larger quantities within hoards – hidden deposits of coins and other precious metals buried in the ground for safekeeping and later retrieval – but the PAS examples are individual coins found in isolation, as casual losses or from a disturbed hoard scattered by a plough. With a typical diameter of around 2.5 cm, these coins are significantly larger than the

Anglo-Saxon coins that were in circulation in the same time period. Made of silver, dirhams have several lines of text on both sides and usually an inscription in Arabic (Kufic) script along the coin's outer edge and in the centre. The coins are often exceptionally informative, typically carrying not only the name and date of the ruler at the time but sometimes also details of the year and location in which it was minted and who it was minted by. They are so important because they are direct evidence of contact and trade with one of the most powerful empires in the world at the time of the Vikings: the Islamic caliphate.

Yet this was a world with which, according to our traditional understanding, early medieval England had very little contact, and certainly not in areas like this, in the middle of rural Derbyshire. Coins such as these dirhams would have been of little use to your regular Anglo-Saxon farmers in the ninth century and consequently there is no obvious reason why they should be found in those contexts. Their presence in England appears to be entirely related to the Vikings and demonstrates not only the vast networks that they were part of, but also something crucial about the global stage on which their actions were played out.

Some two centuries before the Great Army appeared on English soil, an event took place in the Middle East with immeasurable effects on world history: in the year 622, the prophet Muhammad set out across the desert of Arabia with his followers, heading from Mecca to Medina, and this marked the foundation of Islam. Fast forward to the late seventh century, and an increasingly prosperous Islamic caliphate led by Caliph Abd al-Malik began creating silver versions of its gold coinage, the dinar. The new silver coins quickly became an established currency as the Islamic government sought to improve and establish control over its monetary system. It doesn't seem to have taken long before the coins started to circulate far beyond the spheres in which they could be used as legal tender and in the ninth century they were beginning to appear in large quantities in Scandinavia.

It is important to understand exactly what the dirhams represented to the Vikings and why the coins are found in such great quantities in the Viking world: the Scandinavians were interested in the coins' silver content, rather than their monetary value. Throughout the late ninth and tenth centuries, a relentless hunger for silver fuelled much of the Vikings' expansion. You could argue – and many have – that beyond a desire for political conquest and resettlement, a large proportion of Viking raids and attacks was driven by their insatiable need for this precious metal. Silver became a very important part of the Viking dual economy system, in which over time, ordinary coinage began to be used alongside a weight-based payment system referred to as a bullion economy. Much of the silver obtained by the Vikings was melted down pretty rapidly into silver ingots: small bars of metal that allowed for the silver to be saved, stored and traded. Silver fragments – either complete or cut into pieces known as hacksilver, like those found by detectorist Rob – have been discovered in hoards or as chance finds across Scandinavia and wherever the Vikings are known to have travelled.

Occasionally, we get glimpses into the intricate web of connections represented by the silver that the Vikings collected and with that, the networks stretching towards the east. An extraordinary example is the Vale of York hoard that was discovered by metal detectorists, dating to a few decades after the Great Army. In 2007, David Whelan and his son Andrew were out detecting in a field in North Yorkshire. What started as an inconspicuous bleep from a detector turned out to be one of the most important finds of its type discovered in over 150 years: a gilded silver cup holding 617 coins, 67 silver objects and a single gold arm ring. The hoard is thought to have been buried in late 927 or early 928. At that time Athelstan, king of southern England, had just reconquered parts of the country – including York – which for decades had been under Viking control. York had first been captured by the Great Army in 866 and used in part as a seasonal base on and off until 878. Then, from the late ninth century, it became part of a wider region in the north and east of the country that was under Scandinavian control, some-times (though imprecisely) referred to as the Danelaw. In the 920s, though, conflicts between Vikings and Saxons caused insta-bility, which may well have been the cause of treasures such as this being buried in the ground for safekeeping.

The individual items in the Vale of York hoard have highly diverse origins: the cup was made in France, perhaps raided from a Frankish church or paid as enforced tribute. The coins within it, however, varied from locally issued Anglo-Saxon coins to Carolingian currencies from the Frankish empire that dominated much of central and western Europe, alongside unusual Anglo-Scandinavian types. One of the latter is a so-called St Peter's penny, dedicated to the patron saint of York, which features a Christian cross on one side and a Viking sword and Thor's hammer on the other; emblematic of the hybrid identities forged by the early tenth-century Scandinavian settlers. Alongside these a large number of silver ingots and pieces of hacksilver show that the silver economy was also alive and well more than half a century after the arrival of the Great Army.

The international connections in the hoard are even more interesting: it contained fifteen dirhams, including one from a mint in Samarkand, in modern-day Uzbekistan, a key location on the Silk Roads. Another two objects can be linked to the east: a brooch pin similar to those found in a Viking hoard in Gnezdovo, Russia, and a fragment of a more unusual item called a Permian ring. These were given their name because they are most commonly found in an area near Perm in Russia, on the banks of the Kama river by the Ural Mountains.

The Permian fragment is part of a band with an incised design snaking its way around a rounded silver rod. It would once have been part of a large ring, designed to be worn around the neck. Complete neck rings like this have been found in Scandinavia, on islands in the Baltic and in eastern Denmark where many have been dated to the earliest years of the Viking Age. Most of the rings that have been found intact have been wound into smaller spirals, to be used as arm rings by the Vikings. Here's what's so interesting about these, though: while made to be worn either around the neck or the arm, they were specifically used as wearable currency, because the intact rings *always* correspond to a multiple of a specific weight standard. This standard is based on some multiple of 100 grams: Russian examples often weigh around 400 grams and in Scandinavia, lighter versions are found that weigh 100 grams and 200 grams. The Vale of York fragment weighs 26 grams, roughly a quarter of that 100 gram standard. The York fragment also exhibits testing nicks, four in total, showing that the silver had at some point been checked and traded. It's been suggested before that the number of nicks in an item of silver can give you an idea of how long it would have been in circulation, and I wonder if each nick represents a transaction; silver for a slave, four times over.

In the Viking homelands, weight-based and barter payment systems were the norm until the turn of the millennium, as the striking of coinage happened only on a small scale up to that point. Elsewhere in western Europe, the situation was a little different. In fact, between the eighth and tenth centuries, a relatively sharp division could be seen on the continent, with a boundary running roughly along the River Elbe in what is now Germany, by the eastern extremity of the Carolingian realm: to the west of this, a coinage-based economy was the norm while to the east, bullion-type economies took precedence. Intriguingly, the distribution of dirhams across northern Europe corresponds to this division, which suggests that the coins arrived almost exclusively via direct eastern routes and not through the Mediterranean.

In England, while coinage had flourished under the Roman Empire, in the centuries that followed coin production had practically ceased to exist. In the late seventh century a small amount of coinage began to be produced but it was not until the eighth and ninth centuries that coin-based currencies started to form a significant part of the Anglo-Saxon economy. King Offa, who ruled the Anglo-Saxon kingdom of Mercia between the 750s and 790s, reformed coinage through the introduction of the broad silver penny: a coin he used as an instrument of both his political and his economic dominion. Rulers also used coins to assert their power through artistic invention and remarkably Offa even produced a gold coin that imitated an Arabic dinar of Caliph al-Mansur, ruler of the Islamic Abbasid dynasty (754–75), though it is thought that this was mainly to be used for trading purposes in the Mediterranean. In fact, analysis has shown that many gold objects at the time were made from recycled scrap metal.

In any case, up until the reign of Alfred the Great in the last quarter of the ninth century, the use of money in England was generally confined to the eastern parts of the country; on a wider scale, payment was typically made by an exchange of goods throughout these centuries. However, by the time the Great Army arrived on the scene in the middle of the ninth century, the Vikings would undoubtedly have been very familiar with the place coinage had within the prevailing economic system, even if at that point they weren't producing any themselves. This means that they knew of and were part of two quite distinct payment systems, and the dirhams were emblematic of the second.

One way to discover whether artefacts were taken and used for their metal content is by looking for the test marks on silver objects: little nicks or pecks in the surface that show someone has tested the quality of the metal for its purity, no doubt unsure if they could trust the trader standing opposite. The test would both show whether the metal was of the correct hardness and reveal if the object was made of a cheaper material plated with silver.

There are a number of reasons why a bullion economy became so popular among the Vikings. First, it was a straightforward system to use: it enabled the quality and purity of silver to be easily tested and verified, and subsequently weighed out as payment. Second, this type of currency provided flexibility for a very mobile group: it was a form of wealth that could retain its value across the extraordinary distances that were travelled, while also being usable during more settled periods when you might stay in a single location for months or even a few years. Third, silver bullion could be used to avoid taxation. As a pure metal, silver was not a currency that had been issued by a ruler and would therefore not be subject to direct control by a distinct authority; this made it highly likely that it remained outside specific laws, especially in Anglo-Saxon England, and so less likely to be subject to taxation. It is easy to imagine that this would have appealed to the Vikings.

The increasing number of dirhams that have been found is showing us that the connections to the east may have been more frequent than we previously thought. But this still isn't giving us the full picture of just how much silver ended up in Britain and Ireland through the actions of Viking raiders and traders. What about all the silver that was melted down into ingots and bullion? Isotope analysis can finally start to answer this question.

On the surface, silver ingots give no clues at all as to the metal's origin. We can't identify a source by the object's designs: there is no twist of a Permian ring or intricate cast of a Frankish cup to reveal their artistic and geographical starting points. Melted down, none of that remains and until recently it was impossible to determine where the metal came from after it had been turned into a nondescript ingot. Yet, much like chemical signatures in human enamel, metals too retain traces of the environments they came from, leaving us with an opportunity to apply isotope analysis to determine their source.

In nature, silver is rarely found in a pure, native form. Instead, it is usually found in naturally occurring ores that are a combination of several minerals, like galena (lead and a small amount – up to 1 per cent – of silver). To obtain silver from such a combined ore, you would first extract the metals from other impurities through smelting and then separate out the silver through a process called cupellation. This involves heating the metal to a very high temperature, which causes the lead to be oxidised so that it can more readily be removed. However, there are always traces of other elements left – and that is good news because it is precisely these metals that can be used to look for geographical origins. To trace the source of silver, isotopes of lead are especially useful because the isotope ratios measured in a sample can correspond well with lead-silver ores in different geographical regions, meaning that it is possible to differentiate between sources of lead in for example western Europe (England/France) or central Asia.

A recent project is investigating the origins of Viking silver in England on a large scale, focusing especially on whether the silver came from continental sources or further afield. Jane Kershaw, an archaeologist at the University of Oxford who leads the project, has looked at silver ingots found in Viking hoards.[2] The preliminary results show that the main source of silver came from the east and specifically from melted-down dirhams. This means that we may have seriously underestimated the amount of the metal that has come directly from eastern spheres.

NEW DISCOVERIES

It is clear that imported eastern silver forms an extensive collection, not just from the later hoards, but also from the earliest phases of the Viking presence in England. That suggests that those who came to England in the 870s were already part of something bigger, something that stretched far beyond western Europe: a system and a network that was well established and highly functioning. Yet our knowledge of these early connections is recent and much of the evidence comes from new methods like Jane Kershaw's work on silver ingots. To unravel the bigger picture and understand these connections, we need to follow the trail backwards both in time and space and to understand how it fits in with what we know from places like Repton.

When I next met up with metal detectorist Rob, I had a chance to look through more of the finds from the Derbyshire field that he had identified. Among several copper alloy brooches – presumably looted or given as tribute – I spotted a small face: two eyes and a broad nose, likely a fragment of a Scandinavian pendant with a human figure, maybe a representation of Odin. There were also three tiny objects: small and unassuming, with a design that seemed markedly modern, which you could easily mistake for dice from a board game. The objects are called polyhedral or cubo-octahedral weights and are multi-sided measures made of bronze. Each weight has a series of dots on the main sides – between one and six, corresponding to their physical weight. In this way the weights could be used to weigh out small amounts of a commodity, probably silver, used for purchasing everyday items. A trader would have had his or her own set, as this meant that you could be completely sure that nobody was trying to con you. And new research shows that they are likely to have been based on a weight system that had been developed in the east.

Dirhams and dinars were also minted on the basis of set weights of metal in each coin. In fact, the currencies' origins in the pre-Islamic era stem from non-coinage weight standards that were used to measure out amounts of silver and gold. The weight of the dinar was about 4.26 grams, equivalent to one unit of weight called a *mithqal*, and the Islamic dirham weighed 2.275 grams: this was set down in Islamic law. At the same time in the Scandinavian homelands, a weight-based economic system was also in use, which we know about from later medieval written sources. Here the system was built around the *mark*, which was divided into the smaller quantities of *öre*, *örtug* and *pennies*. The *öre* appears to have weighed 24.5 grams, meaning the eight *öre* that made up a *mark* would add up to 196 grams – close to the 200 gram Permian rings found in Scandinavia.

However, it gets even more intriguing. Looking at finds from Sweden, archaeologists have discovered what seems like a combined Islamic/Swedish system because weights have been found that weigh 12.7 grams: three times the *mithqal* unit, and half an *öre*. The implications of this are extraordinary, as it implies a direct link between the two currency systems in use at the time. The reason for developing and using a weight system like this would have been to facilitate trade across different territories. It's tempting to think that the links between the Swedish and Islamic systems were there precisely because of the eastern connections, allowing for straightforward trade across areas in which the different systems were used.

The timeline here is important. The evidence from Rob's discoveries and from other sites in England makes it clear that these polyhedral weights were used by the Great Army, in the mid to late ninth century. For that to have happened, the weights (or at least their prototypes) must not just physically have had time to travel from the east, they must also have become part of an established system of trade. In other words, for it to make sense for the weights to be used by the Great Army, their use, design and conventions must have become both familiar and acceptable to a widespread and broad range of people.

We can't know how much time that would have taken: the timescales are difficult to unravel. Even with related finds like coin hoards, whose burial dates can often be determined fairly precisely, it is tricky to reconstruct a full sequence of events: how did each individual item get to this particular place, and what was its history? An important consideration in using these coins for dating purposes relates to the time it takes for them to travel from the Middle East to somewhere like England. The striking date of dirhams can often be determined pretty well because different issues were produced for very short periods of time, but several time-lags need to be considered. One delay comes from the time taken for coins to move from the place of issue to their final destination, but another relates to what was often a very lengthy period of circulation, especially when they were not solely used as currency in the strict sense of the word. Because coins were so valued for their silver content, they could easily be kept, saved and traded for quite some time after they had been obtained initially.

For this reason, trying to date a hoard or assemblage on the basis of the latest date on a dirham contained within it is unlikely to give you an accurate reflection of the *actual* date that the coins were lost or buried. While we can make an earliest possible estimate for when a coin arrived at a site, that's not always very helpful for single finds. By looking at the distributions of different coins as a whole, though, there seems to be a general delay of around ten to fifteen years between the coins being struck and their earliest arrival in England. What we can't yet answer is whether coins like these moved independently through a series of trade transactions without anyone making the whole journey from east to west or if specific people moved along with them.

Nevertheless, retracing the steps of individual finds and looking at the places that they might have come through might lead to more clues: starting with a better understanding of the site where Rob made his finds. The location was only about four kilometres from Repton and I had driven past it dozens of times, with no idea that the gently undulating fields hid so much new evidence. Here the road passes along the edge of a floodplain, where you can just make out a gentle slope to the right, but from this view-point the river is completely invisible, flowing a few hundred metres away. During the ninth century, it would have flowed right up to where the road is now. Further ahead, there is a steep escarp-ment on top of which you would have had a great view of anyone approaching from the north. The artefacts were found across a large open area and it's possible to imagine how it would have made sense as a place to pull up ships; a gentle beach where land met water. The fields stretch out far and wide, and it is easy to understand how this area could have sustained a large group of people: a whole army group with its hangers-on.

Further ahead on the road a lane goes to the south, revealing dusty red soil leading away from the floodplain to the small church of Foremark, the name of what was once a village. It turns out that the clue was in the name all along: Foremark, known in the eleventh century as *Fornewerke*, is a name that derives from the Old Norse *forn* and *verk*, meaning 'old fortification'. From there, looking to the south-east, you can just about make out a clump of trees that covers Heath Wood, the cremation cemetery with its Viking burial mounds. Until now its location here had made little sense but with Rob's finds, the jigsaw pieces were slotting into place. Other place names around there are informative too, like the neighbouring village of Ingleby, an old Norse name meaning the settlement of the Angles or English. With the knowledge that there was likely a Viking camp at Foremark and a subsequent Scandinavian village, we may have found the missing link between raiders and settlers.

Nevertheless, I am more interested in the early presence and especially the link to the east. Dating the site properly has proven difficult so far, but I do at least have an identification for one of the dirhams that Rob found there. This particular quartered coin was minted in al-Muhammadiyah, also known as Rayy, in the year 768.[3] It travelled from what is now Iran to the south of the Caspian Sea: overland today, a journey of more than four thousand miles. By the time it was lost in Foremark, it was already a century old, which means that it might well have arrived there via Scandinavia. The coin demonstrates a connection between Repton and the east, but to understand what happened, I need to retrace the Vikings' steps, travelling north, following the River Trent to where the Great Army stayed a year before arriving in Repton – a journey that was most likely made by boat.

3.

SHIP NAIL: RIVER KINGS

TORKSEY, C.872

The light is fading rapidly and you're starting to feel the pressure. Smoke from the braziers stings your eyes, the smell of it permeating every pore of your body. Time is running out. It is your responsibility to oversee the repair of the ships and they must be ready by daybreak. The atmosphere in the camp has changed and there is a palpable sense of anticipation in the air; excitement mingling with fear among the new recruits. The traders have packed up their goods, games and laughter have been replaced by the sound of weapons being sharpened and quarrels breaking out. But right now your attention is turned to the vessels in front of you. The salty water and long journeys across the open seas have not been kind to their hulls: timbers have rotted and iron rivets disintegrated, crumbling to orange dust beneath your fingers. The ships need to be in perfect condition as there is no way of knowing when you'll next have access to a safe port. You sigh as the boy running towards you with a handful of iron nails trips over a root and falls headlong, berate him gently while helping him pick them up from the sticky mud.

SEA STEEDS

I am in my study on a rainy afternoon, with every spare surface covered in plastic bags, boxes and reference books. This time the artefacts are those recently uncovered from the new excavations in Repton that I started a few years ago in an attempt to answer some of the unresolved questions about the Vikings. What I'm looking at is an extensive collection of iron fragments: rusty pieces of metal with only a hint of what they once were. We collect, bag and catalogue every single piece of metal we find. For most of them, we record the location in three dimensions, perhaps even photographing them in situ before they are taken out of the ground. I am specifically looking for nails with a square end. There is no shortage of candidates: in my collection there are over a hundred nails, and in the inherited collection from Repton there are an estimated six hundred. They were almost as ubiquitous then as they are today and just as in the twenty-first century, they could have been used for all manner of prosaic purposes. My attention is drawn to a small nail found two years ago, one we got excited about as soon as it came out of the ground. It is only about five centimetres in length, chunky and with a round head at one end and a square plate at the other. It's the latter that makes it interesting because it tells me not just who was there in Repton a thousand years ago, but something about how they got there in the first place.

The origins of the Viking Age and the mechanisms behind those origins have been debated for centuries. A factor usually considered instrumental in both is the development of the Viking ship: the exceptionally well-engineered boat technology that allowed for maritime exploration and warfare on a scale not seen before in northern Europe. The first time one of these ships came to light was in 1867, on a farm in southern Norway. The Tune ship, now exhibited in the Viking Ship Museum in Oslo, is the least impressive-looking vessel on display but in many ways it is the most inform-ative. Well preserved because of the particular soil conditions, the ship was discovered under a vast mound around sixty metres in diameter and at least four metres high.

When it was excavated by Oluf Rygh, a professor who went on to become one of the founders of professional archaeology in Norway, the methods used left a little to be desired by today's standards. The excavation was rough and ready, lasting only two weeks: a wooden frame was fastened to the bottom of the ship and horses were used to pull it out of the ground and on to a barge at a nearby river. From there it was floated down to the Oslo Fjord where it was towed to the capital city. Unfortunately, it turned out that there was no space in the museum so it was left outside until an appropriate space could be built to house it. The ship was later dated through dendrochronology (tree-ring dating) to around 905–910, and although there is evidence that there was a burial inside it, the skeleton and most of the grave goods were lost during the excava-tions. The ship had been used to transport either lightweight goods or, more plausibly, people, making it suitable as a warship. While larger ships like this could travel down shallow waters for riverine manoeuvres, smaller ships would have been far more practical and more commonly used for everyday journeys.

Viking ships were unique for several reasons. The shape of the ships' hulls, facilitated by a type of boat construction technique called clinker-building – a method where each plank overlapped the next – made them superior in stability and speed across rough seas. At the same time, their shallow hulls meant they were suitable for landing on beaches or travelling down narrow fjords and rivers. What's so special is not just the physical flexibility of the hull, but also the new invention of the keel: a structural beam running the length of the ship from bow to stern, stabilising the vessel, meaning that you could rig a sail on those shallow wooden boats. The particular combination of sail and keel allowed for a reach and a speed that were unprecedented. It also made the boats more manoeuvrable at sea.

Viking ships had hugely significant tactical advantages that enabled them to travel vast distances, but also to move through shallow water. The rudder could be pulled up if necessary, so that you could escape from an enemy ship by moving out of reach. They could also quite easily be pulled onto a beach, which makes sense at locations like Foremark. Both home and away, this allowed the Vikings to make use of portage: the dragging or carrying of ships overland in between waterborne routes. This, as we will see, became a critical element of their success in eastern Europe.

Yet despite their pivotal role in the Viking invasions, these ships have left behind little trace of their presence in the places that they travelled to. In fact, to our current knowledge, no ship or boat known to have been used by the Vikings has been preserved in the whole of mainland England. There are some examples from graves in Scotland and on the Isle of Man, but these are invariably small boats, rather than the longships that we presume were used in major attacks by the likes of the Great Army. Even when boats have been found in graves, all that remains of them is usually the ironwork, the nails and rivets, because all the other, organic parts have rotted away in the ground. Bar finding a complete wreck of a Viking ship at the bottom of the sea, our best evidence for their existence in England is, therefore, the metalwork. This is why the ship nail can also tell us about their presence in places like Repton.

The nails were a crucial component of the ships and it's been estimated that on large vessels, like the twenty-two-metre-long Oseberg ship found in Norway, you would have needed at least five thousand nails, meaning more than 125 kilograms of iron.[1] But even that wouldn't have been enough because iron fares very badly in salty seas, rusting and requiring replacement pretty quickly. Ongoing repairs of rivets and nails on the move would have been crucial: not to mention those needed to repair damage a ship might have sustained in other ways, like in a battle or attack. It now seems likely the winter camps were critical for the military success of Viking expeditions because they provided the opportunity to do exactly this, and evidence for that now lay scattered on my office floor.

The ships' sails would also have required tremendous resources. The adoption of large textile sails for ships had developed in the eighth or maybe even the seventh century in Scandinavia, fundamentally transforming connectivity in these northern regions. The sail itself wasn't new – sailing ships had been in use elsewhere for centuries before this – but in Scandinavia boats were typically rowed until sometime in the eighth century and it was only when sails were introduced that open sea crossings finally became practical on a grand scale. Most Viking Age sails were made of wool, because of the material's superior qualities: you could produce heavy-duty textiles that would withstand the harsh conditions encountered as a ship thrashed in the windy, briny waves of the North Sea.

In fact, having an intact and good-quality sail was as important as the ship itself, but this wouldn't have come cheap. According to the eleventh-century saga of Olaf the Holy, for instance, the otherwise hardy Norwegian Asbjørn Selsbane was reduced to tears on having a precious, high-quality sail appropriated by the king's men in partial punishment for illegally purchasing grain. When you look into the logistics of sail production, it's easy to understand why: estimates show that a ship with thirty pairs of oars would have needed a sail that was around 120 m², while a smaller merchants' ship would have required one of 46 m².[2]

Reconstructions have shown that to produce a 100 m² woollen sail with the methods available in the Viking Age would have taken a staggering 1292 days of work – three and a half years with no days off. You'd have needed to acquire 75 kilograms of wool, obtained from about 150 sheep. Clearly, access to these resources, to begin with, was vital for a successful raid. Maintaining sails en route, as well as repair to any damage sustained during a particularly bad storm or in battle, would have been another vital skill. Of course, sails weren't the only use for wool, as it is likely it would also have been used for tents and clothes, with some suggesting that semi-waterproof clothing was particularly desirable for waterborne journeys – understandably so.

Literary sources give us stories of legendary ships, but also useful insights into their making. The most infamous is the ship *Ormen Lange*, the 'Long Serpent', built by the Norwegian king Olaf Tryggvason in the year 1000 according to Snorri Sturluson's saga *Heimskringla*. The story goes that King Olaf commissioned the building of a new ship inspired by another he had captured, but he instructed that this should be superior in almost every way: far larger and more carefully put together, with bulwarks 'as high as in seagoing ships' and thirty-four benches for rowers, which would give the ship space for sixty-eight oars. The glorious *Long Serpent* was richly decorated: its head and arched tail gilded and its sail of magnificent proportions.

Snorri put the success of this ship down to its master builder, a man called Thorberg Skafhog. Thorberg worked on the ship along with teams of others to fell, shape and carry wood, as well as to produce nails: everything used was of the very best. Yet his perfectionism almost lost Thorberg his life. One day he had to leave the building work to the carpenters to attend to some urgent family business. The morning after he returned, the king arrived for an inspection, whereupon the disgruntled workmen informed him that someone had destroyed the ship overnight, chipping into the planks one by one under the cover of darkness. The king got so angry he swore to end the life of whoever had done this, presuming it had been done out of envy.

At that point Thorberg stepped forward and said he'd gladly reveal the culprit: it was, in fact, himself. He had been so disappointed by his team's performance that he had sabotaged the ship, knowing full well that it would anger the king. On pain of death, he began repairing the planks, shaping them in such a way that the ship was declared improved and considerably more handsome. In fact, what Thorberg had done to significantly raise the quality of the ship was to make the planks not just smoother but thinner and lighter as well, and therefore more flexible in the water.

While the story of the *Long Serpent* may not be entirely true, it illustrates the value placed on skilled shipbuilders and tells us something about the craftsmanship involved. Snorri's descriptions of the *Long Serpent* inform us too just how many people a ship like this could hold: at least sixty-eight pairs of oarsmen and thirty extra crew in the fore-hold. This has been a crucial factor in estimating the scale of the Viking invasions. In the 1950s historian Peter Sawyer counted ships mentioned in historical sources, multiplied this by the number of seats in each and used the calculation to estimate the size of the forces.

Larger ships were capable of holding livestock as well, including horses, which would have been of tactical advantage. There's an example in the Bayeux Tapestry, which shows William the Conqueror's invasion of England (William, of course, was a Norman king descendant of Viking settlers in Normandy, so the ships depicted are probably reliable representations of Viking ships). Here ships are shown with horses inside, leaping out into shallow water to take part in battle. There is evidence that the ninth-century Vikings used horses too, though we don't know if they were transported on ships: in a reference in the *Anglo-Saxon Chronicle*, we hear that in 881 the 'raiding army' that left England for the continent was provided with horses by their defeated enemies after a battle.

The use of ships as burial chambers is a reminder that the ship had a place in Viking Age religion too, and not just as a vessel for the journey to the afterlife. Some suggest that the boat was specifically meant to take the deceased to either Hel or Valhalla, depending on your fate. Norse mythology has a place for the boat, in the magic ship *Skidbladner*: this belongs to the god Freyr, the brother of Freya, and was created by the same dwarves who fashioned Thor's hammer Mjölnir. *Skidbladner* was an extraordinary ship, not the largest but considered the best, of the finest workmanship: its sails magically filled with wind as soon as they were hoisted, no matter what direction it was headed in. The ship was so large that all the gods could fit on it, complete with all their weapons and war-gear, yet when it was no longer needed for a voyage, it could be packed up into tiny pieces so that 'Freyr can fold it together like a napkin and carry it in his pocket';[3] a Scandinavian flat-pack creation of the finest variety.

The focus on Viking ships usually rests on their seafaring abilities, which is not surprising considering the impressive feat that travel to places like Greenland and Iceland represented. But we have known that movement along rivers was hugely important for the Viking success. This is evident both from the written records and from the distribution of archaeological sites: take Repton, Paris and Seville – all places where we know the Vikings set up camp or attacked in the ninth century, and just a few examples of sites that would have had to be approached from a river. In continental Europe, in particular, the written sources describe in detail how the Seine was utilised – actively, deliberately and with great success – by an invading Viking army. Conversely, this also required inventive methods for protection by the defending armies, as seen in a dramatic account of the 885 attack on Paris. Among other strategies, the defenders tried to defeat the attackers by throwing a burning, sticky mixture of hot wax and pitch on them, but in response the Vikings allegedly set three of their own ships alight to burn down one of the bridges that led to the towers guarding the city's entrance. So this isn't news: we know the rivers were vital for the movement of the Vikings across many parts of Europe. What we don't know are the actual details; we don't have the physical evidence or the knowledge of *how* this took place. Maybe the river's full significance as an agent in its own right has not been fully appreciated.

THE WANDERER

In the English Midlands, the Trent meanders silently through the Derbyshire landscape. Now the river is little more than a quiet escape from the bustle of modern life, encountered by most people only at bridges or in the occasional glimpse when travelling at speed on an A-road. Yet in the ninth century, the Trent was the source of the bustle here, although we know precious little detail. There are a few ways of tracing riverine usage in the past, with the most obvious being the historical sources in which such travel is directly described. Unfortunately, from this particular period, those are few and far between. There are written sources that are more coincidental, for instance records where ferries and crossing places are described. Indications can also be found in place names, like *Twyford* near Repton, suggesting the location of two crossing places – two fords. But to trace those who used the rivers for trade, warfare, transport or leisure, we need to know where those rivers themselves went in the past, and that is a bigger problem than you might think.

It is made more complicated by the fact that rivers have a clear tendency to change course over time, so that the course today may be entirely different from what it was a thousand years ago. This is clear both at Foremark and at Repton, from both of which the Trent is now far away. In fact, the name 'Trent' derives from a Celtic word meaning 'the wanderer': a wonderfully poetic name reflecting its ability to move and change course rapidly. You can see this clearly on satellite images: the scars of past river courses mark the landscape in the form of serpentine treelines and field boundaries, standing in sharp contrast to the straight lines of modern roads and hedgerows.

The lack of historical information from the early medieval period about the location of the Trent and other rivers presents a real problem. Maps in this part of the world are few and far between until several hundred years later, in the medieval period, and the few early maps that do exist were never meant to be used as navigational tools in the way that we would use them today. Rather, they were a way of illustrating the relationships between places on a more contextual level, making statements to illustrate anything from a historical event to a religious understanding of the world order. Take, for example, the numerous *mappa mundi*, early maps of the world: these typically include a breathtaking range of illustrations, from cardinal directions to flora and mythological beasts. While this can tell us a lot about the medieval mindset, it reveals little about early medieval navigation.

One exception is the so-called Gough Map, the earliest map to show Britain in a geographically recognisable form. What is particularly useful about this map is the way that it illustrates the vast network of rivers stretching across the landmass, which is tilted unfamiliarly onto its side: tentacle-like and swirling, the rivers appear as arteries connecting towns and churches with the coastline. On this map it is the rivers that strike you as the key to communication between one place and another. This must mean that the rivers were key to travel, too.

We are not entirely sure when the map was created, but the consensus is that it's likely from the fourteenth century. The Trent is clearly visible, with Derby and Burton-on-Trent, located just north-east and south-west of Repton respectively, marked out, showing that travel by river all the way from the North Sea coast would not just have been possible but also common at the time. But there is still a four-hundred-or-so-year gap between this map and the ninth century, and the map's lack of finer details means that it doesn't really tell us much about what the Trent would have been like in the Viking Age.

Fortunately, we now have an arsenal of scientific methods to help: from the painstaking observation of the ways in which grits, gravels and sands have moved as sediments through water, using a technique called micromorphology, to the new method of lidar – aerial-borne laser photography. This latter technique is particularly exciting as it reveals detailed imagery of height differences and topography, meaning that we can get a very accurate mapping and survey of the landscape in a way that has been impossible until now. Lidar works by a plane- or drone-mounted device emitting a pulsed laser beam towards the ground, where it reflects off any surface it meets. The pulse that is transmitted back up is measured and the distance that it has travelled is calculated; a bit like the way echolocation or sonar are used to show depths of water and to find schools of fish in the sea. Particularly usefully, the laser beams travel through foliage – in a similar way to how sunlight dapples through the crown of a tree – meaning that a highly detailed map of the lumps and bumps on the ground can be created even in a forest.

For Great Army sites, it's striking. In Foremark, the current meander of the Trent can be seen clearly along this stretch; as can several distinct older channels referred to as paleochannels. Before the river reaches the site, though, a definite bluff rises in the landscape, a steep limestone ridge that even includes a cave that was once an anchorage. The fields where the metal-detected finds were discovered is the first area along the stretch where you could safely have pulled up a boat or, rather, a large number of boats. Looking at the lidar maps, the location makes perfect sense.

TOWNS ON THE MOVE

Retracing the steps of the Great Army and the final leg of the carnelian bead's journey to Repton means that from Foremark you have to follow the river north to Torksey in Lincolnshire. This is the site of the historically attested camp where the Great Army stayed the year before Repton, not far from the Trent's confluence with the Humber – the gateway to central England from the North Sea. It was here, at Torksey, that discoveries made by metal detectorists over the past decade or two really began to rewrite the story of what we knew about the Great Army, forcing us to rethink the ways in which we study the Vikings in England.

Up until the twenty-first century, our knowledge of the Vikings in England, and especially the Great Army in the ninth century,

was surprisingly poor. With the exception of the excavations at
Repton, most of what we knew had come from the sparse historical descriptions of the army's movements, inevitably from the
point of view of the Vikings' opponents. The focus was firmly on
the Vikings' leaders, fleet numbers and occasional references to
'fortresses' or 'fortifications', without any elaboration of what these
actually were.

Those descriptions, combined with the archaeological evidence
of the huge defensive ditch excavated by Martin and Birthe in
Repton, led to a hunt for enclosed and defended camps elsewhere.
Yet for the next three decades, such camps evaded discovery. Several
sites in the Viking homelands displayed very visible defences, such
as at the Viking towns of Birka in Sweden, at Hedeby in what is
now northern Germany and at Trelleborg in Denmark: huge
symmetrical earthworks created by well-organised military units
with time and resources to build and to defend. Surely the force
that caused so much grief for the likes of King Alfred the Great
must have done the same. It turns out that the archaeologists had
been looking for the wrong thing. The discovery of Torksey made
this clear when a vast amount of metal-detecting finds came to
light that could only be associated with the Vikings, such as
dirhams, hacksilver and gold, Thor's hammers, and large quantities
of weights and measures.

The coinage left little doubt that these discoveries should be
linked with the 872–3 Great Army overwintering there.[4] The Islamic
coins date from the 690s at the earliest, in the form of one Arab-
Sasanian-issued coin, and continue to the 860s. Interestingly, the
dates on the ninety-three dirham fragments end abruptly, with the
latest dating to 866–8. This gives us a possible timeline suggesting
that the last direct contact with the east took place no earlier than
866, six years before the Viking camp at Torksey.

But while these dirhams and weights tell us so much about the

Vikings' contact with the wider world, and especially the east, it was something else that metal detectorist Rob had also found dozens of in Foremark that took us even closer to their world. He had found so many of these objects, in fact, that many had not been kept, as he had not realised their significance. A few years earlier, we had found four of them in the ground at Repton: small and rather ugly lumps of lead. The work at Torksey a few years before had demonstrated these to be the real calling card of the Great Army and this made it very exciting to find them in Foremark too.

The lead objects are just over a centimetre in height, usually conical or oval with a flat bottom. Sometimes they are hollow, sometimes solid. Many resemble thimbles both in shape and size and we believe they are gaming pieces used to play board games like *hnefatafl* or similar *tafl* games, which are a bit like chess or draughts. We know these games were popular in the Viking Age, both from historical sources and from the presence of full sets of gaming pieces (though usually made of bone, wood or glass) found in graves across Scandinavia and in new Viking territories and settlements in places like Scotland and Ireland. That games like this were a common feature of Viking life is something we are well aware of and it's also possible that they were part of strategic planning: it's been suggested that the burial of elite warriors with gaming equipment signified a symbolic role in planning military activities (an intriguing hypothesis, but not one I'm sure we can really prove).

However, gaming pieces made of lead seem to have been almost exclusively used or made in England. Most importantly, they appear to be linked specifically to the Great Army, its encampments and the parts of England where we know the Vikings either raided or settled in the early Viking Age. In fact, if you map all the gaming pieces found across the country by detectorists, the distribution matches the Danelaw division and the spread of Scandinavian place-names rather well, showing the predominant focus of Viking settlement in these northern and eastern parts of England. The gaming pieces found at Torksey exemplify how it radically changed our understanding of the Vikings' activities in this period, shifting attention away from a fruitless hunt for fortifications (despite several seasons of excavations and surveys, there are still no signs of any deliberately made defences there) onto something that turned out to be even more important: economy and craft activities.

I first saw Torksey one February on a particularly cold weekend, when the country had ground to a halt following a few inches of snowfall; appropriate conditions, as this was almost certainly the season it would have been used by the Great Army. The largely flat but gently rolling landscape must surely have seemed like a promised land for war-weary fighters ready for rest.

A bank constructed in modern times to protect the fields from the river, in a reminder of its tendency to flood and destroy farmland, yields a real sense of what this place would have been like eleven hundred years ago. The river here is relatively wide, around a hundred metres across, but the banks slope very gently as it snakes away to a well-defined curve in the distance. The water rushes by with surprising speed, the strong winter wind creating small crested waves and a current that makes it clear what an irrefutably good choice the river would have been for swiftly transporting large numbers of people across the country.

It would have been much quicker to travel between Repton and Torksey by river than on foot: experiments using replica Viking ships show they can maintain an average speed of 4–5 knots (approximately 8–9 km/h) and possibly as much as 9 knots for shorter periods. In fact, in 1893 the imaginatively named *Viking*, a replica of the Norwegian Gokstad ship, sailed across the Atlantic to Chicago. The ship carried a crew of twelve and was able to sustain heavy seas, with a keel that was exceptionally well suited to open sea travel. The speed of the ship was an average 10 knots and it travelled at up to 12 knots when the weather was good. The distance between Repton and Torksey along the river today is roughly 120 kilometres, meaning the journey could theoretically have been made in around twelve hours' or maybe even less. This would surely be considerably quicker than making the same journey on foot in muddy terrain.

Across the water, the location of the camp is revealed in a small unimpressive rise in the landscape. The camp seems to have had no defensive ditches, fortifications or other means of artificial protection beyond what was naturally provided by the river. Because of this, it would seem that those who camped here in the winter of 872 to 873 were fairly confident that either they would be left in peace or they were at such an advantage in the case of an enemy attack that they didn't need any elaborate defences. It is clear, too, that whoever had control of the land adjacent to the river would also have controlled movement on the river itself; it is hard to see how vessels could have travelled past this stretch if a large army was situated on either side.

It's quiet here now, but just as at Foremark, I try to imagine what it must have been like if you lived along this river, becoming aware of an approaching fleet of Viking ships sailing downstream towards you: the majestic, bow-shaped hulls, perhaps with elaborately carved heads at the stern – dragons and mythical beasts leaving you in little doubt that this was a force to be reckoned with. Or maybe they would have been simpler, more utilitarian: made for speed and efficiency. But they would no doubt have been colourful sights too, with vivid sails in white and red. We have found evidence for this in ship graves and from the sagas, some suggesting that the kings' or chieftains' vessels were marked out in a display of wealth and power. There would have been shields too, resting against the side of the ship, reminding you that these were not peaceful visitors arriving only for trade.

The choice of Torksey as a location for a winter camp was not coincidental but rather a very deliberate and strategic choice by the Great Army. Torksey, like so many other early Viking sites and encampments, was positioned at an important nodal point: where the Trent met a Roman road heading towards Lincoln, which in due course connected all the way down to London, or north-east towards York. This was like an early medieval motorway, with the Trent itself like a waterborne highway. Taking control of this part of the landscape meant that you would essentially be in control of two major transport routes. In fact, it has been argued that it was the strategic use of winter camps as bases with a combination of mobility by ship and by horse that set the Vikings apart, in terms of their military success, from other groups in this period.[5]

The use of the *wintersetl*, to use the Old English word for a winter camp, as a strategic element of Viking warfare makes a lot of sense when you see the site at that time of year. Flooding and mud would undoubtedly have made the movement of troops numbering in the thousands a challenge: marching for days on end in the unpredictable British weather could easily have jeopardised the success of a raid. The use of Roman roads in the post-Roman period is well known and if you drive any distance through England today, the chances are you'll come across one. They are recognisable, first and foremost, by being incredibly straight. Having been well built in the first place, it is not surprising that they continued in use. The importance of being able to move people around in a military context in this period can also be seen in King Alfred's late ninth-century efforts to create not only defences but also a network of roads known as *herepaths* – 'army roads' – to aid the movement of his forces.

Another thought that strikes me when I look out over the landscape around Torksey is a statement from the *Anglo-Saxon Chronicle*. The entry for Torksey for 872 says that here the heathen army 'made peace with the Mercians', meaning that an agreement of some kind was struck. Seeing how the site is placed in this landscape, and especially how well it relates to the river, some of this likely came down to access. Perhaps violence wasn't a necessary means of taking control here and it was more a matter of practicalities. We know from other sources that the Vikings were particularly apt at extortion: from the later examples of Danegeld, whereby the Anglo-Saxons were blackmailed into paying vast sums of money in order to keep their homes safe from attack (a case of 'either you give us your valuables now and you all live, or you give them to us after you're dead'), to the endless written examples of hostages taken only for ransom. If you were dependent on the river to transport goods or people in any way, you would be particularly vulnerable to taxation for its use. It would have been a little like a modern-day toll road, but with more dire consequences for non-payment.

There are many unanswered questions about daily life among the Great Army and those associated with it. Still, our understanding of it has changed, and we know that it wasn't purely a camp with military associations. As well as the army itself, there was a large group of hangers-on; camp followers who provided essential services like repairing weapons, mending clothes, and producing and supplying craft objects. In some reconstructions, camps are filled with tents lined up with military precision, much like you might imagine a Roman camp to have been. The reality was likely something far less organised. Perhaps it was more like a cross between a migrant camp and a music festival; the Calais jungle meets Glastonbury, but on a harsh day with icy rain.

One of the very few descriptions we have of a Viking camp

from this period comes from the continent, in a source from France written down sometime before 877. Here, in the *Miracles of St Benedict*, the monk Adrevald describes a camp on the island of St Florent le Vieil on the Loire. The Viking raiders had it 'organised as a port for their ships – a refuge from all dangers – and they built fortifications like a hut camp, in which they held crowds of prisoners in chains and in which they rested themselves after their toil so that they might be ready for warfare'.[6] Is that what you would have seen if you walked across this field in Torksey in the late ninth century? They must have become like miniature towns, these camps, where you could get hold of what you needed through barter and exchange.

In fact, it's been argued that the camps were a form of proto-urbanisation, a step towards the later development of towns both back home in Scandinavia and in the new territories elsewhere. The archaeological evidence from Torksey, Repton and from camps in Ireland now makes it clear that craftwork took place in the camps too. That repairs to weapons, ships and equipment went on doesn't require too much of a stretch of the imagination: clothes must have been mended and made, shoes repaired and exchanged. Still, some of the finds discovered by metal detectorists in Torksey were more surprising. Among the dirhams, gaming pieces and hacksilver, there was also evidence of bronze objects having been cast, most likely jewellery. We don't know who the intended buyers of these would have been or if they were made for the army members or for sale or trade externally. It's hard to imagine, though, that the finds of half-finished Thor's hammers – some of which match almost exactly the one that hung from a necklace around G511's neck – were not intended for the army members. The music festival analogy comes to mind again, with buyers strolling past stalls with an array of knick-knacks for sale alongside food vendors.

An army would have needed people with other specialist skills too, like medicine: someone to deal with battle injuries or who could help you if you caught an infectious disease, had a fever or needed to have a rotten tooth pulled out. We don't know who served these functions within a Viking army but with so many people living in close proximity, in what were presumably conditions with poor sanitation, it must have been important. A later Icelandic source, Snorri Sturluson's biography of Magnus Olafsson the Good, an eleventh-century king of Norway and Denmark, tells us that he allegedly selected twelve men with particularly soft hands to bandage wounded soldiers after a battle. In other cases, magic and religion could have been necessary fall-back options.

Another crucial consideration would have been food: a key concern for any military group. We don't know what the Viking armies subsisted on; most likely whatever they could get hold of or, rather, what could be stolen. It's been estimated that an army of a thousand men would have required as much as two tonnes of unmilled flour per day, or the equivalent, as well as fodder for horses and fresh water.[7] Sites like Repton would have been deliberately targeted for attack because they were locations where resources and food supplies could be easily obtained. A monastery or royal estate would have had an available store of food, acquired through taxes (known as *feorm*, or 'food rent') imposed on the local population.

In fact, the whole strategy of seasonal raiding, in which you set up camp in the autumn, could relate to this. At that time of year, around harvest time, stores would be full of food and it would be an ideal opportunity to obtain enough resources to get through the winter. In Frankia – the largest kingdom in post-Roman western Europe and predecessor of the modern states of France, Belgium, the Netherlands, Luxembourg and Germany – monasteries and royal estates were specifically equipped to be able to provision armies in addition to food stores they had for their own use: the emperor Charlemagne expected the monastery of St Quentin to be able to offer enough food for three months for a large force should he need it. This type of information must have been a welcome fact for a band of hungry Vikings. Perhaps the choice of camps by rivers was also influenced by the opportunity to catch fish for food.

Before we picture them as entirely pragmatic in terms of their food choices, though, we should consider another account from France, dating to the year 865, in the *Annals of St Bertin*, a chronicle from a Carolingian abbey in north-western France. This contemporary document gives a vivid account of the tribulations of the Franks, as well as the strategies that were employed by the Vikings. In this particular year, a band of Vikings was based on the Seine at Pîtres, just south of Rouen. One day, the annals state, 'those Northmen dispatched about two hundred of their number to Paris to get wine'. Unfortunately for the Vikings, they were unsuccessful and had to return unharmed but empty-handed. It is unclear whether the description is of a raid or some other attempt to get hold of alcohol by violence or if this was a peaceful trading venture, as either would have been a plausible option.

INTELLIGENCE

There is another significant commodity that must have been sought – and even bought and sold – in Torksey as well as everywhere else that the Vikings travelled, yet it is one we know little about: information. This would likely have worked on two levels: a higher, strategic and tactical level, and a more personal basis. Crucially, information would have been needed about navigation, travel, and the movements and defences of the enemy. It is likely that scouting and reconnaissance parties would have been sent out in advance of larger moves and smaller outposts created to facilitate information exchange. This highly important idea has received too little attention until now and it informs the sequence of events that led to the beginning of the Viking Age.

As we've seen already, the start of the period is ordinarily marked by the unexpected and dramatic attacks on Lindisfarne by a group of people who had allegedly never before set foot on British soil. Yet there is a problem with this idea: how would those first raiders have known where to go and what they would find there? A ship crossing the North Sea on a raiding mission would have needed to know the location of an undefended monastery with the significance and riches of Lindisfarne. The Lindisfarne attack and other similar strikes have been compared to terror attacks; carefully planned targets designed to yield maximum impact. And just as twenty-first-century terrorists rely on extensive networks for information and resources, so too would the Vikings.

In western Norway, analyses of grave goods suggest that the earliest contact across the North Sea originated from this region, which makes sense as the distance is relatively short.[8] It is here that the first of the loot from Britain and Ireland starts appearing in the archaeological record: fragments of intricately carved gilt book covers torn from the treasures that they no doubt encased and repurposed into fittings and jewellery; relic shrines, stripped of their holy contents and placed in a heathen grave. It's been suggested that the Northern Isles of Scotland was where the Scandinavians first heard of the riches that could be so easily obtained in undefended monasteries by pagans with no respect for the sanctity of religious institutions.

In fact, we now have an increasing body of knowledge suggesting that the first attacks on England didn't come quite so much out of the blue as we have been led to believe. A big problem with that perspective is that it suggests the Scandinavians were strangers to the inhabitants of Britain and Ireland, which is far from true. Take the letter written by Alcuin to Ethelred, the king of Northumbria, for instance, which so graphically described the Lindisfarne attack. For much of his letter, Alcuin launches a tirade against not just the foreign invaders, but also his own countrymen and women (Ethelred included) for the sins and 'unwonted practices' they are guilty of. Among these is the following admonishment: 'Consider the dress, the way of wearing the hair, the luxurious habits of the princes and people. Look at your trimming of beard and hair, in which you have wished to resemble the pagans. Are you not menaced by terror of them whose fashion you wished to follow?' Alcuin spells it out pretty clearly: people living in eighth-century England were dressing like and following the trends of those vicious pagans who had been subjecting them to terror attacks. How could this be, if there had been little or no contact across the North Sea beforehand? For context, it's worth remembering that Alcuin was writing in a period when much, but not all, of England had converted to Christianity, meaning that his ulterior motive was to use the Viking attacks as a sign of divine retribution.

Other documentary sources show the attack was not the first. We already know from the *Anglo-Saxon Chronicle* that the first properly documented raid on England had taken place six years before, in 787, at Portland on the Dorset coast. A raiding party apparently from Hordaland in south-western Norway brutally slaughtered the king of Wessex's representative who came to greet them on arrival at a windswept beach near a royal residence. However, more obscure documents, like grants and charters, which documented everything from property rights to demands, conditions and agreements between rulers, churches and other well-to-do households, reveal that measures had been taken to defend citizens against the Vikings in eastern England in the late eighth century. In Kent, a text describes privileges granted by King Offa to Kentish churches and monasteries in 792, freeing them from various dues and services but explicitly excluding military service 'against seaborne pagans with migrating fleets'. This included building bridges and fortification for defence. If threats from the sea were not a common and *established* problem, then surely these actions would not have been necessary.

Yet the sources could also suggest that not all those who appeared from the sea were enemies. Take the Portland attack, for example. The representative of the king, a reeve named as Beaduheard, rode down to meet the three ships with the purpose of forcing them 'in an authoritative manner' to report to the royal town, thinking them to be merchants instead of pirates. In other words, nothing in the appearance of these ships – presumably of a Viking type – led him to believe that he should approach armed or with the back-up of a military force. A later charter dealing with property rights in Kent, issued by King Ceolwulf in 822, hints intriguingly that some pagans may, in fact, not have been enemies. The document specifically talks about military service against 'pagan enemies'; the addition of 'pagan' here could be seen to suggest that not all pagans were enemies or even that some enemies were *not* pagan.[9]

It seems, then, that information about what could be found in those isles to the west was readily available when the first documented raids took place. But what about how to get there? It is likely that the Vikings used celestial navigation in some way; that they observed stars and constellations and used them as markers for directions and north points. Yet no written records survive and even the saga literature is silent on the exact use of such technical measures. It's likely that the passing on of information, in lieu of maps, would have been crucial; knowing which markers on land to head for. This is something we do have descriptions of, for instance in the Icelandic Landnáma ('land-taking') book from the twelfth century, a sort of *Who's Who* or telephone directory of Iceland's first settlers. The text also contains directions for sailing from a particular location on the western coast of Norway to Greenland: 'From Hernar in Norway one is to continue sailing west to Hvarf in Greenland. This course will take one so far north of Shetland that one can just sight it in very clear weather and so far south of the Faroe Islands that the sea appears half way up the mountain slopes and then so far south of Iceland that birds and whales will be sighted.'[10]

Likewise, when Ohthere of Hålogaland, a Norwegian seafarer, visited the court of King Alfred around the year 890, he described his homeland and the journeys he had taken along it. Most of his journeys were depicted in steps, based on how many days he had sailed along the coast or in different cardinal directions, using riverbanks and other landmarks to help him with navigation. It's long been discussed whether the Vikings used specific navigational tools too, but without a satisfactory conclusion. One possible candidate is half of a carved wooden disc found at a settlement site at Unartoq in Greenland: this has carved divisions that it has been proposed were not those of a sundial as some believe, but instead some sort of way to determine directions while at sea. Similarly, in the trading town of Wolin on the southern Baltic coast, an object thought to be a solar compass was recently found. More commonly proposed is the use of so-called sunstones, legendary crystals that would allow you to see where the sun was in the sky in very cloudy and foggy conditions. A recent computer-based simulation has shown that in difficult conditions checking your location with a crystal of this kind dramatically improves your chances of reaching your intended destination.[11] Even if there is no proof that the method was used, technically it would have helped.

More realistically, though, what you would really have needed was an extensive and thorough knowledge of the natural elements. In a thirteenth-century Norwegian text, a father offers the following advice to his son for him to become a successful sailor: 'You must observe the movements of the heavenly bodies and make a careful study of how the sky is illuminated, how night is divided from day, and how day is divided into several time-periods. You must also learn how to monitor the sea-surge and understand the significance of its ebbings and swellings, because that is essential knowledge for seafaring men.'[12]

These, then, were the sort of considerations that would have been needed by those who had arrived in Repton.

Back on the trail of the carnelian bead, I assume it travelled through Torksey and tracing the river north brings us to the Humber. Here you come to another junction, an exceptional meeting point of three rivers: the Trent going south, the Ouse going north – an artery connecting all the way to York – and the Humber, which takes you out to the coast and to the North Sea. From the mouth of the Humber, as the crow flies, the distance to the coast of Denmark is around 550 kilometres, about as far as the drive by road from London to the Scottish border. It is possible to reduce the time spent in open water by hugging the coastline north around Scotland, stopping off in Orkney, then Shetland. From there, the distance across to Norway is only 300 kilometres. Whichever route you chose, the Viking ship would have been more than capable of making these crossings and in principle the journey could have been completed in under a week in a ship sailing at full speed.

Nevertheless, it isn't immediately obvious how the goods from the east – the bead, coins and other commodities like silk – would have reached England. If we assume that they travelled primarily by water, there are two plausible routes. First, there's the option of the Mediterranean: we know from historical records that there were numerous Viking raids along the western coast of France, in Spain and the Iberian Peninsula, and that they reached the western Mediterranean through the straits of Gibraltar, raiding the coastline of North Africa in attacks on Morocco. From there they may also have travelled across to the eastern Mediterranean to obtain goods or even to go inland. But we have no direct evidence of this connection; we might, for example, expect to see dirhams that had been minted in Islamic parts of Spain. So far none have been found in the ground in England. Equally compelling is the fact that there are very few known artefacts from the Iberian Peninsula or the western Mediterranean in England. The second, more likely option, is that the goods, and my bead, arrived via Scandinavia.

PART TWO

HOMELANDS

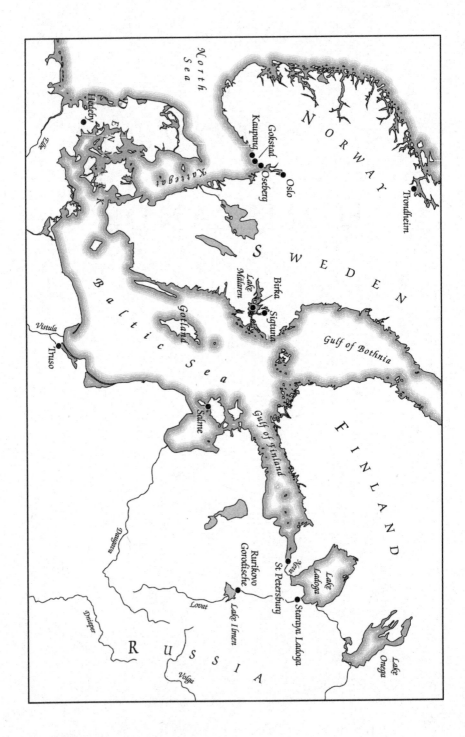

4.

BUDDHA: THE ALLURE
OF THE EXOTIC

STOCKHOLM MUSEUM, 2017

Quiet and serene, he sits looking through the glass from a dark alcove, lit by sharp rays of light that reflect off his shiny, green body. His lips are pursed into a gentle smile and his legs are folded and contorted on top of each other. An air of benevolence and patience radiates from his presence, even here in the small museum space that has been taken over by a rambunctious group of schoolchildren smelling of rain-soaked jackets. The figure stops you in your tracks because he is unexpected. For a moment, you wonder if he has been misplaced or if his presence in the Viking gallery is the result of someone's modern curatorial strategy to surprise and to contrast. He's exotic here, part of another world. Everything about him is different, from his hairstyle to his clothes. The lotus leaf beneath him conjures images in your mind of a culture and a climate you recognise from holidays and the similar statue you recently bought as a garden feature.

IMPORTED OBJECTS

In 1956, a curious and unexpected object was found on a small island in a lake not far from Stockholm. The island of Helgö had once been home to a bustling community of traders, with an emphasis on craftwork. Its name, which means 'Holy island', is testament to some long-forgotten former religious importance. As the small bronze Buddha statuette was pulled out of the ground in an early medieval context, its excavator thought it must be there by mistake: perhaps a souvenir lost in recent times. As it turned out, it really *was* historic and had likely been buried at some point just before the start of the Viking Age. The statue is now so famous that in 2015 it received pride of place on a stamp released by the Swedish postal service: in a multicultural twenty-first century, here was proof that the Vikings of Sweden's past had been the ultimate explorers, already – more than a millennium ago – living in a globalised world with far-reaching networks.

Today the Buddha from Helgö is a curiosity, and it would have been in the Viking Age too. It's unlikely that the Vikings had any knowledge of Buddhism; there is absolutely no evidence in written sources to suggest the religion reached this north-westerly part of Europe until several hundred years later. When it was discovered, the Buddha had traces of a narrow leather strap wrapped around its neck and left arm, suggesting that it had been carried, hung around someone's neck or suspended from a belt.

The Buddha is actually one of three highly exotic items found at this site, the others being a bronze ladle from the eastern

Mediterranean, possibly Coptic Egypt, and a fragment of an Irish or British crozier adorned with a slithering beast and a man's head – a representation of Jonah and the whale, symbolic of the resurrection. The ladle was originally a religious object too, used as a liturgical baptismal implement. Regardless of whether these objects had anything to do with each other or if their religious contexts were even important, they fit into the same category as the carnelian bead and the dirhams: they were exotic imports that had travelled long distances. To understand why a carnelian bead turns up in Repton, we need to under-stand how objects like these fit in to the Viking world in general.

Carnelian beads begin to appear in small numbers in Scandinavia in the first half of the ninth century. Then, suddenly, it's like an explosion: they're everywhere. This particular material and similar beads have been used for many millennia in other parts of the world; they were certainly not exclusive to the Viking Age. Yet it was precisely during this period that their popularity increased so rapidly in Scandinavia, both because of higher demand and a new means of supply. The beads moved along the same routes as the Vikings. For this reason, beads like this are a powerful way to understand trade, networks and the movement of people, especially because of how they reflect rapidly changing fashions.

To find out more, I started searching museum catalogues for other carnelian beads and found many of them in graves all across Scandinavia. In one study, a student had trawled through 266 graves from Norway to look for patterns in who these beads had ended up with.[1] Intriguingly, she noted that carnelian beads were found exclusively in women's graves, usually as necklaces, even though beads in general were worn by men too (the Repton warrior being a prime example). For men, though, the beads were never of imported, luxury materials like carnelian. She also discovered that in many cases, beads in men's graves were found not around the neck but by the hip, which could mean they had been placed in a purse or bag. Sometimes they were found with other things like coins. This, then, could suggest that beads were more of a commodity or means of exchange than they were jewellery.

To better understand what happened with these beads, I turned to the ultimate guide for anyone interested in Viking beads. In the 1970s, Swedish archaeologist Johan Callmer painstakingly gathered, studied and classified almost fifteen thousand Viking Age beads from graves across Sweden. He divided them all into types, classified their colours and shapes, and placed them into a contextual chronological system. In this way, he was able to show how trends had varied over time. Checking the chronology for beads that match that from Repton, a trend was pretty clear to me. Looking at 879 carnelian beads, Callmer showed that the first had arrived in Scandinavia in the period between 820 and 845, in a very small number: only fifteen beads found. A few decades later came a dramatic increase, with a total of 450 dated to between 860 and 885. This is, in fact, almost a quarter of the entire collection of carnelian beads that have been found across the Viking Age. The distribution of the beads then fluctuated, but this was exactly what I was hoping to find. That brief twenty-five-year period matches the timing of the Repton bead's burial in 873 perfectly, and what's more, it fully supports the suggestion that the bead could have reached England via Scandinavia.

So who was bringing the beads into Scandinavia, and where had they come from? All those classified by Callmer had been found in burials but in recent years many more beads have been discovered at trading sites. For example, in Norway in 2012 a brand-new site was discovered through the use of new technology: a ground-penetrating radar (GPR) survey.[2] In this method, a unit sends radar waves into the ground. These reflect back to a computer every time a variation is discovered; this could be anything from a simple change in soil type to a buried wall or even a buried Viking ship. It's one of many methods that allow us to see beneath the soil without digging a hole.

In this particular case, the GPR identified a new settlement or marketplace at Heimdalsjordet, near the Gokstad burial mound that was home to one of the most famous Viking ships ever discovered. The survey revealed a street lined with buildings, and a subsequent metal detector survey unearthed vast quantities of objects in the plough soil. This included craftworking residue as well as, importantly, trading weights like those found at the camps in England and large numbers of dirhams. Oddly, there were very few European coins: almost all the coins discovered were linked to the east. Not only that, several carnelian and rock crystal beads were also scattered across the area. All the signs suggest that this was some sort of coastal trading site where exotic goods may have been traded and exchanged, perhaps including slaves – a site like that where Hǫskuldr bought Melkorka.

TRADING TOWNS

When the merchant Ohthere visited Alfred in 890, he described his journey to a place called 'Sciringes healh'. It has now become clear that this was the site of Kaupang in Vestfold, Norway, on the western side of the large bay of Viken (the Oslo fjord). Viken has even been suggested by some to be the origin of the word 'Viking', though that interpretation seems a little spurious. Kaupang, on the other hand, literally means 'trade bay'. During the Viking Age, Kaupang was probably as urban as you could get in what is now Norway. Its location is no coincidence. This western side of the fjord forms the chief sailing route along the coast while just a few kilometres east of Kaupang lies the mouth of the River Lågen, the main route inland. This coastal zone is among the most fertile regions in the whole of Norway. Further inland, you could reach areas that were big producers of trading goods important for export, like soapstone, minerals for whetstones, and iron.

Kaupang was established around 800 and at the time of its emergence it belonged to the realm of the Danish king in a border zone with the territory of the Northmen, which would later become Norway. There's plenty of evidence for craft activities having taken place there, like blacksmithing and glass bead production, with the land divided into individual plots including permanent build-ings that would have been in use for several years. The craftworking was specialised and refined, one plot yielding substantial evidence for the casting of metal to produce jewellery and mounts in both lead and precious metals. Outside this zone, another area was used more temporarily; tents may have been set up there whenever markets were held, giving space for transient seasonal traders. Finds from Kaupang include dirhams and carnelian beads, even if only a few.

Now here's what's really interesting: Heimdalsjordet, which was more or less contemporary with Kaupang, contained far more objects with links to the east, including imported beads like carnelian and rock crystal – 24 per cent of the total as opposed to only 2 per cent at Kaupang. Could this mean that different people were based here, people who had more of a direct link with eastern networks?

Knowledge of sites like this is relatively new, comparatively speaking: excavation work at Viking towns such as Birka in Sweden and Hedeby near the border between Denmark and Germany started properly in the 1970s and from this point, radical new information about urban growth in Scandinavia started to come to light. Previously, attention had been focused firmly on rich graves, raids and warfare, but in the latter part of the twentieth century, archaeologists were more eager to emphasise the less violent side of the Vikings and, specifically, their involvement in trade. As a result, we've gained significant information about how the exotic imports fit in. But to appreciate this fully, we need to understand the world that the Vikings as we know them inhabited.

In Scandinavia, what we refer to as the Viking Age was the final stage of the period known as the Iron Age, which stretches back as far as 500 BC. Scandinavia had never been part of the Roman Empire and for this reason, classical writers like the historian Gaius Julius Caesar described Scandinavians (along with all other Europeans north of the Rhine) as 'barbarians' who were both culturally and economically inferior. In his opinion, the problem was that they lacked centralised institutions, as well as the bureaucracy and wealth that came with the cities and superior social order that had shaped western and central Europe since the beginning of the first millennium.

The reality of life in the north wasn't quite as dismal as Caesar described. Even if direct engagement with the Roman Empire was relatively limited, information trickled through and many new technologies were adopted in the borderlands with the Empire, reaching Scandinavia through long-distance exchange and networks. There is evidence of influence from the Roman world in Scandinavian agricultural and production technologies, social organisation and even military tactics, which all fed into later developments.

However, it was during the Viking Age that urbanism first took proper hold in Scandinavia. Up to this point the region had been characterised almost entirely by rural settlements, despite urban communities being commonplace elsewhere in Europe at the time. Even around the year 1000, only a handful of towns in the true sense of the word were in existence, until a second and more extensive wave of urbanism hit Scandinavia thereafter, resulting in the establishment of new towns like Sigtuna (Sweden), Roskilde (Denmark) and Oslo (Norway). But in the eighth century, Scandinavians would already have been well acquainted with the larger communities in existence a short distance away in continental Europe. Even though it led to only a tiny proportion of the population living in towns, the change in settlement patterns had a huge impact, not least on trade, and thereby also on developing economic practices. The towns were also instrumental in changing society as a whole from a series of tribal communities into the three kingdoms of Norway, Sweden and Denmark that emerged towards the end of the Viking Age.

This is important, because the political structure of the society influenced not just the success of the towns, but also the dynamics of trade and contact with other regions. The early part of the Viking Age was characterised by political instability; in later years power became more institutionalised, with greater dependence on an established legal system. Earlier on, local rulers' successes had been measured in their ability to attract and retain allies. This had become an essential part of a chieftain's ability to sustain local control over an extended period of time. The saga literature is filled with examples of just how important this was and how precarious life could be; the intrigues and soap-like dramas reveal an undercurrent of power-plays on a massive scale. Having access to ample resources was key not just for the straightforward reason of being able to feed your family, but also in order to keep those under your control happy by providing feasts and supplying essential commodities like beer.

Beer was, in fact, the key to a successful feast and the feast was a pivotal social and religious event, which could help you to establish and to maintain power. If your crops failed, there could be a lot at stake. Take the story of Asbjørn, for example, who was the son of a chief in northern Norway. One year he had such bad crops of barley that he had to buy grain from friends in order to hold his annual pagan winter feast. Otherwise he wouldn't be able to brew enough beer, and a Viking feast with no beer was no party at all. But Asbjørn's bad luck ran deep. The king intercepted his precious purchase and appropriated the barley. Seeing his predicament, a rival chieftain invited the beer-less Asbjørn to join his feast instead, but Asbjørn was forced to decline. If he accepted an invitation to another's feast rather than arrange his own, he would be admitting that he didn't have the resources to act as an independent leader.

The crux here – and the moral of the story – is that in Viking Age Scandinavia, land-based resources were crucial to success, but they were also very limited. Take a look at a map of Scandinavia and you will quickly see why: with its mountainous interior and dramatically narrow fjords and valleys, Norway is not geographically suited to agriculture on a large scale and Denmark, while flat and suitable for farming, is minuscule in comparison. Those who were successful would have increasingly sought ways to demonstrate this to those around them, as can be seen at the wealthy chieftain's farm at Borg in the Lofoten Islands, with its eighty-metre long hall – one of the largest-known buildings from Viking Age Scandinavia. The contrast between the resources available there and those somewhere like England would have been clear; when Ohthere described his wealth to Alfred, the latter was shocked at how little land Ohthere had and how few livestock he possessed (merely twenty cows, sheep and pigs, in addition to his strange collection of wild reindeer). At the same time Ohthere described himself as a wealthy and prosperous man. However, precisely because land-based resources were so limited, alternative sources of wealth included not just raids and trade but also taxation and control of exports, as well as the control of transport routes inland – especially along rivers.

It is crucial to understand that increasing urbanism had its roots in trade – both to the west and to the east – and, importantly, in seaborne networks. Proto-urban trading sites known as *emporia* had developed in the period leading up to, and in the earliest phases of, the Viking Age, always near water, either a river or sea. There is a string of these around the Baltic Sea, especially on the northern coast of what is now Germany and Denmark, sites like Hedeby and Ribe, and along the coast of modern Poland. These were places where objects could be traded and where craft activities sprang up, not to support a population that was already there, but instead for one that had arrived precisely to take advantage of new opportunities.

The emporia became part of a large network and were known stopping places in strategic locations: for example where a river met the sea or somewhere you would stop because of difficult travel conditions. Hedeby, near the border between Germany and Denmark, for instance, was located by an inlet leading to the Kattegat strait and the Baltic to the east, at the narrowest part of the landmass – a distance of eight kilometres overland would connect you to rivers taking you straight to the North Sea. In these places you could sell your goods or get hold of the provisions needed for the onward journey; stop to make repairs to your ship; or maybe even recruit new members for your crew. The Viking camps we see in England in the ninth century must surely have acted very much like this but on a smaller scale.

Early emporia were not only found in Scandinavia but on the coasts of north-western Europe, including in northern France, the Netherlands, and in England at sites like London, Ipswich and York – locations where they originated as early as the seventh century. The sites also sprang up elsewhere around the Baltic Sea.

It's likely through these that exotic goods started to find their way into Scandinavia, and what they all had in common was their maritime links. Geography, after all, had a huge impact on this region because nature could be as much a barrier as a connector. Incidentally, it may have been through the emporia that knowledge of sites prime for raiding was obtained. Portland, the site of the first recorded Viking raid, is only a short sailing distance along the coast from the trading settlement at Hamwic – now Southampton. Perhaps this explains why the reeve Beaduheard wasn't alarmed at the sight of Scandinavian ships and why Alcuin was tired of the negative influence of pagans on the Saxons.

When trying to understand exotic objects and their appearance at sites like this, there is one place above all that is critical to understand. Not far from Helgö, where the Buddha was found, once lay the bustling trading town of Birka: one of the most significant towns in Viking Age Sweden. Located on a small island in Lake Mälaren – now a freshwater lake thirty kilometres west of Stockholm – Birka could be reached by boat from the Baltic Sea. The town emerged sometime in the eighth century, probably around 750 or just before, as an important site linking inland places like Uppsala with the vast trading networks that could be reached across the Baltic. It either developed from a smaller seasonal trading post or could have been founded by a king to try to control and to expand trade. Despite covering only an area of around five to six hectares, its townsite, the Black Earth, was surrounded by a complex defence system including a rampart, an underwater palisade and a hillfort, making it clear that this was somewhere worth defending. It is notable that from the very beginning Birka was fortified: clearly, a vital part of its existence. This was a town controlled by a political authority whose power was there to be seen, even more so in its later life.

Over time Birka became quite heavily populated by Viking

standards; its cemeteries are extensive and contain a staggering two thousand burial mounds along with a substantial number of unmarked graves – maybe as many as five thousand burials in total in the town's two-hundred-year lifespan. Many of the graves were richly equipped with objects from far and wide, testament to a wealthy population. Some of them were elaborate chamber burials: subterranean rooms for the dead, in which their final resting place had been carefully and deliberately arranged with objects needed for the afterlife. Birka seems to have focused on trade and craft production in what has been described as a complex early urban society. Excavations in the settlement area yielded specialist craft workshops and evidence of household activities, while the town appears to have been supported by a considerable hinterland beyond the lake, with plenty of opportunities for agriculture, the collection of raw materials and the exploitation of wild game, especially animals from which furs could be produced and exported. Birka's contacts with areas around the Baltic were extensive. In its earliest phases, in the late 700s, these seem to have been focused to the south-west, trading with Denmark and beyond to the Rhineland.

Around the end of the 800s, something changed dramatically at Birka and contacts with the east were clearly established. Silks and silver appear, and it seems that Birka was one of the earliest places in which the eastern-based weighing standards were used. This happened in the 860s at the latest.[3] Just as in the study of the origins of silver in England, it has been possible to look at the isotopic variation in lead found at Birka as well. The results have been surprising: the majority of the metal in the Birka lead weights turned out to have come from England, and from Derbyshire to be precise.[4] In other words, it's likely that they were made of metal mined somewhere near Repton. We can't know, of course, whether the objects themselves were made in England or manufactured back in Scandinavia from recycled lead.

It transpires that the weights weren't the only objects made from Derbyshire lead that have been found in Scandinavia: the same was the case for a set of pewter mounts from a horse harness that was found in the Norwegian Gokstad ship burial, which dates to 895–903.[5] This is real evidence of the metal having been taken from the west back to Scandinavia and it's very possible that the Great Army, and the conquest of Mercia and Repton, in particular, was instrumental in this trade. It seems that the monastery at Repton was, if not in charge of, then at least influential over the lead mines at nearby Wirksworth and perhaps this was part of what the Great Army had been aiming for upon taking control of the monastery. Now that we have so much new information about the ways in which weights were used in the Vikings' English camps, we should reconsider whether in fact they were manufactured in England rather than in Scandinavia.

EASTERN CONNECTIONS

There is a series of objects from Birka with undeniable links to the east, and one in particular is very compelling. In the nineteenth century, Swedish archaeologist Hjalmar Stolpe excavated a large number of the town's richly furnished graves. Over the years many have tried to interpret whether the grave goods and types of burial in Birka could tell us whether they were those of locals or of immigrants, but this has proven a futile task.

One of the graves is that of a woman in a rectangular wooden coffin. Based on the clothing and jewellery she was buried with, the grave could be dated to around 850. In addition to brooches, she had a row of beads including glass, crystal and carnelian, while her clothing remains showed that she was dressed in typical Scandinavian fashion. Remarkably, she also had a finger ring lying on her chest, made of a white metal and set with a violet-coloured stone: one of four similar rings found in Birka of a typical Arabic design. This one, though, left no doubt of its eastern connections as it had an inscription in Arabic that read 'for Allah'. Rings like this, with Arabic writing, are rare in Europe and this is the only one found in Scandinavia. Was this, too, a traded object?

That's what has been assumed up to now, but recent scientific analysis of the metal has suggested a different story.[6] A 3D model made from photographs was combined with images from a scanning electron microscope – giving an extremely close-up view – and elemental analysis to detail precisely what materials it was made of: very high-quality silver, with, importantly, very little wear. The filing marks on the inside remained, traces of the original mould that had been used to cast the ring; the marks of the craftsman had not worn away through use. This was unusual: most objects found in graves, such as bronze jewellery, have evidence of wear. The inscription on the ring was in an angular, early Kufic style showing its clear association with the Islamic world. This new evidence suggested that the ring had passed from the silversmith, maybe somewhere in the caliphate, to the woman buried in the grave with very few steps in between. Could this mean that she, or one of her family members, had migrated and brought the ring with them?

A twist in the tale is that others have argued that the inscription isn't in an Arabic script at all.[7] This is because, it's claimed, it doesn't fully resemble Kufic script and even if it does, a proper interpretation of its message renders it meaningless. Instead, it's possible that it's something called 'pseudo-Kufic', a type of imitation of an Arabic inscription much like what Offa placed on his gold coin back in the eighth century. This would make it more likely that the object was made outside the Islamic world. But in many ways, the veracity of the inscription – whether it's genuinely Kufic or not – doesn't really matter. Objects like these carried very specific meanings in Viking society, but those meanings may not have had anything at all to do with their original purpose. The inscription could likely not be read by its wearer. Instead, the ring was important as a marker of the *exotic*, showing that you had links with those external worlds and an ability to travel, or to obtain imported goods. This, then, could be a way of securing your social position at home or even of elevating it. A similar example can be seen in the pseudo-Islamic designs on trading weights found at Heimdalsjordet that would have invoked not just the exotic but associations of eastern silver, which was of very high quality.

We haven't always understood the power of small objects like beads, rings and pendants to inform us of wider trends and cultural phenomena. For a long time beads were considered mainly as adornments; objects to be classified, described and catalogued in order to tell us about trade and the import of goods, maybe even to give us a hint at dating. Now, we understand better how well placed they are to tell us about cultural customs and connections, things like gift-giving, symbolism and social stratification. What did it mean to wear a faceted carnelian bead imported from a distant and exotic part of the world, as opposed to a cheap glass one that had been made locally?

We don't know at what point the *exotic* became quite so fashionable in Scandinavia. Was it a case of demand encouraging supply or was the demand caused directly by the sudden availability, something that changed during the Viking Age, of goods from the exotic east? The desirability may have lain purely with the objects themselves for their artistic value, or they may have symbolised something else, namely a link to the places abroad. When this happens, neither the coins' original value nor their silver value matters. Many dirhams turn up as necklaces: pierced or with a loop attached, they adorned the necks of women in fledgling Scandinavian towns and even on rural farms. These objects were all *luxuries*; opulent and rare, and as one description has it, 'simultaneously extravagant, inessential but highly desirable, and difficult to obtain'.[8] They signalled not just wealth but connections. Their value, whether financial or symbolic, was recognised by those who used them and by those who saw them, in the same way that today we might recognise luxury brands and status symbols.

In the case of the dirhams that were transformed into necklaces, the original monetary value of the coins had been subsumed not once, but twice: first when they left their Islamic starting point, where they could be used for their face value, and second when the coins were transformed into a wearable object of art. Necklaces like this are found quite often in Scandinavia, usually in graves, but now a small number of them have even been discovered in England: here discoveries include a coin minted in modern-day Afghanistan in 905–6, later gilded on both sides and fitted with an extra pin to be used as a brooch after a previous existence as part of a necklace.[9] These dirhams-turned-jewellery are typically found in women's graves.

Prior to the Viking Age, exotic, imported objects were almost exclusively found in elite graves in high-status contexts. For instance, Swedish archaeologist John Ljungkvist studied amethyst beads in Sweden and observed that objects like these were clearly the trappings of higher social strata. While this is not surprising considering how expensive and difficult to obtain they must have been, the important point is that this changed during the Viking Age. Objects like exotic beads became much more commonplace. Clearly, these displays of wealth and luxury became irresistible for those with social ambitions. For many, later on in the period, they also became emblems of experience and new influences. Luxuries could have an even more overtly political role if they were used as part of armour, weaponry or horse gear; not only would these mark out the wearer's political power but this very wealth would be used to intimidate rivals.

It's notable that aside from all the foreign coins, the most common category of luxury items seems to be that of beads and dress accessories. Silks, ornaments, and trimmings like ribbon and gold thread are all categories of things that were highly visible in daily life and for a broad range of people. This emphasises the interpretation of them as traded objects, symbolising elite status, but it has also been suggested that they mark out incoming people, largely traders, whose use of the objects expressed their own personal link to other customs and to distant lands. For it is certain that foreign traders were present in Scandinavia, possibly in large numbers. Those itinerant traders first seen in the early emporia would have had a natural home in towns like Birka as well.

Take, for example, Gilli, the trader who sold Hǫskuldr the Irish princess Melkorka in the *Laxdæla saga*. We know too that a Jewish-Arab merchant or traveller, a man named as Ibrahim ibn Ya'qub al-Tartushi, visited the town of Hedeby in 950. He described it ('a large town at the very far end of the world ocean'), its inhabitants' despicable customs ('the people often throw a newborn child into the sea rather than maintain it'), their appearance ('there is also an artificial make-up for the eyes: when they use it beauty never fades; on the contrary, it increases in men and women as well'), and, finally, their beliefs ('its people worship Sirius except for a few who are Christians and have a church there').

Sites like the early emporia, towns and trading places were melting pots not just of people but also religions. Anyone resident somewhere like Birka may have come across eastern religions, including Islam, to some extent. In fact, some have gone as far as to suggest that Islam was not only known but also a religion that was actively followed, albeit on a very minor scale: twenty years ago, it was already being suggested that Muslims living and trading in Birka may have needed someone, 'a Mullah, to lead the prayers and speak for them in front of the king'.[10] Could Muslim missionaries have reached Scandinavia too? Elsewhere in the world, Muslim traders and other officials served as important agents for spreading Islam to the ever-expanding borders of the caliphate. The dirhams with their religious inscriptions, reminding the reader of God's greatness, can also be considered minor missionary objects, at least to those regions where their meanings could be read and understood. Still, it would be grossly incorrect to use this as proof that the Vikings in any way respected or even understood this on a large scale, though curiously a particular form of graffiti may suggest otherwise. Arabic coins found in northern Europe are sometimes inscribed with graffiti, ranging from simple non-decipherable signs to runic inscriptions, pictures of weapons and boats, and various magic symbols. A study of over fifteen thousand Arabic coins found in Sweden showed that a small number of them had been inscribed with Thor's hammers and some even with what might be Christian crosses. Similar Thor's hammer graffiti was found on a coin in Kaupang. There's an intriguing chance that this might actually have been a statement aimed at neutralising the coins' original religious messages. In any case, it's quite clear that religion was a contentious issue during the Viking Age, not least because this was a time of transformation that would eventually lead to the adaptation of Christianity across Scandinavia. We need only to pick up one of the western written sources to confirm this: the *Anglo-Saxon Chronicle* makes very clear just how much of a nuisance the invaders' pagan beliefs were and, indeed, how much of a cause for concern the lack of adherence to Christianity was for the leaders in early medieval England.

In the west, conversion was used as a deliberate political tool in the interaction between Vikings and Saxons. After leaving Repton, for example, Guthrum, one of the leaders of the Great Army, agreed a truce with King Alfred at Wedmore in the year 878. As part of the deal, Guthrum agreed to convert to Christianity and be baptised by the king. Whether he really kept to the Christian ways he swore to that day is unknown. Only a decade or so before, however, the Great Army may have specifically targeted the beliefs of their Saxon enemies, if we are to believe the legends: in one King Edmund, ruler of East Anglia in the 850s and 860s, was killed on 20 November 869 and, according to the sagas, his death came about after he refused to denounce his Christianity. His killers, led by Ivar the Boneless, tied him to a tree, shot him full of arrows, beheaded him and threw his head into the forest. A compelling story, but most likely another example of medieval propaganda.

We do know that Christian missionaries made the effort to go to Scandinavia to try to convert those northern heathens. The first of these described in some detail in a broadly contemporary source is Ansgar, the first archbishop in Hamburg-Bremen, who travelled to Birka twice in the ninth century. The first time, he succeeded in converting a royal steward to Christianity and building a church. Apparently, the locals weren't too impressed and soon reverted to paganism, forcing him to return a couple of decades later to make a second attempt. While this story may not be entirely true, it is very likely that such attempts at conversion were relatively common. Yet detecting evidence of religious belief in the distant past is difficult, especially without written sources.

Forms of burial may give us a clue to past religious beliefs, but these are often mis- or over-interpreted. A traditional view is that burials without grave goods represent Christians, and those with, pagans. But the real picture is far more complex and nuanced.

While the Christianisation of Scandinavia happened towards the end of the Viking Age, the process took place in different ways and at different rates across Scandinavia: this was not one overarching event, but a gradual spread. So although, for example, in Denmark King Harold Bluetooth is credited with the final, full Christianisation of the country, no single event made it all happen. In Norway it's assumed that Christianity largely came from the west, through contact with England and Ireland, and in Denmark and Sweden that it came through contact with Germany.

For most people, religions may even have persisted side by side in an overlap period. Sometimes we find symbols of religion that may suggest as much: like graves containing both a Christian cross and a Thor's hammer – maybe because the owner believed in both or maybe because the objects had no religious meaning to them whatsoever. The most pragmatic and perhaps most likely explanation for the presence of small items like the Buddha statue and the Allah ring, which may or may not have had religious significance, is that they were traded, exotic items. It is nevertheless important to remember that ideas could easily spread along with the objects too.

If we are to understand how both exotic objects and ideas went back and forth, a key consideration is that of the *people*: who they were and how much they moved around. In the Viking Age objects from the outside are thought to have been brought in almost exclusively by raiders or maybe traders returning home, which is in contrast to many other periods in history, where it's often thought objects were brought in by migrants. An excellent analogy that shows how complicated such assumptions are has been provided by Susan Oosthuizen, an archaeologist studying the emergence of the English in the middle of the first millennium.[11] What if, she suggests, two thousand years from now, our written records have disappeared, and all we have is archaeology and you start to look at the distribution of IKEA stores around the North Sea as a way to understand migration? You'd notice just how much of an impact IKEA had on British furniture design, but the further you got from the shops, the number and concentration of IKEA sofas, crockery and tea lights would diminish. This might lead you to conclude that sometime in the late twentieth century a significant number of Swedes had colonised Britain and the shops were 'central places designed to state and preserve Swedish identity'. But as Susan argues, flat-pack furniture isn't linked to Swedish ethnicity in Britain and even where Swedes are living in this country, there isn't a high percentage of them working in IKEA stores. This reaches the root of the difficulty that we have in understanding the spread of objects, ideas and people in the past. It's very easy to look for correlations, but it's equally easy to misinterpret the distribution of objects as evidence of past population movements.

THE SCANDINAVIANS

So who really were the Vikings, these people of Scandinavia, and how much do we know about their migration patterns? It is often thought that prior to the Viking Age they had little contact with the outside world, and that even throughout the period the main, if not the only, direction of movement was *out* and not *in*: in other words, that people from elsewhere did not come to settle in Scandinavia. The make-up and ethnic background of the Vikings has been notoriously abused. The concept of an ethnically superior and racially homogenous Scandinavian past was at the forefront of Nazi Germany's Aryan race policy: in Nazi-occupied Norway, the Borre Viking Age burial mounds provided the backdrop to public propaganda meetings held by Vidkun Quisling, leader of the fascist *Nasjonal Samling* party in the 1940s. The party deliberately drew parallels between its efforts to create a new superior state and the unification of Norway by Harald Finehair towards the end of the Viking Age.

The glorious blond-haired and blue-eyed Viking warrior was, of course, a very fitting poster boy for Hitler's ideals. In fact, the Nazis were so engaged with revealing the superiority of the Vikings that in the 1930s Heinrich Himmler's *Ahnenerbe der SS*, Nazi Germany's think tank, funded major excavations at Hedeby as one of its main research projects.

Recently, though, new bioarchaeological methods have begun to provide answers in a different way. In 2020, the results of the first-ever detailed ancient DNA study of bones from the Viking homelands was published.[12] A team based in Copenhagen had scoured museum collections to put together an extensive collection of material in order to try to define, genetically, what the population of Scandinavia looked like during the Viking Age, as well as to say something about those who migrated. Studies of modern DNA focus on what populations in the world look like today: if you decide to have your own ancestry analysed, you can easily order a kit on the Internet, swipe a cotton bud along your inner cheek, and send it sealed in a little tube to a lab. A few weeks later you will get your results as a percentage, or you may even get a map, that tells you *where your ancestors came from*. Except, strictly speaking, this information isn't true: what it really tells you is where in the world people matching your genetics are living *right now*.

This doesn't necessarily represent an ancient population. We are, after all, a species that has been on the move since day one. In other words, if we simply look at present-day patterns we can't quite know what the influence of later migrations has been: this could, for example, explain the discrepancy we saw between the modern and ancient DNA studies of Iceland's settlers, in terms of the proportion of male and female migrants from Scandinavia and Britain, where the ancient DNA suggested more of a balance in numbers from Scandinavia than the modern dataset. It also explains why it is so difficult to pin down an exact number of Scandinavian Viking Age migrants in England: genetically, most are so similar to those we refer to as Angles and Saxons, who migrated from regions in and near southern Scandinavia just a few hundred years earlier, that we cannot disentangle the separate migration events.

The results of the Danish study of ancient DNA confirmed much of what we thought already, but it brought a few surprises too. The researchers found groupings in the dataset that they referred to as 'Norwegian-', 'Swedish-' and 'Danish-like', yet these genetic patterns didn't accurately reflect the country boundaries we see in Scandinavia today. Genetically speaking, for example, the ancient populations of south-western Sweden were more similar to those of what is now Denmark than they were to groups who lived in eastern parts of the Swedish mainland at the time. Intriguingly, the researchers also found representatives from what they described as a 'British-like' or, more accurately, a 'North Atlantic' ancestry group in Scandinavia. The suggestion is that these were individuals originally from Britain or Ireland who had at some point moved to Scandinavia. This indication is compelling because it shows geneflow coming *into* Scandinavia, a story that we typically aren't told.

One explanation is that these people could be the slaves we struggle to identify but, as before, we have to consider whether such enslaved people were likely to have passed on their genes to a detectable extent. More probable is that these are either straight-up migrants who had headed east or the result of alliances; intercultural marriages.

What's more, the Danish team also found individuals dating to the Viking Age with large amounts of South European ancestry in both Denmark and south-west Sweden, something that is entirely new. Maybe it shouldn't surprise us, knowing as we do how much people moved about at the time, but this evidence isn't mirrored in written sources. These people could have been born in those areas and subsequently migrated north, or they could have been the descendants of someone who had. In any case, the finding is important because it proves Scandinavia to have been a place that people came to from the outside – not just the other way around. This, of course, has implications as well for all those exotic objects that came into the Viking homelands, because it makes it less likely that they arrived through trade alone.

The genetic study isn't the first proof of migration in the Viking Age, however. Isotope analysis at the site of Sigtuna in Mälaren, the town that came to take over from nearby Birka when it declined at the end of the tenth century, showed that among those analysed, a full 50 per cent were not from the local area.[13] Likewise, at Birka, strontium isotope analysis showed a mix of people who could have grown up locally and many who were clearly immigrants: as at Sigtuna, they were about half and half.[14] One particular burial was that of a man and woman together, in a chamber grave with rich grave goods including weaponry and gilded jewellery, and a leather bag containing gilded silver mounts of a type known from eastern Europe. There were trading weights, a fine set of scales and, nestled among the other objects, a beautiful set of glass gaming pieces and bone dice. The isotope analysis suggested that the man was not local to Birka, but that the woman could well have been of local origins. Whoever these two were, they clearly had international connections.

In fact, the genetic diversity seen in the late Viking Age cemetery at Sigtuna was greater than in many prehistoric groups and,

according to the researchers, on a par with that found among
Roman soldiers in England, a result that is surprising for a population often considered to be unusually homogenous. The bad
news is that although we can be certain that these people were
not local, we can't pin down exactly where they were from. Just
as in Repton, the information boils down, quite literally, to a single
figure which corresponds to a form of geology, and there are
numerous places across Europe that could yield such a value. Yet
with all we know about the eastern contacts we should undoubtedly consider those regions as possible sources: eleventh-century
Sigtuna is rich in imported goods too, including glass finger rings
of Russian origin, and even a ceramic so-called resurrection egg
from Kyiv – a high-status religious artefact. Pottery from western
Slavic territories was also found in Sigtuna, though it is far more
likely that much of it was made locally by potters working in
Slavic traditions than to think that everything was imported.

Intriguingly, the Danish ancient DNA research team found cases
where ancestry from outside Scandinavia was detected in individuals buried in what we would consider a distinctly 'Viking' way:
burials that we would otherwise have no qualms about identifying
as Viking. For example, at three sites in the Orkney Islands, typically considered to be culturally Viking, only a small proportion
of the individuals had Scandinavian-type ancestries while the rest
were considered local, genetically speaking. Examples of Sami
ancestry – the indigenous population of northern Scandinavia –
have been found in typically Viking graves in Norway too.[15] This
shows that genetics is not going to give us the ultimate answers:
cultures and identities are far more complex and there is no such
thing as a 'genetic Viking'.

Amid all this new information about migration, there is a
particularly curious finding, and it relates to sex: the Sigtuna dataset
showed that among those who were migrants, as many were women

as men. This is important information because for such a long time Viking migrations have been seen as almost exclusively male affairs. Nevertheless, the Sigtuna study was not the first example of female migration. Elsewhere in Scandinavia evidence has been found not just of female migration but also of significant power and status among women. The most notable example can be seen in one of the richest and most elaborate Viking discoveries ever made: the Oseberg ship. Today the ship is housed in the Viking Ship Museum in Oslo, a building designed in the 1920s to resemble a church. The museum's arched ceilings and whitewashed walls form the perfect backdrop to let you take in, spectacularly, three ships that are displayed in the cruciform arms of the building. The Oseberg ship is arguably the most beautifully crafted, with a sleek, streamlined hull made of oak, elaborate carved decorations, and a spiralling prow. Measuring twenty-two metres in length, the ship has fifteen pairs of oars and a thirteen-metre-tall mast. In or around the year 834, it was buried in the ground as part of an elaborate funerary process, as testified by the extensive list of grave goods: as well as everything you'd need to rig and row the ship, the burial included cooking equipment and food – even buckets of apples and blueberries – clothes, chests, boxes, six beds, tents, sleighs and a cart. Animals had been sacrificed as part of the funeral, including two cows, fifteen horses and six dogs.

Soon after its initial burial, the mound was robbed (evidence includes eighteen wooden spades thought to have belonged to the thieves), which probably explains why there were no items of jewellery, precious metals or weapons. Nevertheless, the grave contained several exotic objects. Among these were imported silks from the eastern Mediterranean, most likely Byzantium, and the so-called 'Buddha bucket': a bucket with a fitting in the form of an enamelled, seated figure with crossed legs. Although he looks very much like a Buddha, the consensus now is that this object was made in Ireland. In any case, it too fits the category of 'exotic' very well.

The Oseberg grave is completely unique and this, the richest of all Viking burials, was the grave of two *women*. Considering the extensive wealth displayed by the burial, they must have been of very high status. The two were both relatively old – the younger was likely just over fifty and the older seventy to eighty. For a long time, it has been debated which of the two was the main burial and it was thought that the older woman was the younger's attendant or even slave, or perhaps the other way around. Because they both died at the same time, it is often assumed that one may have been sacrificed to accompany the other, a practice that some argue took place in the Viking world. Then, in 2006, an article was published that described the results of an ancient DNA study of both of the women's skeletons. While the genetic signature of the older woman couldn't be determined at the time, the results showed that the younger woman carried a mitochondrial haplotype most commonly found in the Black Sea region. The implication is important: could one of the most significant Viking burials be that of a migrant woman from the east – or was this an indication that the younger woman had been a slave?

As these tests were carried out in the early days of ancient DNA analysis, they will be refined in the future, not least to look for a family relationship between the two women.[16] Whatever the outcome, this whole burial and the genetic evidence forces us to rethink the roles that these women played – or at least it should – and not just in Viking Age society, but in the movements to and from Scandinavia. Should the River Kings also include River Queens?

5.

VALKYRIE: RIVER QUEENS?

DENMARK, 2012

*H*e had almost given up when the tell-tale high-pitched sound caused him to pause. Unmistakable, the numbers on the display panel made it clear that this was not another scrap of iron but bronze at the very least – possibly even silver. Taking off his gloves, he propped his metal detector against the spade dug into the ground and carefully loosened the dirt on the surface. The object came to light quickly, buried only a few centimetres down in the frozen soil: a small, stylised silver head looked back up at him. As the icy earth had created a hard shell around the rest of the figure, he decided to take it home and leave it on a radiator to thaw. Later, he patiently removed the remaining soil. A neck and shoulders appeared, and hands holding a double-edged sword and a shield, in a style that clearly belonged to the Viking Age. The figure had long hair, with a face that was unmistakably feminine. There was no doubt that this was a woman, bearing arms. Who was she? A Valkyrie, shield-maiden, warrior; mythical or the representation of someone real?

IN SEARCH OF VIKING WOMEN

The Viking Age, as we are used to hearing about it, is over-whelmingly filled with men. With his grizzly beard and gritted teeth, the Viking warrior is imprinted on the modern mind: the Repton warrior with his hammer and sword fits precisely the image we have in our heads. The very word Viking is by definition male; its old Norse origins are gendered to make a *vikingr* a man. Even so, as one researcher put it, although this makes the Viking *woman* a linguistic impossibility, she is also a biological necessity. Of course there were Viking women too. Yet surprisingly, it's only relatively recently that the Viking woman has been given much attention; now, in the twenty-first century, she seems to have come back with a vengeance.

For much of the study of the Viking Age, women have been waiting faithfully back home on the family farm, passively watching a migration process going on around them. There's still a lot we don't know about their roles and agency, but many new discoveries and a new way of thinking are beginning to change things. Repton remains one of the very few burial sites with undoubted Viking associations in England and, probably, one of the most significant outside Scandinavia. So if we can understand who the women from Repton were – and why they were there – that is a great place to start.

If Viking excursions were almost exclusively male ventures, you would expect to find evidence of mobility both into and out of Scandinavia – i.e. people who had migrated at some point in their lives – to be found only among men. That, however, turns out not to be the case, as I discovered a couple of years before I started working in Repton. As a student in Norway, after months of application letters, ethical committees, training and preparations, I had finally been given the golden ticket: permission to sample the remains of forty Viking Age skeletons that were kept in the basement at the anatomical department of the University of Oslo. I had become interested in studying *mobility*, wanting to find out how widespread migration really was among those who died during the Viking Age. Especially the women.

When I was finally given access to the Schreiner Anatomical Collection at the University of Oslo, I ventured down the metal stairs to find the skulls of seven thousand people, their anonymous faces staring out from behind glass-fronted, timber cabinets. That day I spent some time just walking up and down the rows of cabinets containing shelf upon shelf of skulls, each gingerly placed in a shallow cardboard box with its accession number handwritten in ink across the front. I had a list of numbers preselected from a database, corresponding to individuals that fitted my strict criteria of time, place and age. I would take the skulls with me back upstairs to the preparation lab, put on a white coat and goggles, and as carefully as possible sample what I needed before returning them to their shelves.

Just as in Repton, the samples were sent to a lab for strontium and oxygen isotope analysis and I played the waiting game until the list of numbers came back in a spreadsheet. Some of the results were quite unexpected. The majority of those showing evidence of mobility – in other words, those buried in a very different location from where the isotopes indicated that they grew up – were women. Two of the women seemed unlikely to have grown up in Norway at all; their tooth enamel fitted with values from either elsewhere in southern Scandinavia or, intriguingly, in Britain. While I was looking at only a small sample, it didn't fit with the common idea of the housewife who stayed at home.

I also wondered if this couldn't demonstrate that some of those grave goods from far and away had travelled with the women after all. Infuriatingly, I wasn't able to match up anyone who'd clearly migrated with an imported artefact: most of those graves did not have bones and teeth that were well enough preserved to analyse. So I began to look elsewhere too, at studies that others had carried out, to see if the results were the same. It turns out that they were: of all the strontium and oxygen isotope studies that I could find at the time, where both sexes were present in the burial record there seemed to be as high a proportion of migrating women as men. The biggest problem was that there appeared to be far more male graves from the Viking Age than female (another hot topic of debate: more on that later). Nevertheless, this was new information, albeit on a small scale.

Within the next few years, more studies began to back up the early results, and the first ancient DNA analysis of Viking Age skeletons from Norway also found evidence of mobility among women. In this study from 2015, DNA was extracted from burials and their mitochondrial haplotypes (mtDNA) were established. The genetic material that is passed down solely through the female lines, mtDNA is especially interesting: while you inherit the mtDNA in your body from your mother's side, you can only pass it on to the next generation if you are a woman. This means that the data from studies like this can say something about gender-specific ancestry, something that is especially useful if you are trying to work out whether men or women (or both) migrated in the past. The study found that several individuals had mtDNA haplotypes that were inconsistent with what you would have expected from Norway, meaning that either they or one of their near ancestors had most likely migrated there. One of the women sampled in the study was even more intriguing than the rest.

In 1927, on a small farm by a river running east from the

Trondheim Fjord, a team of workmen were digging trenches to extend the railway across a plain. In the process they came across some artefacts: a woman's brooch, a sword and part of a horse harness. Finding no more evidence of a grave, they continued their work until, four hundred metres further on, they came across more artefacts, this time associated with a body. There were two very well-preserved oval brooches of a typical Viking type, laid out in position on the deceased's chest. Further down were two beads, one made of brown glass and the other of a ceramic material. All that was left of the skeleton was, according to Trondheim Museum's archives, 'the cranium, thighs, and shins, reasonably preserved, and it is hoped that also the remaining bones will be obtainable'. The bones and artefacts were donated to the museum, with the former finding their way into the Schreiner Collection.

There the woman remained, anonymous and unremarkable, until 2015, when the Norwegian study's analysis of her bones showed that her mtDNA lineage most likely belonged to a group known as Hg A*.[1] Very rare in Scandinavia and also in Europe, the haplogroup is more common in the Black Sea region, including among Turkish populations. This is, however, almost all we know about her. Nothing about her grave stood out; the osteological analysis carried out almost a century before had classified her skull as of 'Nordic type' (although now we know that this type of classification is meaningless at best and racist at worst). Her grave goods were typical and unelaborate.

This might actually be what I find the most intriguing: here we have a woman who, somehow, genetically, has ties to the Black Sea and presumably to the movements east, but absolutely nothing from the traditional evidence supports this. She is not mentioned in any of the history books, nor is her story one that we might recognise from many other examples. We don't know if it was actually she who migrated from those regions or one of her maternal ancestors; nor do we know in what capacity. Independent traveller, wife, daughter, warrior? This, the role of women in the Viking world, is one of the key questions we need to answer, especially when it comes to those who travelled abroad.

WARRIOR WOMEN

There are no burials at Torksey that we know relate to the Great Army, so the objects are all that we have to go on. The presence of a spindle whorl there has been taken as evidence that women were present as textile manufacture was considered more or less exclusively a female task.[2] There is good evidence that jobs, on the whole, were gendered in the Scandinavian homelands, so there is no reason to assume that they wouldn't have been when away from home, too.

It's almost certain that there were women in the Viking camps: it's hard to imagine a group of thousands of army members and hangers-on gathering without a single woman among them. Yet there are two important issues. First, if we accept that women were there, taking part in what were essentially military operations, who were they? Had they accompanied the group from Scandinavia, such that we can confidently label them as 'Viking' women? Alternatively, could they have been hangers-on who had joined the group along the way, either voluntarily or through coercion? Would that still let us define them as *Viking* women in the same way? Second, we have to consider what their roles were. If the presence of spindle whorls is what leads us to think that women were present, a corollary is that we assume these more domestic tasks were what they were there to do. This is where the women in the Repton charnel come in. Now that we feel quite confident that the mass grave relates to the ninth-century Great Army, we can reconsider their presence there.

When Martin and Birthe published their analysis of the bone deposit, they concluded that roughly a fifth of the bones belonged to women. We don't know if that truly represents the whole group because you can only work out sex when certain parts of the skeleton remain: usually a pelvis or a skull, because this is where there are clear sex differences like broader mandibles and pronounced brow ridges for men, or a pelvis broad enough to allow for child-birth in women. This means that the 20 per cent is probably a minimum, and in fact the DNA analyses that Lars Fehren-Schmitz and his colleagues carried out showed that at least one of the Repton jawbones that was thought to be male is in fact that of a woman.

In the original analysis, it was thought that these women were likely of local origins because of their comparatively shorter stature. The conclusion was no doubt also affected by the fact that at the time the original work at Repton took place, it was overwhelmingly assumed that women did not take part in the raids. It's now not clear if the statistical analyses relating to stature still stand up and, infuriatingly, the isotope evidence has been inconclusive. The women in the charnel who have been tested are certainly not *local*, but it's not obvious where they've come from. Two of them, though, seem very unlikely to have come from England at all, as they have strontium values that are very rare here, and in Britain can only be found in highland areas of Scotland or possibly Wales, though they would equally be at home in inland Scandinavia and many other places in continental Europe.

The isotopes show that those women could have migrated like the men and could just as well have come from Scandinavia. However, this doesn't tell us what their roles were. Is it possible that rather than being wives and hangers-on, they were part of the Great Army fighting force – that they were female warriors? Women warriors certainly do feature in the Viking world, but we don't know if they are real or mythological. Yet very recently one particular Viking woman might have changed that, making a major mark on the world more than a millennium after her death: she is the now rather notorious 'Birka warrior woman'.

In 2017, researchers from the University of Uppsala published a study showing that the skeleton in the grave of a warrior from Birka was, in fact, that of a woman and not a man as previously thought.[3] Using ancient DNA, the team had reanalysed a skeleton, Bj.581, that had been excavated in the late nineteenth century, concluding that the body had two X-chromosomes and was therefore biologically female. This was surprising because for more than a hundred years the grave had been considered that of an archetypal warrior, very much as that of G511 in Repton has been – and still is – described.

In Birka, the burial circumstances are even more compelling. The deceased was placed in an underground chamber, cut out of the earth and lined with wood, creating a rectangular room. Near the centre, the body had been carefully arranged by the mourners, probably seated and facing east. On a small platform at the foot end of the chamber lay the remains of two complete horses, nestled tightly together and facing their former owner. The horses seem set for action; one of them is bridled and ready to be ridden. All around the body, objects had been placed: two large shields, a sword, an axe, two lances and a fighting knife, along with twenty-five arrows of a type specifically designed to pierce chainmail. Whoever mourned this person had made a concerted effort to equip her with whatever might be needed in battle by someone with a wide range of military skills, from hand fighting to mounted archery.

Such a richness of objects was rare even in Birka, despite its many burials. In fact, Bj.581 was one of only two from the entire site that contained a full complement of weapons. For these reasons, it's not surprising that in 1878 the occupant of the grave was thought to be a man. Yet when the genetic study was published in 2017, the news hit the headlines worldwide and went viral on social media. Here not only was the proof that twenty-first-century sentiments hungered for – that women too could demonstrate martial prowess in the past, just as the media depict – but this evidence had been provided by that holy grail of scientific endeavours: DNA. The Birka warrior made her re-entry into the world in a perfect storm of circumstances. Even so, not everyone was enthusiastic about the new findings. The main objections were twofold.[4] One: just because this woman was buried with weapons, did that make her a *warrior*? And two: this was only a single individual; could she really be used to say something about the roles of women in Viking society as a whole? In other words, did that really mean there were a lot more like her?

To answer the first question, many turned to the bones. I got to see Bj.581 in Stockholm during a visit to the Swedish History Museum with Dr Charlotte Hedenstierna-Jonson, the archaeologist who had led the new study. Laid out carefully on a table in a bone lab, the unnamed woman had been reunited with many of the artefacts she was buried with. Her bones were fragmented and brittle; and her skull was still missing after it had been mislaid by an unnamed antiquarian at some point in the last century. The one thing that the researchers had searched for (and the same question that I am repeatedly asked about the Repton charnel women) was if there was any evidence of violence or traumatic injury. Bj.581 yielded none. There was no axe wound to her pelvis; no sword marks slicing a lower arm raised in defence: nothing like the injuries G511 had sustained. In fact, we have no idea at all how

she died, aged only in her late thirties. But here absence of evidence is not evidence of absence, as the missing skull and poorly
preserved bones could easily be hiding past injuries.

Equally, many have searched for evidence of the repetitive strain
that would have been caused by typical 'warrior' activities, like
signs of stronger arms from wielding heavy weapons, in a similar
way to how a professional tennis player's serving arm will be
considerably larger than the other. Archery, for example, causes a
considerable strain on the body because the repetitive movements
require a strengthening of muscles that, when used repeatedly,
cause the bones to modify in the places where the muscles are
attached. Evidence like this has been found among tenth-century
Hungarian burials, in men buried with extensive archery equipment, showing that we can look for such evidence in past
populations too.[5]

Bj.581 was buried with arrows and probably a bow to go with
them, but her body exhibited no definite evidence to suggest that
she had used them repeatedly. For this reason, many have argued
that the objects were symbolic of her role rather than actual,
physical evidence of it. In other words, they might signal how
someone wanted to present her in death rather than a demonstra-
tion of what she did in life. Comparing her with G511 from Repton,
it seems that the only major difference between the two – apart
from their gender – is that the Repton burial has severe injuries:
there is no doubt that he met a violent end and therefore at some
point took part in fighting. This could make it seem as if injury
is what defined you as a warrior; though that seems a little unfor-
tunate, because surely those who were either successful in battle
or simply very lucky would not be represented in this way.

If you accept the interpretation of the Birka woman as someone
who held a martial role, that has strong implications for the Repton
women too. Although she dates to the tenth century, several decades

after Repton, she shows that this type of role was at least possible for a Viking woman: she could, certainly, have been part of a fighting force. This shouldn't have come as such a surprise, because she wasn't the only one. There are other female burials with weapons in Scandinavia, although they are relatively rare. But if we look elsewhere in northern Europe, there are contemporary examples of women wielding military power, the best known being Aethelflaed, Lady of the Mercians, who was the daughter of Alfred the Great: possibly the only woman from Anglo-Saxon England known to have led military forces (though ironically, in this context, her main foes were the Vikings). Meanwhile, on the continent, another woman was in charge of a fight against Vikings too: Gerberga of Saxony, the sister of Otto I of Germany, organised the defence of Laon in northern France in 945–6 when her husband, Louis IV, was captured. What both Aethelflaed and Gerberga have in common is that they independently led forces and attacks and organised defences in a tenth-century environment, which is typically thought of as a time when only men could hold power. In both cases, these women owed their political position to a family connection, but at the same time, both are described as well educated, intelligent and possessing the ability to lead military strategy with the support of their contemporaries.

It's tempting and not unrealistic to place the Birka woman in the same sort of context. We should also remember that power was certainly afforded some women in this period, the Oseberg burials being a prime example. Neither of the two women there has been associated with military roles because the grave didn't contain any weapons. However, as the Oseberg mound had clearly been robbed, we can't be sure if there were originally weapons that were stolen. A curious, arrow-like wooden object described in the early twentieth-century catalogue of the grave has been interpreted as a *hærpil*, a so-called war arrow or bidding stick used to alert or rally people for defence and warfare. Perhaps this was indicative of a military role after all. In any case, isn't it likely that someone with so much wealth and no doubt a lot of power would also have been in charge maybe not of a military force, but at least of fighters capable of defending land, wealth and resources? I would certainly think the Oseberg women commanded power in some way, even if they themselves didn't fight.

Nevertheless, such examples are rare, both in the historical record and in the archaeology. Could that 20 per cent finding in Repton represent an actual proportion of women who were part of an army – if that's what they were – when we have so little evidence from anywhere else? There are some intriguing historical sources to look to as well, the most famous being the Danish historian Saxo Grammaticus, who wrote in the twelfth and early thirteenth century. In remarkably negative tones, he describes the following:

There were once women among the Danes who dressed them-selves to look like men, and devoted almost every instance of their lives to the pursuit of war, that they might not suffer their valour to be unstrung or dulled by the infection of luxury. For they abhorred all dainty living, and used to harden their minds and bodies with toil and endurance. They put away all the softness and light-mindedness of women, and inured their women's spirit to masculine ruthlessness. They sought, moreover, so zealously to be skilled in warfare, that they might have been thought to have unsexed themselves. Those especially, who had either force of character or tall and comely persons, used to enter this kind of life. These women, therefore (just as if they had forgotten their natural state, and preferred sternness to soft words), offered war rather than kisses, and would rather taste blood than busses, and went about the business of arms more than that of amours. They devoted those hands to the lance which they should rather have applied to the loom. They assailed men with their spears, whom they could have melted with their looks, they thought of death and not of dalliance.[6]

We don't know if Saxo's descriptions are true and it is clear from the tone of his account that he really didn't approve of the concept of female fighters, writing, as he did, from a very religious perspective. As a Christian cleric, for him these sorts of actions did not fit into a feminine sphere.

He doesn't give details such as the number of female warriors or how common they were, but he does go on to name specific memorable women and their actions. Here, they are listed in far more complimentary ways, like Hetha and Wisna, two female captains, who he describes as having the bodies of women on whom 'nature bestowed the souls of men'. Even if his writing is exaggerated, perhaps the takeaway message from Saxo is that being a fighter and part of a military force was a possibility for a woman during the Viking Age, even if it wasn't quite as common as some fictional twenty-first-century representations would have us think.

The Icelandic saga literature also features fighting women, and although these stories date to the twelfth and thirteenth centuries, they may have some roots in reality, even if the characters are largely fictional. While none of them leads armies specifically, there are several examples of women who knew how to handle weapons and who you definitely wouldn't want to anger unwittingly. One of the most fascinating characters is Freydís Eiríksdóttir (even if much of her behaviour is quite shocking): the daughter of Erik the Red and sister of Leif Erikson (who according to the sagas first reached North America), Freydís travelled west from her home in Greenland to the new settlements set up in Vinland, probably somewhere on or near the coast of Newfoundland. Unfortunately for those travelling with her, her journeys all ended in violence. In one case, she demanded the murder of her co-settlers, picking off the women herself when the men refused to do it for her. In another story, her expedition group, having made it to Greenland, was attacked at night by the native population armed with strange weapons (possibly catapults). The men in the group, roused from sleep in this new and hostile territory, were terrified by the missiles being launched at them and fled, but Freydís, who was clearly not fazed by this unexpected turn of events, admonished them for their cowardice. Picking up a sword, she engaged in battle and – the best part – exposed one of her breasts, slapping it with her sword, and giving a loud and piercing battle cry. The attackers were clearly terrified at this, for they turned and ran. It should also be mentioned that Freydís was heavily pregnant. While her morals are questionable, she is portrayed in the sagas as both fearless and brave, taking action – including violence – that is no different from that of her male counterparts. It might be that this is more a reflection of a romanticised, thirteenth-century idea of brave women than a genuine reflection of a Viking Age reality, but it could also be taken to show that such behaviour was not wholly unexpected, nor was it unlikely that women could use weapons, regardless of whether or not they'd fit into our 'warrior' category.

A problem with attempting to use accounts like those of Saxo and the sagas as historical sources is the heavy influence of religion: all the stories recount a world viewed through a Christianised lens. Such descriptions communicate an often admonitory view of the pagan past, where women do *unwomanly* things, often with dire consequences, that a good Christian woman would never do. This makes it difficult to assess the extent to which they reflect reality. Another source is different: John Skylitzes, an eleventh-century Greek historian, describes a battle which took place in 971 at

Dorostopol, part of a war of the Imperial Byzantine Empire against the Rus', eastern Vikings we will hear more about later. In an offhand remark, Skylitzes describes how, after defeating the Rus', the Byzantine soldiers scour the battlefield for anything they can scavenge from their enemies' corpses. Among these, they discover the bodies of women wearing armour, who had clearly been fighting alongside the men. Unlike so many of the other near-contemporary accounts, this information isn't given in an admonishing or preaching way, which increases the chances of it being an actual description of a real circumstance rather than something that was written with an ulterior motive.

Finally, we have the women who feature so prominently in our understanding of Norse mythology, often with crucial roles pertaining to the violence and warfare that are so familiar: the Valkyries. Made even more well known and popular by Wagner's opera cycle *The Ring of the Nibelung* (where fictional horned helmets make their first appearance), for more than a century the Valkyries have captured people's imagination as a highly romanticised image of warrior women. The operas are loosely based on what is known from written sources, but with plenty of creative licence. In Norse mythology, the Valkyries were the choosers of the slain: after a battle these flying figures would sweep down to the battlefield and select who among the defeated would make it to Valhalla – Odin's hall in Asgard. One source describes them riding through the sky in full armour: as they pass through, the sweat from the horses' manes falls as dew in the valleys and as hail in the forests. In Valhalla, the lucky warriors could eat and drink from an endless supply served to them by the Valkyries, when they were not engaged in leisurely fighting among themselves. A benefit of Valhalla was that if you died in one of these battles, you would automatically be revived at the end of the day – all of the fun, none of the risks.

The Valkyries are shown as 'tragic warrior women, doomed by

The carnelian bead
discovered in Repton.

The mass burial
in Repton, found
underneath a
mound inside one
room of a partially
destroyed Anglo-
Saxon building.

OPPOSITE: Grave 511, the 'Repton warrior', buried with objects including a Thor's hammer pendant and a sword by his left leg.

The juvenile grave from Repton, containing four young people buried together outside the mound.

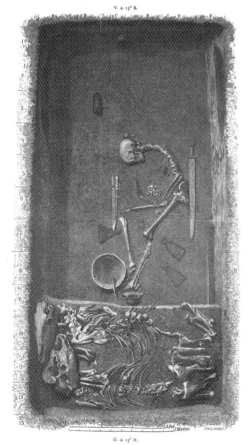

The chamber grave of Bj.581, the 'Birka warrior woman', surrounded by weapons and with two horses at her feet.

The tenth-century Vale of York hoard, discovered by metal detectorists in 2007.

A ring with a Kufic-style inscription found in a woman's grave in Birka.

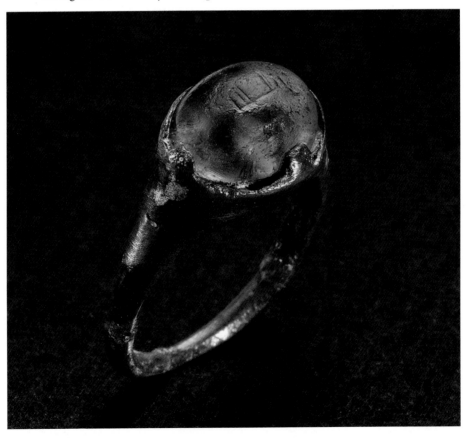

A silver cap mount from Birka grave Bj.581.

Another cap mount found in a grave in Shestovitsa, Ukraine.

A selection of silver arm rings and other objects found in the Spillings hoard from the island of Gotland in Sweden.

Excavations of the Oseberg ship burial, 1904–5. This was the final resting place of two women buried in AD 834.

The Oseberg ship, now displayed in the Viking Ship Museum, Oslo.

The so-called 'Buddha bucket' with a fitting of possible
Irish origins found in the Oseberg grave.

A runestone found on Berezan Island in Ukraine, raised by a man named Grani in memory of his business partner Karl.

A runic inscription from Hagia Sophia, Istanbul, with the name Halfdan.

Four views of the figurine of a woman bearing weapons, possibly a Valkyrie, discovered in Denmark.

their love for mortal men'.⁷ They often become the protective, supernatural lovers of mortals, shielding their chosen man on the battlefield and existing as a form of spiritual wife; sometimes so passionately in love that they continue their relationship in the afterworld. With names like Geirskǫgul (Spear-Shaker), Sigrlǫð (Victory-Hostess) and Randgríðr (Victory-Urger) to entice you into their world, it's perhaps not surprising that this image captured the imaginations of later writers and composers. The Valkyries embody the powers of Odin, including the ability to cloud the mind, induce confusion and freeze limbs: in short, essential skills to ensure the opponent loses both the battle and his life.

The Valkyries aren't the only women in Norse mythology who count among their attributes strength on the battlefield and feminine charm: they are matched (or rather, surpassed) by the powers of the goddess Freya. Freya is closely linked to the Valkyries because when they swoop down on the battlefield to choose their dead for Valhalla, those who don't make it to Odin get picked for Sessrumnir, Freya's hall on Folkvang (the Field of Folk). In fact, according to the poem *Grímnismál*, the true order of events was the opposite: it was Freya who got the first pick of the fallen warriors. Freya herself ventured into battle on a chariot drawn by two cats, though don't let that fool you into thinking she wouldn't be a fearsome opponent, with her sword and shield held up in front of her and her hair in a long, flowing ponytail. How much these myths and legends reflected a reality in which women took part in battle is unclear. But what *is* clear is that in the Viking world, we do come across fighting women and women perfectly capable of wielding a sword or an axe; some real, some imaginary. So when new objects come to light, like a small silver figurine found by metal detectorists in Denmark in 2012 of a woman with a ponytail, sword and shield, we can't know if she is a fictional Valkyrie or a representation of a real-life fighting woman.

I try to understand what this means for the women found in the charnel in Repton. I'm not convinced that we'll ever be able to answer whether they were *warriors* or not, but cases like the Birka woman are important. Thanks to her, and the almost contemporary Aethelflaed, there's no reason why the Great Army could not have had women within its ranks. I wondered if there were any other objects in the charnel building that might be informative. Clearly, many grave goods had originally been mixed in with the bones and these would usually be how we identify and interpret gender in past burials, though as Bj.581 so wonderfully demonstrates, this can be deeply problematic. There was a spindle whorl mixed in with the bones in the Repton charnel: could that provide evidence of women acting in more domestic roles there, as has been assumed at Torksey? I wondered too about the carnelian bead. Who would have worn it, a man or a woman? Yet trying to say something about whether or not women travelled abroad based on the objects that they might have worn can be very problematic, as such interpretations have had deep repercussions to date.

MIGRATION

Until recently it has been assumed that in similar cases in the Scandinavian homelands, exotic and imported artefacts buried with women were gifts from men. This is especially so in western Norway, where artefacts looted from Britain and Ireland have mostly been found in women's graves. But the new isotopic and genetic evidence on migration has forced us to rethink the interpretation of these burials. The recurring problem is trying to work out whether it was the object or its owner who travelled.

When it comes to women in the Viking Age, the conclusion has almost always been the former, which has had an enormous impact on how we have viewed women's agency – their involvement and individual participation – in the entire period. Partly the issue is that the interpretation of the objects has been based on a number of assumptions that lead to circular arguments, a serpent biting its own tail, going right the way back to the start of the Viking Age.

The traditional story that begins with ferocious, unprecedented and vicious attacks on monasteries like Lindisfarne is backed up by the presence of exotic looted objects, often from ecclesiastical settings, in eighth-century graves in western Norway. Most of these artefacts are clearly not things that would have been sold or peacefully traded: fragments of stunning chip-carved book covers repurposed into brooches or a near-perfect reliquary shrine are extremely unlikely to have been taken from a sacred place such as a church without some loss of blood, or at least the threat of it. What is peculiar is the appearance of these early artefacts from Britain and Ireland almost exclusively in women's graves. Every textbook describing this will tell you that the objects were gifts from brothers, fathers and husbands who found success and wealth overseas on a daring raid in the west. The assumption is that all these exotic goods came to Scandinavia through violent raids that women would surely not have been part of.

This may well be true, but looking at the evidence more carefully reveals something interesting: many of the foreign objects in women's graves are not things that must necessarily have been stolen. In fact, graves often contain items like bowls, ladles and serving equipment, objects that related to feasting and to social occasions.[8] These would have been suitable as gifts bestowed in the making of alliances: the sort of thing you might have taken with you as a dowry. Could the women with whom the objects were buried not have travelled as well? The isotope evidence from the Norwegian skeletons in the Schreiner Collection revealed a number of non-local immigrant women, some of whom may well have come from Britain. This should make us reassess the objects as well.

The remarkable shift in the way we are learning from the past and the scientific evidence – the osteological analysis, isotopes, DNA – is having a tremendous impact. Still, it's not always a straightforward relationship and we have to be very careful how we interpret the new evidence. The Birka woman is a key example: while the debate centred around the sex of this individual, it soon returned to the concept of a 'warrior'. Just because this woman had been buried with weapons, did that really mean that she had had a martial role in life? Yet if we weren't asking questions like this for a *male* burial, why should we do it for its *female* equivalent?

There has been a recent shift in the understanding of women's roles in the settlement of England too. Until very recently it was assumed that the Viking or Scandinavian migrants who came over to settle were overwhelmingly, if not exclusively, male. What changed this view was – again – metal-detected artefacts, this time female jewellery. Dr Jane Kershaw at the University of Oxford collected evidence from the Portable Antiquities Scheme database because previously only a handful of Scandinavian women's brooches were known from England.[9] Metal brooches were a common feature of women's fashion, maybe even as ubiquitous as belts (at least among those who could afford them). Some are exceptionally intricate and beautifully ornate; oval and shaped like a tortoiseshell with snaking designs, worn in a pair high on the chest. In fact, tortoiseshell brooches are so commonly found in women's graves in Scandinavia that they often become the *definition* of womanhood, their presence or absence determining whether we believe the occupier was a woman. It follows, then, that if you find these objects abroad, women must have been there to wear them. And that's exactly what Jane found. Her trawl through the database showed a twenty-fold increase in the number of Scandinavian-style female jewellery and dress accessories found in eastern England over a twenty-five-year period.

Of course, we don't know if the women who wore the brooches had obtained them through trade or if they were local women who had been given them by Scandinavian relatives. But Jane could quite convincingly show that over time the sort of designs and fashions that were available very closely mirrored changes seen in Scandinavia, which is something that would be far more likely to have happened if the brooches arrived along with the women themselves, rather than on the ships of a trading merchant. The question, then, isn't only whether the Viking women were there (either at home or abroad), but also what roles they had. Were they 'just' wives and daughters, or slaves and concubines? Or did they take more of an active part in their journeys and what was going on there? Importantly, were the women who did accompany the River Kings also from Scandinavia originally, or did they join along the way?

There are examples of travelling women in the sagas who are not specifically fighters. There's Aud the Deep-Minded, for instance: daughter of a Norwegian chieftain (the unflatteringly named Ketill Flatnose), who according to the sagas became infamous as one of the first settlers of Iceland. Married to a Norse king of Dublin, Aud lost both her husband and son to fights, at which point she decided to make it her task to move to the new, green, promised lands, marrying off her granddaughters along the way. Clearly a woman of means and ability who was highly respected, Aud prepared a ship in secret for this mission and had twenty free men accompany her.

The problems with our current knowledge of Viking women

are important because they relate to current thinking about the origins of the Viking Age. One issue is the major bias in the archaeological record in that there seem to be far more male burials than female in Scandinavia.[10] This was first discovered in the 1980s, when the search for Viking women started in earnest. Looking at the statistics of male versus female graves, it was discovered that in some areas of Norway male graves outnumbered female by a staggering seven to one. Over the years this has been taken very literally to suggest that there were more men than women around in the Viking Age. But that is problematic. It's extremely uncommon for there to be a big sex difference in a population without very particular circumstances – for example, large numbers of men dying in battle. Even so, this would only explain the discrepancy in an adult population, and shouldn't cause such a difference in the numbers of burials. If equal numbers of girls and boys are born in the first place, equal numbers of women and men should be buried at death.

The most likely explanation for the difference in Scandinavia, it has been argued, is that selective female infanticide was carried out. This could have led to a situation much like that of modern-day China, where the one-child policy and a strong cultural preference for sons have caused a profoundly skewed sex ratio in favour of men due to an increase in selective female abortion, infanticide and abandonment. Unfortunately for the Viking Age, we don't have the evidence either to prove or disprove this claim, rendering it mere speculation. It's almost impossible to prove that infanticide took place on a large scale: infant burials rarely survive, and even if they do, determining the sex of an infant skeleton has only been possible with recently developed DNA techniques.

In fact, the only supposed evidence we have that infanticide took place at all is from the saga literature dating to the twelfth or thirteenth century, in which one story includes a female infant who was left exposed to the elements to meet her death because a female child was less valuable than a male. This is unconvincing as evidence that the practice was so common almost five hundred years earlier as to cause a major imbalance between the sexes. Even more importantly, in the sagas, male infanticide was at least as common as female, so this really cannot be used as convincing proof that more girls were murdered than boys.

The implications are serious, because it has been proposed that the lack of women in Scandinavia was one of the main drivers of the start of the Viking Age in the first place. The first time this was suggested was in the Middle Ages, when Dudo of Saint-Quentin, a French historian who wrote a *History of the Normans* sometime in the late tenth or early eleventh century, proposed that the Viking raids had started because of an excess of unmarried young men. Presumably in Dudo's time, much like now, this demographic category was over-represented in the crime statistics. His idea was taken up more earnestly in recent times; first, in a suggestion that perhaps what drove these men abroad was the fact that at home they had to compete to get a wife, as there simply weren't enough women to go round.[11] Therefore, to stand out as an eligible bachelor, you'd have needed wealth, quite literally: bridewealth, a sort of payment due to the bride's family (the opposite of a dowry), which was common in many cultures. A second and more recent suggestion has taken the idea further, proposing that an additional lack of women came about because of a common practice of polygyny, i.e. the taking of more than one wife, leaving fewer women available to marry.[12]

While at face value these suggestions seem plausible, they have serious flaws. The first relates to the archaeological evidence. Does the seven-to-one difference proposed for some parts of Norway reflect a genuine lack of women overall? I think the answer to this question is no. But to understand why, we need to look at how these graves are identified in the first place. In many cases the sex of a burial in a grave will have been determined solely on the basis of grave goods, at least if the bones are not well enough preserved for this to be done osteologically. That means that the grave goods are assumed to reflect a specific gender: this is typically done by taking weapons and tools to represent men and textile-working equipment to indicate women, though sometimes it's more specifically about dress, like women being buried with certain types of brooches, which might be more reliable than the former items. So if a grave where the bones are either poorly preserved or lacking altogether contains a single sword, for example, it is taken to be the grave of a man.

In most cases this is likely to be correct; but as Bj.581 demonstrated, not always. What about when there are no grave goods, or when grave goods can't be associated with a particular gender, such as a single knife? This was actually quite common, and such graves are typically not included in the statistics. If it was common for women to be buried without any grave goods whatsoever, that would significantly skew the results. It's also worth remembering that in Norway in particular, there aren't many big communal cemeteries in this period. Instead, graves are often found underneath mounds on the outskirts of farmsteads; these would have been family burial grounds, but not necessarily ones that every member of a household was buried in. This gives us another way in which our dataset could be skewed: if only the heads of the household were buried there, this may well have precluded women. Even more interestingly, in the infrequent cemeteries that have been excavated using modern methods, the ratio of men and women has been closer to 1:1.

The second problem with the bridewealth and polygyny hypotheses is about numbers and statistics. One thing we do know is that throughout the Viking Age a huge number of people left

Scandinavia: some to settle in new lands, who would certainly not come home again, and many to take part in raids and battles. Many of those would not have returned either, at least if we believe the numbers of dead listed in historical accounts: just a couple of examples include the 840 men killed in Devonshire in 878 and the four thousand Danes killed with the Danish king's son at the Battle of Brunanburh in 937. If most of those who departed were men, this should have left an *excess* of women back home. If there really were *fewer* women, the imbalance to start with must have been extreme, unless large numbers of women left their homelands too. From the evidence for female migration, that now seems very possible. But even so, the hypothesis really doesn't stack up.

Warfare, then, may have involved some women – certainly as camp-followers and maybe as fighters or, in some cases, commanders. Yet as the evidence from the camps in England shows, trade was part and parcel of the Viking phenomenon. Most of the time the individuals who engaged in trade are invisible to us. The trader who stored precious goods in a lockable chest, who knew the products obtained in minute detail – in order to be able to assess their worth when both purchasing and selling – and who measured out the exact quantities at the market rate in exchange for silver cut from an armband, that trader remains anonymous, a shadowy character whose life went by unrecorded. We find out more about them only when scales and weighing equipment are found in graves, as we can fairly safely assume these objects relate to the role the deceased had in life. This is how we know that women were also involved in trade. In Birka, there even seems to have been a majority of women traders: 32 per cent of all finds of weights in graves were from women's graves, compared to 28 per cent in male graves – the rest were in graves where sex could not be determined.

Unusually, it seems to be different in other regions, like Norway,

where only about 17 per cent of all weights could be associated
with the graves of women.[13] Could this mean that there were
regional differences – that the norm in Norway, for example, was
not the same as in Sweden? There's also a high proportion of
Viking Age women's graves in Russia that contain weighing equipment: as much as 50 per cent according to one study.[14] Infuriatingly,
even this has been explained away by some as evidence of 'farewell
gifts from husbands'. However, it's more likely that trading in the
region would have been a family venture in which women could
participate fully. Even in Scandinavia there is evidence that women
may have been actively involved in trade in eastern territories: a
woman in Birka, for instance, was buried with a weight and a
purse containing Islamic silver coins, and with jewellery including
carnelian and amber beads and gilded silver pendants that may
have come from Hungary.[15]

Putting the debate about the Birka woman's warrior status and
occupation to one side, there's another point that has been largely
overlooked but which, in many ways, is even more significant
for understanding the world that she was part of. Although most
of the organic materials in her grave have long since rotted away,
some proof of what she was dressed in when she was buried
remains. Just above her head, the archaeologists found five small
artefacts that formed part of a hat or cap. These are four plum-
shaped objects best described as tassels, made from very fine
silver thread embroidery and braiding, with edgings of silver foil.
They would once have hung from ribbons on the hat and would
have been filled with some sort of organic material. The fifth
item is even more striking: a pointed cone made of silver foil,
decorated with patterns of granulation – tiny beads of silver
arranged in a geometric chevron-like arrangement. Traces of silk
were found inside the cone, which suggests the entire headdress
could have been made of the material. The contrast with her

military equipment is striking; the delicate beauty of the silver and silk against the violence inherent in the iron designed to cleave flesh.

Headdress decorations like this were unusual in Sweden at the time. Based on other comparative examples, it seems almost certain that the cap was made in the Dnieper region of what is now Ukraine. This could mean one of two things. Either this woman wore the hat in death because it was a high-status item, something that set her apart from others buried around her and linked her to the upper echelons of Birka society. As such the garment itself could be a symbol of exoticism and wealth, her ability to obtain it and to wear it the most important signal. Or it could directly symbolise her own connections to the east and to the Dnieper region – presuming that we rule out that it was a gift from her husband. She could have lived there, or maybe even grown up abroad: strontium isotope analysis of her tooth enamel showed that she didn't come from Birka, although the exact location of her childhood could not be ascertained. Long before Bj.581's body was determined to be that of a woman, it had been proposed that caps like this were given as rewards for service in the guard of the rulers of the Rus', the eastern Vikings we will hear more about later. Does her gender change or challenge this interpretation, or does it, conversely, work to support the martial interpretation of her role in life?

When you look through all the evidence it is clear that she is not the only woman who has links to the east, the woman with the Allah ring being just one other example. Recently, it was discovered that the axe in the grave of a woman from Denmark was of a Slavic type, a fact that saw her identified by some as a Slavic woman. In light of the Birka warrior debate, this sort of identification should certainly be cautioned against. But just as there are a high number of women in Norway with links to the west, there are many women in Sweden in particular who have links to the east. Combined with the scientific evidence that women were part of the migration both into and out of Scandinavia, we really can't exclude their agency from those worlds any longer. We have to carefully consider what roles they had; whether they were warriors, wives, traders, slaves (or slavers) or explorers. Or, more likely, people with a combination of identities that changed over time. Some criticise those who emphasise such points for going too far in the wrong direction, creating a fictitious female-dominated society in the Viking past; a matriarchal fantasy fuelled by twenty-first-century desires and sentiments. Yet this criticism is unfair and it is unnecessary. We can't deny those women a place in the Viking world and we have to seriously and rigorously assess the ways in which we consider their agency. Whether or not they were River *Queens* is undecided, but they were undeniably *there*, an active and instrumental part of the phenomenon, and especially the part of it that was heading east.

6.

KING PIECE: HEADING EAST

SALME, ESTONIA, C.750

I remember, more than anything, one game he played years ago, against another chieftain after one of the lavish feasts held in honour of our visit. We had all had far too much to drink. That night the long hall was loud with chatter and music, singing of dubious quality, and vigorous gesticulation. Most of us couldn't understand each other, but somehow the mead seemed to solve that problem. I was sitting next to him as they started playing the tafl game. I knew his gaming pieces so well, having watched him carve them out of bone on a previous expedition. He said they had never once brought him real bad luck: they had made him win when he needed to and lose when the gods decided it was better for his opponent to win. This time it looked to be a draw and the game was so intense that a silence settled all around them, a circle of faces waiting to see the outcome. I knew he let the chieftain win, because just before he made his final move and his king piece was captured, he caught my eye and the corner of his mouth rose up in a tiny smile.

AUSTMARR: THE EASTERN SEA

That exotic goods found their way into Scandinavia isn't surprising, and these goods seem to reflect the directions people have travelled. While most artefacts from Britain and Ireland are found in Norway, Sweden has the highest quantity of Islamic dirhams in the whole of Europe after Russia. Nor is it surprising that certain Scandinavian objects – like the female jewellery discovered in England – followed travellers abroad. What *is* surprising is that outside Scandinavia, *more* artefacts of Scandinavian origin have been found in the east than in the west.[1] This is an extraordinary fact when so much of the emphasis in our usual discourse on the Vikings relates to their westward exploits, but this information implies that the movement of people and goods east from Scandinavia may have been far greater in magnitude than that moving west. To understand why and how this happened, we need to consider the first steps of that movement, across the Eastern Sea.

The Baltic Sea today is a true connector just as it was in the past. The oldest geographical descriptions of this far northern fringe of the world come from the classical writers Tacitus, Ptolemy and Jordanes, who talked about the barbarian tribes inhabiting the 'islands of the Baltic'. While it is clear that this in part referred to actual islands like Gotland, located off the south-east coast of Sweden, the descriptions also included what the second-century Egyptian geographer Ptolemy described and showed on a map as the island of *Skandia*, which was in fact the Scandinavian Peninsula.

After that the written records are largely silent on these islands in the Baltic until Ohthere's chat in 890 with King Alfred, along with the accounts of another traveller who also reported on his journeys to the king, namely Wulfstan.

Wulfstan was a merchant and traveller thought to have come from Hedeby, and his account of the so-called 'Eastern route' is preserved in Alfred's translation of the Roman historian Orosius's *Historiae adversum pagano* – the 'History Against the Pagans'. Here Wulfstan describes a journey starting in Hedeby and ending in Truso, another emporium in what is now Poland. The journey apparently took seven days and Wulfstan describes whose lands he passed along the way. Similarly, according to the chronicler Adam of Bremen, writing in the middle of the eleventh century, sailing from Wolin in Poland at the mouth of the River Oder to Novgorod and Russia took fourteen days. Clearly, these were well-known travel routes that could take you from one part of the Baltic to another at an impressive speed. There, in that sea once known as Austmarr, one location more than anywhere else demonstrates the Vikings' thirst for silver and what both triggered and fuelled so many of their exploits: the island of Gotland.

In 1999, on a quiet rural farm at Spillings in the north of the island, an astonishing discovery was made: two hoards containing a staggering sixty-seven kilograms of silver. Nearby, a third hoard was found, this one holding twenty kilograms of bronze, mainly pieces of jewellery. The find was sensational, and all three hoards had been buried in or around a building, probably a barn or a storehouse, in the Viking Age. The silver hoards included no fewer than a jaw-dropping 14,295 coins, most of them Islamic. The most recent coin had been minted in 870–1, just a couple of years before the Great Army plotted its attack on Repton. The bronze objects, mainly jewellery from what is now Estonia, Latvia and Lithuania, had been placed in a wooden chest made of spruce, protected by a heavy iron padlock. What's more, the Spillings hoards aren't unique: incredibly, they are just three of around seven hundred hoards that have been found on the island. The total amount of silver dating to the Viking Age found on Gotland now exceeds a thousand kilograms – the weight of a compact car – and includes 168,000 coins. Among these is a rare discovery of twenty-three coins from Persia, linking the island directly to the Silk Roads. The silver from Gotland makes up a large proportion of Sweden's Islamic coins. So why was so much silver buried in the ground, and why here?

The first part of this question is perhaps easiest to understand. It looks as if many of the silver objects were hidden in the ground almost immediately after whoever brought them arrived on the island, rather than after having circulated for some time. The most pragmatic explanation – both here and elsewhere in the Viking world, as with the Vale of York hoard – is that this was the most straightforward way of keeping your wealth safe from others: particularly important when you were overseas in hostile territory or in times of conflict. Curiously, in some places like Spillings, several hoards have been buried in what was presumably someone's home, suggesting that there might have been one hoard for each generation. Did this mean the owners were spectacularly unlucky, or that they were so wealthy that they never needed to retrieve them? There is an alternative explanation for why we keep finding these hoards in the ground: according to Snorri Sturluson, Odin decreed that when someone died and travelled to Valhalla, he could take not just what he had with him on his funeral pyre, but also what he had *hidden in the ground*. In other words, if you were about to go into battle, burying all your silver in a hole in the ground didn't just have the benefit of making sure it was there when you returned if you were successful, it would also let you bring it to the afterlife, should that be the outcome.

The second part of the question is more complex, but relates to the island's geographical location. The Baltic Sea saw key traffic between Scandinavia and the east both before, during and after the Viking Age, and this small island is strategically located just off the coast of Sweden. Some 90 kilometres from mainland Sweden and about 130 kilometres from Latvia in the east, the military importance of the island would have been obvious; so would its usefulness as a stepping stone between east and west. If you travel to Sweden, it'll take you just over three hours to get a ferry from the port near Stockholm across to the island that was centre stage during the Viking Age.

Gotland is like a little world of its own, albeit a very quiet and somewhat isolated one. The island is relatively flat, the highest point only eighty-two metres above sea level. It's ringed by a rocky shoreline, even more dramatic in places than those you commonly find in southern Scandinavia. Occasionally, sculptural standing rocks – sea stacks – jut from the shallow waters, like nature's own natural art installations covered in spots of white and green lichen. You might find a gem of a hidden, sandy beach, and inland you can walk through lush conifer forests, reaching the odd shallow lake near the shore. In the summer the island transforms into a bustling tourist destination, where Swedes and more far-flung travellers rub shoulders on its winding and narrow cobbled streets. Its history is highly visible, from the medieval city wall surrounding the town of Visby to the Viking graves and runestones dotted throughout the interior.

While clearly connected culturally to the Vikings in Scandinavia, Gotland was very much its own cultural sphere, even during the Viking Age. Because of its geography, the island could be more or less self-sufficient, as the soils and flat landscape allowed for farming. It is littered with picture stones: carved sculptures of a type that aren't found anywhere else in Scandinavia. These show graphic illustrations of ships laden with travellers, warriors and horse-mounted Vikings, and mythical creatures flying overhead. The stones represent some of the best contemporary images of the Vikings and they are also one of the few places where Valkyries are depicted. One stone shows a woman – most likely a Valkyrie – waiting on shore with a flaming torch while a fully rigged sailing ship packed with feisty warriors heads towards land. Another shows Odin's eight-legged horse Sleipnir ridden by a figure who is either Odin himself or a dead warrior arriving in Valhalla, being offered a drinking horn by a Valkyrie.

Gotlandic society was remarkably stable and wealthy, showing no sign of a king or an aristocracy, but with a population that knew how to take advantage of their position as middlemen in a well-adjusted and fine-tuned trading system. With so much material coming in from abroad, researchers have been keen to find out if foreigners arrived here too. A few years ago, a team of Canadian and US scientists wanted to investigate the origins of the Viking Age Gotlanders by using strontium isotopes to study burials.[2] They sampled sixty adults from the seventh- to eleventh-century cemetery of Ridanäs, one of the island's trading ports, to find out how many of them had been immigrants. The results were surprising: the researchers concluded that only three of the individuals had grown up elsewhere and the remainder were local. The result was at odds with the archaeological evidence; surely the high proportion of imported artefacts on the island would also have brought with it people from the outside? The suggested explanation was that very few of those who came to Gotland as traders took up permanent residency there; they were transient, mobile visitors. It has also been suggested that the distance across the sea would have been too great for many to make such an extensive move – an idea that is improbable, knowing what we do about seaborne travel at the time.

However, when an analysis of ancient DNA was used to study the Gotlandic Viking Age population it revealed something else altogether. The team from Copenhagen, who had worked on the large-scale ancient DNA analysis of the Viking homelands, examined Gotland's graves too and came to a very different conclusion. Compared to the rest of the Viking sites that they had studied, they found that the island environment displayed the greatest genetic variation: the researchers even described it as 'extreme', relatively speaking. This means that the island had far *more* diverse communities, with a bigger influx of people from the outside, than had been seen in most of contemporary Scandinavia. That result seemed more in keeping with what we know from the archaeological record: with so many objects having been traded far and wide, surely people must have come along with them too; we just hadn't been able to prove it before.

The genetic evidence suggested that these foreign visitors weren't always transient, but that many stayed and settled. One particularly intriguing conclusion was that the genetic signals on the island were much more like those found in Denmark, Britain and Finland than among Swedish populations. In other words, this was a location where people didn't just hail from the neighbouring Swedish mainland, as you might have suspected. Interestingly, a similar pattern of diversity can be seen on Öland, another island off the coast of Sweden.

So why was the Gotlandic result so different from what the isotopes had suggested? There are two possible explanations. First, the strontium evidence could be misleading. What the researchers were able to show was that these individuals fitted within a range of values that could be expected from the island. However they *weren't* able to exclude the possibility that those people had grown up in other areas with similar geology and therefore similar strontium values to the soils and waters found on Gotland. In fact, the vast majority of the burials from Repton could also fit with the Gotlandic dataset, meaning that we can't exclude the possibility that immigrants are disguised in plain sight. Second, the genetic data give us information that could go back many generations, making it unclear at what point in time these individuals migrated. Nevertheless, the combined bioarchaeological evidence does support a diverse and cosmopolitan population living on Gotland in the Viking Age.

Thinking about all this silver coming in, and the assumption that slaves were being exchanged for silver elsewhere, one question we need to ask is whether Gotland was involved in the lucrative slave trade. If we assume that the silver in the west was directly related to the slave trade, this could be the case here as well. Like other long-distance traded commodities, enslaved people must surely have passed through Gotland and the Baltic port regions. We know slaves were part of the Gotlandic societal structure because the Guta Law, a law code of the island that was written down sometime in the early thirteenth century, discusses various situations involving slaves and details how they should be looked after. At that time, for instance, you had to be extra sure that if you were enslaved you didn't work on a holiday (this was, of course, after conversion to Christianity) because your master would be fined and you would have an extra three years added to your servitude. In another part of the law, a returns policy is spelt out: you could buy a slave to try out for six days and if you weren't entirely happy you could return your purchase, in an arrangement that essentially treated enslaved people like inanimate objects. Although these laws date to the thirteenth century, the practices may well have continued from origins in the Viking Age.

You could also argue that the exceptional wealth of Gotland seems rather suspicious, even for a society of successful farmers, traders and middlemen. One author has likened Gotland, and especially the town of Visby, to a northern Venice where a mercantile oligarchy grew rich on dominating the trade that flourished across the Baltic Sea. What's clear is that Gotland and the Baltic served as crucial connectors for both goods and people between east and west. It is from here that we can start to see how the River Kings fully engage with the network that is key to understanding not only how but also why, ultimately, a carnelian bead ended up in Repton: the Silk Roads.

TOWARDS THE SILK ROADS

The term 'Silk Roads' has been in use since the nineteenth century, when a German geologist, Ferdinand von Richthofen, gave the name to a network or web of trade routes and connections that had been in existence for millennia. Described as 'the world's central nervous system',[3] this network was one that had a profound impact on the development of world history but also one that, at least in the west, has often been neglected. Yet when we study developments in eighth- and ninth-century Europe, and especially the eastwards expansion from Scandinavia, it is vital to understand that those movements didn't develop in isolation. Instead, the Scandinavians very skilfully tapped into something that had been successfully established thousands of years before. Entrepreneurship formed a key part of their success, as did the ability to respond to a specific system of supply and demand. Violence played a crucial role too, of course.

The origins of the silk trade and thereby the Silk Road networks as we know them lie with the Asian empires of Persia and China in the first millennium BC. Key catalysts were the conflicts and trade relationships between the Chinese empire, especially the Han dynasty (206 BC–AD 220), and various nomadic tribes in the steppe territories – the vast plains stretching across central Asia – whereby payment of tribute was common: luxury gifts would be given by the emperors to tribes on the steppes of Mongolia in exchange for peace.[4] These gifts included large quantities of silk, which was treasured for its unique, fine qualities and which China could produce in substantial quantities. Subsequently silk became more than a luxury item: it began to be used directly as a currency, which was far more useful in regions where coins had little or no use-value and perishable items, like grains or other foodstuffs, could be vulnerable to the elements. Further to the west, silk would be first introduced to the Roman Empire some time during the first century BC. Its continued popularity as a luxury item was one of the main drivers of growth for the trading routes that stretched from the far east to Europe. However, although silk was significant in the development of these networks, it soon became just one of many commodities that were traded far and wide along the routes. Importantly, the Silk Roads were instrumental in transporting not only goods but also ideas, culture and religion from east to west and back again.

Of course, the Vikings weren't the first northerners to connect with the Silk Roads or the regions in the eastern Mediterranean. Yet what is clear is that this inroad from the Baltic formed a route east that had not been previously utilised by western European powers to any degree. While the advent of the so-called Dark Ages meant that the networks established in the Roman Empire would no longer exist in the same form, this did not mean that post-Roman England and continental Europe were unable to trade and make contact with the east; far from it. In England, the seventh-century Anglo-Saxon ship burial at Sutton Hoo in Suffolk contained elaborate pieces of Byzantine silverware, while garnet from India and Sri Lanka was relatively abundant in the fifth and sixth centuries in north-western Europe. Stunning examples of these bright red jewels adorn weapon fittings in the elaborate seventh-century Staffordshire hoard, possibly the finest collection of early medieval artefacts ever discovered, and they are a common sight among other Anglo-Saxon jewellery too. The garnet trade at this time came through the Mediterranean and relied on links with continental Europe – Frankia, in particular. Much as with carnelian, luxury commodities like garnets are particularly well placed to help us track down long-distance connections.

In Scandinavia, the roots of contact with the Silk Roads run deeper still and can be traced back to the so-called migration period that preceded the Viking Age. Yet at the beginning of the Viking Age something happened to propel it further east. So what caused such a knock-on effect that it was felt all the way north to the Scandinavian Peninsula?

While this period is often (unfairly) referred to as the Dark Ages in both England and in much of western Europe, owing in part to the apparent loss of wealth and development in the wake of the collapse of the Roman Empire, the situation in the east was very different. There it was an age of gold. Important to this prosperity was the foundation of the city of Baghdad in 762 as the capital of the Abbasid caliphate, which had overthrown the Umayyad caliphate just over a decade earlier. Baghdad rapidly became a central hub for the Silk Road trade. This was a multi-cultural and multilingual capital: somewhere that information and knowledge could be exchanged and obtained, where merchants and trading partners with information about lands as distant as China and east Asia could mingle with those who wrote and read the works of illustrious scientists, geographers, historians and other scholars. The west soon engaged with this culture and extensive trading and exchange networks across Europe came into existence, nicely symbolised by a gift sent to Charlemagne of Frankia when he was crowned Holy Roman Emperor* in 800 by the pope: he received an Indian elephant from the Abbasid caliph Harun al-Rashid, which had been shipped to Pisa from a North African port after originally belonging to an Indian raja.

Coin hoards, like those found on Gotland, are what really allow us to track how change affected the dynamics of faraway places in the cold and dark north: it's been said that the dirham finds are the manifestation of the beginning of Viking expansion to the east and, therefore, the first established contact with what is now Russia. Over the years much time and energy have been spent by numismatists cataloguing and classifying the dirham hoards found across Scandinavia. The coins have been divided into groups, the earliest of which, discovered in Russia and Scandinavia, mainly contains dirhams struck by the Abbasid dynasty. These coins come from a range of places in the Middle East and central Asia, as well as from North Africa, for example from al-Abbasiyya in what is now Tunisia. Another group of finds is dominated by Samanid coins originating from the Persian dynasty from central Asia. When studying hoards, much of the numismatist's time is spent attempting to reconstruct particular journeys and degrees of contact from the content of one particular collection. However, this can be problematic. There was no control over the circulation of dirhams within the caliphate, which meant that coins struck almost anywhere could be used as legal tender, thanks especially to their consistent weight and high silver content.

---

* The Holy Roman Empire was a complex of territories and political institutions in central and western Europe, largely what is now parts of France, Germany and Italy, that was in existence from 800 to 1806. Technically, Charlemagne's title was 'Charles, most serene Augustus, crowned by God, great and pacific emperor, governing the Roman empire'.

The first Islamic coins reached eastern Scandinavia by the late eighth or early ninth century: in Birka, Sweden, Ribe in Denmark, and Staraya Ladoga in Russia around 786 – the latter being the earliest collection of eastern coins known to have reached the area around the Baltic. The very first Islamic coins found in the border zones of Europe, though, are from the Caucasus, i.e. southern parts of modern-day Russia and what are now the countries of Armenia, Azerbaijan and Georgia. This may well have been the first link in what was to become the chain of exchange between the Islamic caliphate and eastern Europe.

This, then, is where the expansion eastwards began, and there's a good reason why it took place in the second half of the eighth century. At this time trading relationships were able to develop in this part of Eurasia because the political situation there was becoming more stable, with peaceful relationships developing between the Khazars in the northern Caucasus and the Arabs of the caliphate.[5] This meant that trade between the Abbasids and places like Armenia could flourish, which led to vast quantities of dirhams produced from mines both there and in North Africa circulating in the region.

That political problems could impact on relative coin numbers found in the north is clear, as the availability of each type would have been affected by ebbs and flows in coin production. In the first half of the ninth century, for example, the number of coins struck in the caliphate decreased dramatically because a war was raging internally between Caliph Harun al-Rashid's sons: this particular caliph (who, incidentally, may partially have inspired the tales of the *One Thousand and One Nights*) decided to apportion his empire between his two sons. That turned out to be a spectacularly bad idea, because after his death in 809, civil war broke out for a prolonged period of time as the brothers fought one another for supremacy. At the same time the Islamic world was bearing the brunt of religious conflict between Sunni and Shia

Muslims. The ripples from both events were felt far up in the north when the disruptions affected the minting of coins. Consequently, the lower number of hoards found at that time reflects not a lack of contact, but rather a lack of supply.

Similarly, changes in supply could take place for more natural reasons, as at the end of the ninth century when huge silver deposits were discovered in Afghanistan. In 892, the Samanid emirs began mining for silver in central Asia on a massive scale and this had a positive impact on the overseas silver trade. Huge quantities of coins were produced in the trading cities of Bukhara and Samarkand, which both lay north of the Oxus river. The silver used for minting in the caliphate was usually derived from the nearest mines and the quantities involved were enormous. Mines in Yemen, for example, could produce an estimated twenty thousand dirhams every week, or about a million each year.[6] The export of silver continued until about 965, at which point the mines seem to have been more or less exhausted. With silver supplies from the mines in the caliphate decreasing, the moneyers began to debase their silver, reducing the coins' silver content to make it go further. The testing nicks seen on coins found in England and Scandinavia are testament to the Vikings' knowledge of these practices.

SALME

The numismatic evidence makes clear that by 800, some seven years after the Viking raid on Lindisfarne, the route to the east lay open: a fact that is far more significant than reports of sporadic attacks to the west. Albeit on a smaller scale than what we were to see later, by this time nodal points around the Baltic Sea had been well established and trade had already begun along the rivers of the east, the trade that would eventually bring those vast quantities of silver to the north. But who were the people involved in the travel to and transactions with the east? There is a reference to this region in the legendary *Ynglinga saga* by Snorri Sturluson: in it King Yngvarr, one of the Swedish kings, raided the Baltic Sea and went to Estonia, where he fought a battle. The Estonians were so numerous that Yngvarr was defeated and died: he was buried there in a mound close to the sea. The place where he died is named as Sýsla, likely an abbreviation of the Old Norse name for the island of Saaremaa. And it is precisely here, in a small coastal village called Salme, that a recent discovery has given us some important clues about those early travellers to the east, if in a gruesome way.

Saaremaa sits near the coast on the eastern side of the Baltic Sea, nestled like a too-small bottle top over the Gulf of Riga. This gulf marks the entryway into the riverine networks through the River Daugava, which was one of several ways you could move inland towards the eastern waterways. Bar a Soviet-era monument commemorating fallen soldiers of the Red Army, there is little to see as you arrive on Saaremaa, leaving visitors to take in the woods and the constant presence of the Baltic; Sweden and Finland are less than a day's ferry journey away.

Until 2008 there was little of archaeological significance to be found, but a chance discovery during roadworks that year put the sleepy village of Salme on the map with an extraordinary find: not just one but two ships filled to the brim with artefacts and human remains.[7] The two ships turned out not to be shipwrecks but deliberate burials: they had been dragged about a hundred metres inland from the beach, and would once have been marked by a mound or some other identifier. Storms battering the coastline over the years had ensured that they were eventually completely covered by marine sediments that had been washed ashore. If they were originally visible from the surface or marked in some way, any knowledge of their presence had been lost over time beneath the sandy deposits.

When the ships were excavated, it became clear that they were both of clinker-built types that have come to be associated with the Vikings. The first of the two, the smaller vessel, was a rowing boat with six pairs of oars: within it, the remains of seven tall young men had been buried inside the hull. At least two of them had been placed sitting up, as if still on a journey, with objects around them (though disappointingly, the overzealous construction workers who first found the boat had moved the artefacts without recording their locations). There were the typical items you'd expect from this kind of grave: two swords, spears, arrowheads, knives and axes, and even decorated antler combs. Animal bones were found nearby, perhaps the remains of a funeral feast or offerings to take to the afterworld. Remarkably, these included two decapitated hawks.

Two years later, excavations of the second ship began, and this turned out to be one of the most spectacular ship graves ever discovered. The ship itself was larger, approximately 17.5 metres long, with a keel for sailing, a size that would typically have held a crew of around thirty. After more than a millennium in the ground, most of the ship had rotted away, so all that remained were several rows of rivets, just like those ship nails discovered in far-flung places like Repton. The ship's skeletal outline reflected the harrowing discovery inside it: the remains of no fewer than thirty-four individuals, their bones stacked at one end in four layers 'like firewood', the bottom layer of skeletons lying across the ship and the remaining three layers at right angles to the one before. This truly was a mass grave, evidence of a catastrophic and tragic event. The bodies were all those of tall and relatively young men, with many displaying injuries from sharp blades. Others had been decapitated.

There was no doubt that they had met a gruesome end, yet their burial showed that great care had been taken to give them a respectful interment. The bodies, although stacked, had been arranged neatly and in both boats any displaced or damaged body parts had been carefully put back in their correct anatomical positions, sometimes in an almost theatrical display. One of the men, aged around twenty-five to thirty-five, had been buried with his head turned to the left, his left hand placed underneath his head and his right arm outstretched: underneath that, the excavators found the beautifully decorated hilt of a sword, made of gilded metal with a pommel containing precious stones, alongside the head of a sacrificed dog. Was this man its owner, taking his loyal friend with him to the next world? Strontium evidence showed that both this and several other dogs buried in the ships had travelled with the men. Whatever the reason, there is no doubt that the manner in which they were buried was a crucial part of a belief system relating to their destiny after death. Perhaps, too, it had been done to communicate a message to those who observed the funeral performance.

If the circumstances of the burial were exceptional, so too were the grave goods. In total, the second ship contained forty swords, many of them gilded or bejewelled. The burials were covered with iron bosses from shields and large pieces of woollen cloth that may have come from the sail. Combs, shears, beads, padlocks, even bear tooth pendants were found among the remains, while a second dog skeleton, cut in half, was also inside the hull. There were multiple arrowheads, many of them still stuck in shields or in the wood of the side of the ship, in an echo of the fateful final journey of the men on board. Interestingly, scattered among the bodies were also a number of gaming pieces made from whalebone and walrus ivory. In the smaller boat, at least seventy-five pieces from two sets or more were found, along with three antler dice. One of the men buried in the bottom layer of the larger ship had an entire set in his lap; another had a collection of several pieces near his head, with the final piece, one that had a metal pin in its top, probably the king piece, in between his teeth. All in all, the ships contained 326 gaming pieces.

It's probably not a coincidence that there were so many in a burial of this type. While games may have been an important part of passing time on dull, lengthy ship journeys or when camped out during the winter months in a muddy field in Derbyshire, they also played an important role in Viking Age society, both strategically and diplomatically; the fact that they are often placed in weapon graves and in boat burials attests to this. At Birka, Bj.581 had a complete set too, which has been taken as evidence of her role in planning military strategy. The Salme burial with a king piece in his mouth is evocative; was this the body of a leader or did the piece signify a captured enemy? Even Norse mythology includes board games: in *Völuspá*, an Icelandic poem that describes the beginning and end of the world, the Aesir, the gods, can be found playing with golden gaming pieces at the dawn of creation until their game is rudely interrupted by giants. After Ragnarok, the end of the world, the gods discuss whether golden playing pieces will be found in the grass of a newly created earth. Games could be taken deadly seriously by the living too. According to the sagas, the eleventh-century Cnut, king of Denmark, Norway and England, had his brother-in-law Ulfr murdered after a board game turned sour.

So who were these men? The artefacts buried with them weren't of local origin but had parallels across Scandinavia, many being similar to those that had been found in inland Sweden. In an attempt to find out, scientists used strontium isotope analysis, and the results were pretty conclusive.[8] First of all, it turned out that most of the men came from very similar geographical backgrounds to one another and certainly weren't local to Estonia. Their values did indeed match origins in inland Sweden (maybe the Mälaren region, where Birka is located) just as the artefacts suggested. We know that there were links with Sweden in later times, as several runestones dating to the eleventh century describe people who either travelled to Estonia (sometimes they are nicknamed *Eistfari*, 'Estonia-traveller') or died there. An exception was a group of five men who could either have been local or, the scientists concluded, have come from Gotland.

A few years later the bones were to give up even more secrets, when the team from Copenhagen analysed their DNA as part of the large-scale Viking study. This revealed that the general ancestry of the men was of types common in Scandinavia; importantly, just as with the isotopes, their profiles were very similar to one another. In other words, the men had belonged to a very homogenous group of people, fitting the profile suggested by the isotopes. Yet it was when looking for evidence of kinship among the dead that the geneticists made the most unusual discovery: four of the men were in fact brothers, and not only that: the four had been buried side by side. Not far from them lay the body of a third-degree relative – a cousin, perhaps. As with the father and son in Repton, here was proof that these raids had been family affairs. It is tempting to suggest that the burials can be linked to the death of the Swedish king Yngvarr, but there is no way of finding proof.

The Salme graves did not seem to be the end result of an ordinary battle. The men were accompanied by ornate and beautifully decorated, high-quality weapons; they were kitted out in finery, taking gaming pieces of precious materials like whalebone and walrus ivory with them. The animal remains were important too, the hawks and the dogs. Would such animals have accompanied a group on an ordinary war raid? The excavators didn't think so. They believed this was a diplomatic mission of some sort, perhaps one carried out or accompanied by an elite warrior group.

Systems of diplomacy and negotiation would undoubtedly have been well established at the time, something hinted at in several western sources from the eighth century. For example, after the attack on Lindisfarne, in the second of his two letters, Alcuin the scholar wrote to Higbald, who was the bishop of Lindisfarne at the time. He said that he would go to Charlemagne to ask for help to recover youths taken captive by the Vikings who had attacked the monastery. This reveals two things. First, that hostage or slave taking by the Vikings was common and well known. Second, and more important in this context, that Charlemagne had some way of negotiating to help get them released, quite possibly through diplomatic contacts.

Even outside crisis situations, the use of interlocutors and intermediaries must have been common. They would also have acted as translators, both in a literal sense and as guides to local customs, religion and cultural traits. Objects would likely have been shared as diplomatic gifts; gift exchange has always been an important part of establishing and maintaining relations. Exotic objects from the decades prior to the Viking Age have been interpreted in exactly this way, such as the Coptic bowl found at Helgö in Sweden and objects from Anglo-Saxon England – even the Byzantine finds in the Sutton Hoo grave in Suffolk. Along similar lines, marriage alliances would often have been made for diplomatic reasons: there are countless examples of this from historical records. After all, what better way was there to establish a bond than to create a literal one, written in blood through a new and subsequent generation? Nothing says alliance quite like the word *family*.

This brings us back to the many female graves that have been found containing associations with the east – could they have been the result of deliberate alliances, formed in the name of diplomacy? Where we have written records, there is no shortage of examples of marriages like this in the higher social strata. Take Sithric, for example, the Viking leader of Dublin, who was the grandson of the notorious Ímar, founder of the Irish Uí Ímair dynasty that came to rule much of the Irish Sea region from the ninth century onwards. Sithric later became the king of Northumbria and in 926 he married the sister of Aethelstan (who was dubbed the first king of England) in a deliberate move to forge an alliance between the Vikings and the Anglo-Saxons.

Regardless of who those buried in the ships were, what's especially important about them is the date. The ships date to a period at the cusp of the Viking Age, around AD 750: a few decades before those fiery red dragons appeared in the sky above Lindisfarne. This is key for two reasons. First, because the larger ship is quite possibly one of the first to have used a sail in this part of the world, an adaptation of technology that is often considered instrumental to the Viking Age. Second, because this grave manifests so much of what we think of as classic Viking traits, but it is early, and it is in the Baltic, not the west. As the coin evidence shows, the trade routes that began to emerge and were very rapidly developed and extended at this time all had their foundations in established networks that operated on a more local level. What started as a quiet trickle of silver in the late eighth century soon turned into something more akin to a tsunami. This was like a gold rush. During the Viking Age, these areas in the eastern Baltic were not so much destinations in themselves but rather gateways to the east. The trading sites were more than convenient stopping-off points, they were *nodes* in an established, extensive network and part of its wider coordination. The very existence of those smaller trading sites around the Baltic Sea from long before the Viking Age is essential to understanding how the long-distance networks could arise so quickly.

EASTERN SETTLERS

Here, then, at the rim of the Baltic Sea, is the gateway to the older eastern routes that could take you along the rivers across eastern Europe and to the south. By the eleventh century this system appears to have become a continuation of the Baltic itself, because in Adam of Bremen's description of it he says the sea stretches to the regions of the Scythians and even to Greece. The Greek historian Herodotus said of Scythia (broadly meaning the lands to the north-east of the Black Sea and towards central Asia) that it had 'few really remarkable features, except its rivers, which are more numerous, and bigger, than anywhere in the world'.[9]

If you look at the map today, it seems impossible to travel all the way from the Baltic to the Black Sea by boat. Though the thin, spidery veins of the river network reach through the forested plains, there isn't a single, clear route that you can trace with your finger from north to south: certainly not one that it would seem plausible to move an entire fleet of ships through. To get to Ukraine from Scandinavia, you would have to travel through trading towns in the eastern Baltic, through Novgorod and using an extensive network of rivers like the Neva, Volkhov, Lovat and Dvina. The route requires you to traverse, in many places, from one river to another by portage, whereby boats are transported overland. The same was true in the ninth century; yet by the time of Adam of Bremen's description, these routes had become so well established that they had developed into the two main arteries feeding the silver trade: the Volga and the Dnieper routes.

It all began, in more ways than one, at the site known as Staraya Ladoga or, in the Icelandic sagas, Aldeigjuborg/Aldeigja. This was the starting point for both the route that went down the Volga and towards the Caspian Sea and the Dnieper route that led to the Black Sea. It was also the first truly eastern settlement with evidence of Scandinavian input. Today Staraya Ladoga is a sleepy inland village on the bank of the River Volkhov, about two hours' drive east from St Petersburg. If you wanted to travel here by boat from Scandinavia, you could sail to the easternmost Baltic to find the mouth of the Neva river, nipping across to Lake Ladoga and south on the Volkhov. As you were sailing you would see burial mounds dotted along the riverbanks; differently shaped ones representing separate burial traditions.

Aldeigjuborg was a melting pot of people, cultures and ethnicities from the very start. The first settlers here were Slavic and Finno-Ugrian people, many of whose livelihoods were dependent on the densely forested areas stretching towards central Asia. By the mid-eighth century, as trading and the movement of people began in earnest, Staraya Ladoga developed to become one of the first connectors between the Vikings and the Silk Roads. There's evidence for a Scandinavian presence here from around 750, and extensive evidence of craftwork: there are large timber houses that may have been used as workshops for craftsmen working with materials like glass, bronze and antler. There would have been itinerant craftsmen, such as a comb-maker who worked at different sites around the Baltic. Fragments of fabric have been discovered, from clothes like those that would have been worn by Scandinavians: for instance, leather shoes of types that match those worn by the women who were put to rest on the Oseberg ship in Norway. There are gaming pieces scattered about in Staraya Ladoga too. Later on, in the ninth century, somebody dropped an object here, an enigmatic spindle whorl of wood that was discovered in 1950, with a runic inscription whose translation no one can agree on.

The first evidence of long-distance trade at the site comes in the form of dirhams and imported glass beads. Later, carnelian beads turn up as well as curious dung beetle-shaped carnelian pendants, matching examples found in Birka and in Dagestan by the Caspian

Sea, evidence of contact with both the north and the south. Intriguingly, the early settlement here seems to have been peaceful, as there are no signs of fortifications around the town in its first 150 years of existence. There is no defended garrison like that at Birka, and few weapons have been found. Early life in Staraya Ladoga appears to have been quiet.

The importance of all this evidence is that in the eighth century, in a region that has far-reaching contacts, we have a settlement with a clear Scandinavian identity where both craftwork and trade were taking place. Not long after, similar outposts started popping up along the river routes. If you continue south from Staraya Ladoga along the Volkhov river, you will eventually reach Lake Ilmen: small, grassy heights on the riverbank mark your arrival, appearing like an archipelago of little islands. These are precisely what gave this region its name to the Vikings in later years: Holmgardr, after the Scandinavian word *holm* meaning 'island', 'islet' or 'peninsula'.* In the ninth century the settlement of Rurikovo Gorodische was established at a major crossroads where the Volkhov meets Lake Ilmen.

But by this time things had changed. In stark contrast to early Staraya Ladoga, Rurikovo Gorodische was heavily fortified from the word go. This, then, was no longer a time of peaceful trading and the exchange of craft goods: the reality had stepped up a notch. Staraya Ladoga became fortified around the same time and fortified settlements appear elsewhere too. From Lake Ilmen there are two directions to travel: either east, reaching the Volga and eventually the Caspian Sea, or south to the Dnieper in the direction of the Black Sea. Either way, we are deep into the world of the River Kings or, as the written sources refer to them, the Rus'.

---

* Later on the name was to be transferred to the better-known site of Novgorod ('new town').

PART THREE

EAST

7.

NECK RINGS: THE TALES OF THE RUS'

VOLGA RIVER, C.938

After getting dressed she puts them on carefully, one at a time. She has made sure the latest additions were made slightly bigger so that each neck ring stacks alongside the others, resting neatly against her chest. She runs a finger slowly along their spiralled surface, each in turn, taking care not to leave greasy fingerprints on the polished metal. She loves seeing them on evenings like this, knowing the effect their reflections have on everyone who sees her in the dim space lit only by the fire; the glint of metal sparkling across the smoky room. They'll all know how much each is worth, and she can't resist the opportunity to show them off. She's expecting several more when her husband arrives back from Miklagard. They should be back before long as the leaves have started to turn, and the air is sharp; this morning the pail of water outside the house was covered in a thin, glassy layer of ice. The scouts have been sent on horseback downriver as there are rumours that something is brewing near the rapids. They won't be the only ones expecting ships laden with wealth.

THE RUS'

W hen you start to study the Vikings' journeys eastwards, one thing immediately becomes obvious. On the map, sites stretch across the region showing a clear distribution along the rivers that snake their way through the landscape, reaching inwards to the vast expanse of land from the Baltic Sea in the north and the Black Sea in the south. It appears unquestionable that these realms belonged to those who controlled the rivers and, importantly, to those who knew how to navigate them.

We understand a fair amount about these journeys, although not from the archaeological sources but from semi-fictional written accounts. Here, unusually, we can observe the River Kings from two perspectives. The sagas, mostly Icelandic stories written down in the twelfth and thirteenth centuries (which may or may not have been inspired by true events), provide tales of journeys to places that seemed exotic to me when I learnt about them at school: Garðaríki, Miklagard and Serkland, known now by their modern names Russia, Istanbul and possibly the Abbasid caliphate. In the minds of the medieval writers, these were places filled with riches, wealth and beauty. Here exotic animals, pungent spices and colourful fruits could be found in sumptuous palaces and markets; people wore unusual clothes and spoke mysterious tongues.

In contrast, there exist accounts written down by Islamic travellers who encountered tall and fair-haired northerners along those riverine routes across eastern Europe. In some Muslim sources, the Vikings are referred to as *al-Madjus*: 'Fire-worshippers', a common term used to describe heathens. The accounts describe these people from an outsider's perspective, often emphasising the barbaric and unusual customs that shocked the writers, and stood in stark contrast to the comparably sophisticated behaviours that they were used to in the (to them) more civilised east. From these tales, we learn of how the Vikings conducted their trade and even of how they earned dirhams to buy jewellery – including beads – for their women; of how their women wore neck rings of silver; and of an elaborate chieftain's burial with human sacrifice. Crucially, we also learn about the slave trade and the Vikings' exceptional ability to take advantage of a gap in the market to fill a niche as middlemen between steppe tribes like the Khazars and the prospering Islamic world.

But in both the east and in the Arabic accounts, the northerners are no longer known as Vikings. They have morphed, seamlessly, into a group with a new identity: the Rus'. As it happens, this terminology has, to a significant degree, separated east from west in a way that is intricately linked with modern-day politics. The question of whether the Vikings and the Rus' are one and the same has been of national importance for decades in eastern Europe, but it is also, arguably, one of the main reasons why up to now Vikings in the east have been so detached from the Vikings in the west. New discoveries are starting to challenge this state of affairs. But before getting that far, we need to consider those written sources.

The first time the Rus' appear in a written document is in an account from an unexpected source: the *Annals of St Bertin*. According to the *Annals*, on 18 May 839, an envoy arrived at the court of Louis the Pious, the emperor of Frankia. At the time Louis was holding court at the Ingelheimer Kaiserpfalz, his imperial residence in Ingelheim am Rhein near Mainz, an opulent palace furnished with riches befitting the Holy Roman Emperor and son of Charlemagne. The envoy who walked through the palace doors that day came from Byzantium and was accompanied by a group of men who called themselves *Rhos*.

With them, the group brought magnificent gifts and a letter from the Byzantine emperor, Theophilus. The letter contained a special request regarding these men who had travelled with the Greeks. Apart from the usual effusive praise and proclamations of continued love between the two reigning sovereigns, Theophilus requested that the Rus' be allowed to travel safely through Frankia, as they had been sent there by 'their king' to seek friendship. He also requested Louis to give them help to get home if they needed it because, Theophilus described in the letter, they had reached Constantinople by an incredibly perilous route, 'through the most fierce and savage primitive tribes'. We don't know who these tribes were, but we can safely assume that they had travelled the riverine route through eastern Europe.

Louis the Pious was suspicious. Despite his Byzantine ally's apparent faith in the men, he questioned their motives for travelling to Frankia, suspecting that rather than being friendship-seeking travellers, they were probably there to spy on his kingdom. Interrogating their backgrounds further (having never heard of these *Rhos* before), Louis eventually discovered that they belonged to the people of the *Sueones,* or Swedes. In other words, those we would call Vikings. Louis decided to keep them in Ingelheim for a while to be on the safe side until he could discover their real motives. He wrote back to Theophilus to tell him as much, threatening to send the men back to the Byzantine emperor to deal with should he discover that they had dishonourable intentions.

At this point the sources fall silent on the fate of this particular group. It is not known if they made it home safely, nor where these particular Rus' came from: the statement that they belonged to the Swedes was how ethnicity would have been commonly described at the time. While Louis clearly wasn't familiar with the Rus', he was definitely familiar with Vikings and Swedes: he had supported the missionary Ansgar in his travels to Birka when he had attempted to convert them to Christianity only a few years earlier. Perhaps it was this understanding, that he was dealing with pagans resisting conversion, that aroused his suspicions.

Most now believe that the name Rus' derives from the Old Norse word *róa*, meaning 'to row'. Eventually this was simplified via an Old Finnish version of the word, used by Finns to describe rowing crews, *roðsmenn*: migrant, boat-based Scandinavians whom they encountered in eastern territories. In northern written sources, like the sagas and skaldic poetry, the destinations eastwards were jointly known as the *Austrvegr* – 'the eastern route'. The term is used in runic inscriptions found in Scandinavia, many of which include either *austervegi* or simply *austr*, 'east', mostly without any further geographical explanation: in most contexts, this description would clearly have been enough.

The name for much of what we now think of as Russia is known from the Icelandic sagas as *Gardarike*, where the first element *gorod* comes from the Russian word for a fortified town (which, again, is based on a Norse word meaning either 'stronghold' or 'settlement'); *-rike* means 'kingdom' or 'realm'. In other words, the kingdom of cities. Later the name *Garðar* becomes shorthand for the whole of this eastern region: in one definition, 'the entire area between the Arctic and the Black Sea and between Poland and the Urals'. Another name sometimes used is *Greater Svitjod* – or Greater Sweden: in the *Ynglinga saga*, Snorri Sturluson explains that this territory extended from the north to the Black Sea, claiming that some said the territory was no smaller than 'Saracenland the Great', i.e. North Africa. Either way, the territory of the Rus' was impressively extensive.

A relatively contemporary description of the Rus' and their

territory is given by the tenth-century Arabic writer Ibn Rustah, who largely based his work on an anonymous account thought to have been written down in the late ninth century. The account goes as follows:

> [Their centre] is an island around which is a lake, and the island in which they dwell is a three days' journey through forests and swamp cover with trees and it is a damp morass such that when a man puts his foot on the ground it quakes owing to the moisture... They make raids against Saqalaba [the Slavs], sailing in ships in order to go out to them, take them prisoner and carry them off to Khazar and Bulgar and trade with them there ... They have no cultivated lands; they eat only what they carry off from the land of the Saqalaba ... their only occupation is trading in sables and grey squirrels and other furs, and in these they trade and they take as price gold and silver, and secure it in their belts (or saddlebags).[1]

Although it is not an island, it is often thought this quote refers to Staraya Ladoga or, more likely, somewhere around Lake Ilmen.

This, then, was the starting point or perhaps the heartland of the new Viking territory for trading, raiding and settlement. It seems almost certain from the written sources that the Rus' had established themselves in these areas by the beginning of the ninth century, which matches the archaeological evidence. But what the evidence from the ground doesn't tell us is that it was the trade in slaves and furs that particularly attracted and propelled them, ultimately causing vast quantities of silver to flow northwards. The regions they encountered here contrasted starkly with the territories they would come across in the west: most importantly, these plains did not contain the same kinds of riches as could be found in France or in Britain and Ireland. Here were no wealthy churches or unguarded monasteries rich with gold and precious jewels. Instead, to succeed here the Vikings turned their attention to something else: lucrative resources that could be traded and exploited, things that could give them access to the silver they so hungered for elsewhere. The east paved the way for the most enterprising among them, who could rise to success rapidly. This was a place for entrepreneurs.

STEPPE ROADS

The lands to the south of Lake Ilmen, Novgorod and Staraya Ladoga have a different geography; the forests peter out and are replaced by a belt of grassland known as the Eurasian Steppe. The region reaches as far as Hungary to the west and continues through Ukraine and central Asia, stretching all the way east to Mongolia and China, a distance of some 2500 miles from Europe to Asia, a division that in this continuous landscape makes little sense. There are mountain ranges interrupting the belt in several places, like the Caucasus, the Urals and the Altai mountains, but the regions beyond are all accessible via passes. On horseback, you can travel relatively unhindered from west to east over the grassy territory, which is dotted with trees that grow along riverbanks and streams. For this reason, for thousands of years the steppe allowed for extensive travel and trade, the so-called Steppe Roads being an early precursor to the Silk Roads.

The steppe was inhabited by a large number of different nomadic tribes driven by geography and climate to a lifestyle on the move: the region proved very suitable for the movement of animals, with temperatures and rainfall patterns dictating the availability of grazing, while agriculture became, the further east you went, ever less economically viable.

According to one Islamic traveller, this broad region was home to a bewildering array of people, customs and religions, including tribespeople with customs that shocked in their lack of refinement and not least their lack of modesty and hygiene. But that was the view as seen through the eyes of a missionary, much like those of Christian travellers to the north. The reality was that these nomads and agriculturalists, whom external commentators considered disorganised and haphazard, were part of a network of people whose interactions were well defined, and whose practices made sense in the harsh winters and hot summers that characterised these wide areas of wilderness.

Scandinavians who travelled to these regions would have encountered the Slavs, a people that at the beginning of the Viking Age had already settled in large parts of eastern Europe. Besides the Slavs, they encountered and traded with a wide range of nomadic groups – some more peacefully than others. The major trading partners, and often enemies, were the Khazars, but the Rus' also frequently interacted with other culturally Turkic groups like the Volga Bulghars, the Pechenegs and the Magyars. The Khazars were originally a Turkish people, specialising in the breeding and trade of horses. The Khazar state emerged as the main successor of the Western Turkic Khaganate, which had been the predominant power on the western steppe since the 550s. At its high point the Khazari empire stretched all the way from the lower Dnieper region in the west to the Volga Bulghar state in the north. With a capital in Itil at the north-western corner of the Caspian Sea, the Khazars were able to take advantage of all the traders coming through the lands that they controlled. Ultimately, they became crucial connectors between parts of Europe and the Muslim world, and the Vikings were part and parcel of the growing trade links.

The Pechenegs were another nomadic Turkic group that caused much grief to both the Byzantine Empire and to the Rus'. They were ferocious and feared by most of those who encountered them as enemies, although this at times led to them being hired as mercenaries by the Byzantines. Occupying territory in the Pontic steppe (a large area stretching roughly from the shores of the Black Sea to the Caspian Sea and the Ural mountains) from the late ninth to the mid eleventh century, the Pechenegs were actually a group of eight different tribes with individual rulers tied together by a loose tribal federation. In the tenth century, these tribes were living on both sides of the Dnieper river, which allowed them to assert a certain amount of control over trade in the area. Because these territories were ideally suited to pastoralism and animal herding, groups like the Pechenegs bred and traded horses on a large scale; an important commodity for buyers across a wide territory. Apart from animal husbandry, their main form of income came from plunder and they were very good at it.

Most of what we know of how these groups interacted with the Rus' comes from written accounts. The first such Islamic account that mentions the Rus' is the ninth-century *Book of Roads and Kingdoms* by Ibn Khurradadhbih, who was the director of the Abbasid caliphate's Bureau of Posts and Intelligence. Ibn Khurradadhbih was concerned with describing trade routes used by an organisation of Jewish merchants, the Radhaniya. They followed four routes, stretching as far as Frankia in the west and China in the east, and alongside these he also noted the routes that were used by the Rus'. According to Ibn Khurradadhbih, these people travelled from the furthest reaches of the Slavic lands down to the eastern Mediterranean, where they sold swords as well as furs and pelts, paying 10 per cent tax to the Byzantine emperor.

He explained that on the way back they would travel a different route, across the sea to Samkarsh, located at the Kerch Strait that separates the Black Sea from the Sea of Azov, before making their way up to Slavic territory again. Alternatively, Ibn Khurradadhbih wrote, the Rus' could take another route through the capital of the Khazars – where they would again have to pay 10 per cent taxes – before heading to 'a point they know' by the Caspian Sea. From here, they might transport goods from the city of Gorgan in Iran overland by camel to Baghdad.

That the waterways were essential to the Vikings is clear from the *Ynglinga saga* too. After describing the different territories, Snorri names the great river flowing through Svitjod down to the Black Sea: the Tanais, better known to us as the River Don, which flows from the Dnieper basin. This, Snorri proclaims, divides the world into thirds: Europe to the west, Asia to the east, and in between, in the land of the river delta, the Vanaheimr – the world of the Vanir. The gods, then, from whom all the Scandinavians had descended, lived right there on the floodplains of eastern Europe. A more helpful description in practical terms comes from another source: the Byzantine emperor Constantine VII Porphyrogenitus, who described the travels of the Rus' from Novgorod to Constantinople and these treacherous routes down the Dnieper in some detail, with a focus on how to get through the difficult rapids.[2] His description is spellbinding and clearly based on first-hand accounts and intelligence.

The journey went as follows: first you came to a rapid named Essoupi, a name that means 'do not sleep', for reasons that will become obvious. He explained that the rapid was 'as narrow as the width of the polo ground'. Right in the middle of it was a series of high rocks standing out like islands around which the water 'wells up and dashes down over the other side, with a mighty and terrific din'. Apparently, this was too much of a challenge to travel through by boat, so the Rus' put most of their men on to dry land, while the rest went barefoot in the shallows, feeling their way with their feet and punting with poles from the edge of the riverbank to guide their boats through the danger. The next challenge was the rapid called 'the Island of the Barrage', where travel overland was again necessary. The third rapid was named Galandri, which means 'Noise of the Barrage', while the fourth was the big one called Aifur. This rapid was tricky, explained Constantine, because when they got out of their boats, they had to keep a vigilant watch for the Pechenegs who were likely to attack. We hear that those who were not standing guard took the goods that were on board and walked six miles overland, alongside the slaves they had captured tied up in their chains. Finally, the boats were carried across to the far side of the rapid before they could load up their cargo and sail off again. Several more rapids were encountered on the journey, including the 'Little Barrage' and the creatively named 'Boiling of the Water'.

Remarkably, there is a runestone on Gotland that refers to one of these rapids, that of Aifur: it is a stone raised by four brothers in memory of a man called Hrafn, who died somewhere in the region. The inscription states that they all 'came far and wide in Aifur' and that they also raised stones in memory of Hrafn south of a place called Rofstein, which is thought to have been somewhere nearby.[3] This inscription shows that the names of the rapids were well known back in Sweden, and I can't help but be reminded of those four brothers identified as having died together on the Salme ship: they had obviously travelled together as well. More evidence that journeys out of Scandinavia were clearly family ventures.

Constantine VII Porphyrogenitus goes on to explain that when the end of the river was reached, sacrifices were made on the island of St Gregorios, now known as Khortytsia. Here birds were sacrificed to the gods, with the boat crews casting lots to decide whether or not to eat the birds as well, and predictions were made about the future. Not far from this location five swords were found in the riverbed during the building of a hydroelectric dam; these weapons may well have represented symbolic sacrifices.

The extensive use of and adaptation to overland travel in these portages may have implications for what was happening in the west as well. Could it be that portage was required there too, allowing the Vikings to make overland connections? It was common in Scandinavia. The coastal route along western Norway, for instance, had several stretches where sailing was simply too dangerous or slow. The route, *Leden*, included places where you would instead take an inland course, often via portage overland.[4] This is something that is rarely considered but which could, perhaps, have allowed for more extensive riverine travel in places like England too.

The maritime skills of the northerners were noticed by many observers. In the account by Ibn Rustah, he makes a point of saying that these people didn't raid from horseback, but raided and fought in ships. It seems the clinker-built boats were superior in these territories too. Many have argued that full, keeled Viking ships could not have been used on these rivers and it's certainly unlikely that larger ships were used here, as the rapids and portages clearly would not have been suitable for them. But while it's very possible that local boat types may have been used for some of the journeys, if you were going to cross larger seas, like the Baltic, the Black Sea or the Caspian, you could not have managed with a small river vessel. This is where the design of the smaller boats and Viking ships come into their own; their shallow hulls are easy to drag in and out of the water and can even be taken apart if need be. It's likely that those used by the River Kings were smaller vessels known as karvs, essentially a kind of barge. Tenth-century

Byzantine writers use the word *karabos*, from which *karv* is derived, to describe Rus' ships in the Byzantine fleet. We also hear the same name in many accounts of travel to Constantinople, which suggest that it was particularly suitable for river transport.

A useful source dating to the eleventh century is a runestone from Uppsala in Sweden. The stone was erected by a captain named Ljótr in memory of one of his sons who had died abroad: he was called Aki and had steered a cargo ship, referred to in the runes as a *knorr*, in Greek harbours (the 'Greek' referred to here is the word used in Scandinavia for the Byzantine Empire).

Constantine VII Porphyrogenitus, in his description of the travels of the Rus', gives another perspective as he talks about *monoxyla*, which are a form of log boat (from the Greek *mono* meaning 'single' and *xylum* meaning 'tree'), being used on these journeys. He describes how the boats were cut up in the mountains in wintertime and brought down to the neighbouring lakes in spring when the ice melted; from there, they entered the Dnieper. Next they were taken to Kyiv where they were finished off and sold to the Rus'. The Rus', in turn, bought them as 'bottoms only' and fitted them out with oars and all the tackle needed to travel the Dnieper in June. This could mean that what started as a log boat was also fitted out with strakes, turning it into something more like a Viking-style boat: this was, after all, how those ships are thought to have developed in the first place. Expanded log boats or dugouts are known from Scandinavia and what is described here is very similar to boats depicted on picture stones from Gotland around AD 500. While they would have been no substitute for a full-sized Viking ship, such vessels would have had obvious benefits. They were light and strong enough for the rapids and some have even argued that they could hold a substantial number of people.[5]

In one of the sagas, the protagonists launch thirty ships from

Sweden, travelling all the way to Gardarike 'without lowering a sail'. However, looking at the map and at the vast distances being talked about here, it is hard to believe that it would have been possible not just to bring your own ships all the way from the Baltic across these natural barriers, but also to have enough boats of a decent size to launch attacks like those described later on. Over the years a few people have tried their own experiments to see if it was really possible. The first came in the early 1980s when a Swedish expedition attempted to travel all the way to Istanbul using an eight-metre-long boat based on one of a Gotlandic design. Unfortunately, the mission was hampered by a lack of permission to travel through Soviet territory at the easternmost Polish border. The team successfully reached their destination by travelling the rivers of a more westerly route, eventually reaching Turkey through Bulgaria.

After the Iron Curtain was raised in 1991, numerous other voyages were carried out in the 1990s and early 2000s, mostly on selected legs of the journey from the Baltic. None, however, made it all the way in one go and all had to resort, at some point, to modern conveniences like towing by truck or taking a car ferry across part of the Black Sea. One particular journey from Sigtuna in Sweden to Novgorod, while successful, took a full forty-one days, although it could perhaps have been completed much more quickly with more experience and in better conditions. Even so, the implication is that to travel from Scandinavia to Constantinople in one go would have taken the best part of a season, and that was before you started to worry about attacks by unfriendly locals.

Having in-depth knowledge of the local river conditions would have been essential to success. Apart from the obvious problems of knowing where a stretch of waterway was wide or deep enough, you'd also have needed to keep an eye on the water table: this could change radically from year to year, and from season to season.

In the spring, as the snow thawed, the currents would have run more swiftly and the rivers would have filled with meltwater and autumnal rains, making travel more straightforward. On the other hand, a warm and dry summer could lower the water table significantly, which would make the risk of hitting the bottom, even in a shallow vessel, a genuine threat. You'd also have had to make sure that your journey was completed before winter set in and the waters froze solid.

Travelling overland for part of the route would clearly have been necessary, just as many of the written sources suggest. This may have required the use of horses to help pull both the ships and their cargo. Taking slaves with you would have been convenient, as they could be used to carry goods and supplies and to move the vessel. Some archaeologists have proposed that sledges could have been an alternative mode of transport in wintertime, taking advantage of the snow and of frosty, ice-covered rivers. Historically, travelling 100–150 kilometres by sledge in a day was not unusual in Russia, which would have made this a perfectly viable way of moving long distances. Archaeological evidence backs this up; as for instance in Novgorod a near-complete sledge dating to around 1000 has been discovered along with hundreds of parts of others, some as long as three metres.[6] Other pieces have been found in Staraya Ladoga, right from the early phases of settlement. Three elaborate sledges – likely used for ceremonial rather than practical purposes – were found with the Oseberg ship burial too. Clearly, this technology was available, and it was used for travel and to transport goods too.

A BRUTAL LIFE

L ife out in these territories could be harsh, not least because of the extreme temperatures and conditions that had to be endured in the winter. This, however, was something the Scandinavians would have been used to, so it's not surprising that they were able not only to succeed, but also to thrive in such an environment.

Apart from information on logistics, the Arabic texts tell us about certain customs and details of everyday life that are absent from any other sources. The most famous account is that of the tenth-century traveller Ibn Fadlan, whose enthralling narratives include vivid details of the customs of all those he encountered on his journey. His accounts are riveting reading; first-hand obser- vations of an almost ethnographic character that describe the customs of the Vikings in the east, although this was far from his intention. Ibn Fadlan's journey had essentially been a missionary one. His convoy had been tasked by the Abbasid caliph Al-Muqtadir to travel to the Volga Bulghars to instruct them in the Islamic faith. Ibn Fadlan was also meant to help them build a mosque to worship in and a fort to defend them against rulers who opposed them. This was in response to a direct request from the Bulghar ruler, who had very recently converted to Islam.

The journey started on 21 June 921. Along with Ibn Fadlan travelled a whole delegation, including some who had been chosen because they had first-hand knowledge of both the languages and customs in the places they were to encounter along the way. It's unclear exactly what Ibn Fadlan's role was, but it seems to have been an important one. It turned out that the actual mission was nowhere near successfully accomplished – in fact, it became a bit of a comedy of errors, in which money that was meant to be delivered never was, and the intended correction of aberrant religious practices didn't go quite to plan. Regardless, we have been left with an invaluable travelogue and anthropological study that may have been intended as an official report to be returned in some formal capacity to Baghdad.

Ibn Fadlan's account is at times sober and descriptive, at other times personal, odd and downright peculiar. There are sections that are clearly embellished, filled with exaggerations and the supernatural, yet at the same time vividly dramatic and humorous. Ibn Fadlan provides us with the only surviving contemporary eyewitness description of a Viking funeral and in this there's little doubt of the link between the Rus' and the Vikings.

Much of the time Ibn Fadlan describes what he sees with quite some horror. The Vikings are dirty, have no sense of even basic hygiene and display some particularly dubious idolatry of their strange gods. In his own words: 'Indeed they are like the asses which err.' Most seriously, he observes that the Rus' don't wash after going to the toilet or after eating or, even worse, to get rid of the ritual impurity caused by having sex. To top it all off, he describes that every morning when they *do* wash, it is with water that is dirty and filthy: a servant provides a master with a bowl of water in which he washes his hair, blows his nose, spits and does 'every filthy thing imaginable'. Afterwards the bowl is passed to the next man who repeats the actions before passing it on once again. For a Muslim used to a high level of personal hygiene and with a strong sense of purity, this would have been an abomination.

An alternative view has been given by Ibn Rustah, another writer (who never actually saw them himself): he says that the Rus' clothing was always clean and they were kind to their slaves, whom they also equipped with good clothes because they were going to be traded. Ibn Rustah described the baggy trousers worn by the Rus' and which are mirrored in images on Gotlandic picture stones. Ibn Fadlan depicted the Rus' as the most perfect physical specimens he had ever seen – tall and ruddy – with green tattoos of trees and figures covering their bodies from their necks to their fingertips.

Of their customs, Ibn Fadlan was particularly outraged by the Rus' sexual practices, which were starkly in opposition to those he was used to back home in a Muslim context. It should be mentioned that it wasn't only the practices of the Rus' that he objected to: he was similarly shocked by the lack of sexual morals and common decency displayed by other people he met on his journey. In an encounter with a Turkish tribe, the Oguz, for example, Ibn Fadlan was horrified to see that while he was in conversation with a man, his wife bared her private parts and scratched herself in front of everyone watching.

Life among the Rus' was brutal and subject to a series of rules that ensured justice was meted out. A thief, for example, would be hung by a rope from a tree and left there, exposed to wind and rain. They were also allegedly a treacherous group among whom mistrust was high: in one account it's stated that none would go to answer a call of nature alone, but would be accompanied by three companions to guard him so that they could protect him with their swords. 'For if a man has even a little wealth,' said Ibn Rustah, 'his own brother and his friend who is with him covet it and seek to kill and despoil him.' Presumably this is why we find so many keys, padlocks and buried hoards across the Viking world.

You would need to trust the people you worked or traded with, but sometimes even that could be difficult: a runic inscription from Gotland describes a man who died on an expedition far from home after he was betrayed by the *blakumen* (possibly the Wallachians, inhabitants of present-day Romania). Presumably, these were people he trusted and had some kind of professional relationship with, and his family back home showed their upset and displeasure through the statement 'God betray those who betrayed Him'.[7]

Other accounts describe the Rus' in more favourable terms as fierce people hailing from a formidable nation, their men huge and courageous. 'They do not recognise defeat; no one turns back until he has killed or been killed,' says the philosopher and historian Ibn Miskawayh. In one story, a group of five fair-faced Rus' took on a large number of Daylamite fighters (from modern-day Iran), each killing large numbers until eventually they were defeated. But even then the last of them climbed a tree and 'stabbed himself in the vital organs' rather than be captured. Clearly, these people were notable for their fighting abilities.

It is in Ibn Fadlan's account that we find a reference to neck rings; those torques – Permian rings – that have turned up in hoards in Scandinavia and England:

> Round their necks, they wear torques of gold and silver, for every man, as soon as he accumulates 10,000 dirhams, has a torque made for his wife. When he has 20,000, he has two torques made and so on. Every time he increases his fortune by 10,000, he adds another torque to those his wife already possesses, so that one woman may have many torques round her neck.

Ibn Fadlan's observation demonstrates two things: first, that silver was used as a portable currency among the Rus', in a way that made an overt statement about your relative wealth (although the 10,000 is likely an exaggeration, as this would make each necklace weigh around three kilograms). In Scandinavia, arm rings often cut up as hacksilver were used in exactly the same way. Second, it confirms that the rings had a weight-based value that directly corresponded to a number of dirhams. This is important because weight systems were integral to the bullion economy, including that used by the Great Army, and this can tell us about the long-distance trading networks. While it's not entirely certain how and where the weight systems used by the Vikings in the ninth century originated, it's clear that they were closely related to those of the eastern worlds. This narrative, then, has left us with some invaluable links between those described as Rus' and those we call Vikings; without Ibn Fadlan's account, we wouldn't have understood the social side to the neck rings' use.

Ibn Fadlan used an interpreter on his journey, as he often described how he got his information in this way. The interpreter translated not only conversations but also customs, so he must have been someone with intimate knowledge of those cultures. In Fadlan's telling we don't know if the interpreters were part of the expedition or locals, although in another ninth-century account we hear that when they travelled all the way to Baghdad, the Rus' used Slavic-speaking eunuchs – slaves – to translate for them.

DEATH OF A CHIEFTAIN

One account above all the others that he wrote has made Ibn Fadlan famous: that of the funeral of a Rus' chieftain. This event was something that Ibn Fadlan observed first-hand by chance because he happened to be present at a camp when a leader died, somewhere near the Volga. The description is grisly and horrific, but at the same time it conveys an intricate pattern of behaviour and ritual that we would never otherwise have been able to reconstruct. The sequence of events that he describes is sleek and well orchestrated; a performance of death rituals carried out as much to the advantage of the dead as to the living.

The funeral took place in the warmer part of the year because the ground was not yet frozen. Ibn Fadlan and his caravan had stopped, and he was observing the Rus', who had come up the river in their boats, camping by the Volga, in order to trade. The boats would have been laden with goods, perhaps saved up for months to take advantage of a strategic and convenient riverine market. There were men, women, children and countless slaves: some slaves were for sale, some were for the traders' own needs; some for whichever purpose was the most beneficial at any given point in time.

The camp was extensive and had grown beyond recognition. Ibn Fadlan walked among them, accompanied by his interpreter, observing how, apparently, upon arriving at the camp, each trader stepped off the boat with offerings in hand: bread and meat, onions and milk, which were taken to an idol. He would have observed and listened to the interpreter describing how the idols – wooden sticks carved with a man's head – represented their god, who would make sure the trader got a good deal and wasn't conned in the process. When Ibn Fadlan sat in his tent at night, quill scratching at the pages as he put his observations down in words, he laughed to himself quietly at the foolishness of these traders. They didn't realise that their gifts of sacrificed animals – heads of sheep and cows placed on wooden stakes driven into the ground to feed the hungry god – were, in fact, eaten by feral dogs at night. The naïve Northmen, he wrote, returned the next morning pleased to see that their god had accepted their offerings.

Then Ibn Fadlan would have been informed, perhaps one morning after he'd noticed a different atmosphere in the camp, that one of the leaders had died. He observed that the preparations for the funeral were lengthy, taking ten days to complete: there were clothes to be sewn and a funeral pyre to prepare. The funeral itself was conducted by a woman referred to as the 'Angel of Death', and Ibn Fadlan described her and her responsibilities as follows:

'She is in charge of sewing and arranging all these things, and it is she who kills the slave girl. I saw that she was a witch, thick-bodied and sinister.'

The 'things' he refers to are the coverings on a bed that had been placed on the boat, dressed with cushions of Byzantine silk brocade. Interestingly, alternative translations state that the Angel of Death was a 'gloomy, corpulent woman, neither young nor old'. Could this be what was referred to as a *volve*, a travelling woman of religion like those we learn of elsewhere in the Viking world? An important part of the ceremony was that someone needed to accompany the dead chieftain into the afterlife. According to Ibn Fadlan's account, a slave girl or concubine volunteered for the task and went through a long series of rituals as part of the event. Initially, she was treated relatively well, being given two attendants to look after her. She was described as merry and didn't seem, at any point, to object to her treatment, in Fadlan's description, in part probably because she was plied with alcohol and maybe drugs throughout the process.

Next the slave girl took part in a curious ritual where she was lifted above a doorframe, claiming to see not just her parents but also her master in Paradise calling to her. According to the description, she didn't seem to object either to having sex with a large number of the chieftain's men who, bizarrely, proclaimed that they only did this for the love of their fallen comrade. It is possible that as a concubine or slave, this sort of treatment may have been commonplace for her. By volunteering for this particular task, her status was also elevated from that of a slave to the bride-in-death of a chieftain. For someone whose life had few prospects, this might not have been as bad a choice as we think. For her to have this level of agency, both in terms of her own future and as someone playing a central role in a significant event, is important if we are to understand the role of women here.

Eventually the slave girl was led into a burial chamber on board a ship that had been pulled from the water, and to which the chieftain had been moved from his temporary grave. It was here that the slave girl was murdered by the Angel of Death so that she could accompany the chieftain: in a harrowing account, Ibn Fadlan describes that she was held down by some of the men while others beat their shields, allegedly to drown out her screams. Finally the boat and all that it contained was set aflame. Afterwards Ibn Fadlan describes how a mound was built on top of the remains of the ship, onto which the Vikings set a wooden post inscribed with the chieftain's name and the name of the king of the Rus'.

Two things are important about this account. First, the description of the funeral is so close to the archaeological record of Viking burials both in Scandinavia and the rest of the Viking world that we cannot possibly deny these people's link to those we think of as Vikings, even though they are described as Rus'. While the funeral was a cremation, it matches very closely the details of ship graves found elsewhere: the burial chamber inside the Oseberg ship, for instance, sounds remarkably similar. The animal sacrifices depicted by Ibn Fadlan are familiar too, and the entire funeral is a good match for the elaborate ritual seen at Salme and the performative elements of the Repton charnel mound. Both cremation and inhumations were common across the Viking world, sometimes taking place side-by-side. The form of burial practice varied enormously too: some dead were placed in the ground with no grave goods, others with equipment needed for the afterlife. Some are in coffins and others, like Bj.581, in elaborate chamber graves. According to Ibn Fadlan, this related to status and wealth. A poor man, he said, would be cremated, whereas a slave would be left where he died, waiting for the dogs and birds of prey to devour him. Another possible reason why it is so difficult to find slaves in the burial record.

Second, Ibn Fadlan's narrative is the most reliable – at least to a degree – contemporary account of human sacrifice during the Viking Age. And it's this description that offers a possible link to the juvenile grave in Repton. Could those juveniles have been killed in a ritual enacted in a similar way? Obviously, the circumstances were very different, but there is extensive drama and an element of performance evident in Ibn Fadlan's account that is perhaps matched at Repton. The burial by the Volga wasn't just a practical process of dealing with a rotting corpse, but an elaborate display of rituals and storytelling, carefully choreographed in a way that made sense to those who watched it. If we are to believe Ibn Fadlan's depiction, each element, from the preparation of the body and the creation of the chamber aboard the boat to the ritualised abuse of the slave girl, was part of a story that had meaning and clear reasons for being carried out. There was something theatrical in Repton too, in the way that the mass grave must have been created: the clean layer of red sand beneath the bones and the stacking of remains, possibly around a central burial. It is possible that a similar performance took place there, in the shadows of the crumbling ruins of the once-glorious monastery.

8.

BEAD: CROSSROADS

VYPOVZYV, UKRAINE, 2018

I've stepped out of the trench for some water, sitting on the parched grass underneath a makeshift shade made from a threadbare tarpaulin. The sun is scorching overhead and we haven't seen clouds for days, digging far from the shaded pine forests that surround the open plain. Shielding my eyes with my hand, I look up towards the hill to the east, making out a person walking barefoot down the sandy path towards me. Up there is the ancient hillfort overlooking the river, with an excavation trench reaching almost ten metres down at its deepest. Home-made, rickety ladders barely support the students climbing down to the bottom where ancient postholes appear as outlines in the sand: all that remains of the fortified structure that loomed atop this hill a thousand years ago. As the figure comes closer, I see that it's Vitaly, his right hand clenched into a fist. He has found something. I push myself off the ground and walk towards him. 'Is this what you were looking for?' he asks and stretches out his hand. And there it was: a small carnelian bead with smooth, flat surfaces, oblong and with facets cut along its sides, identical to that found in Repton.

POLITICAL MINEFIELDS

The tales of the Rus' provide a colourful background and a convincing and compelling description of the people you would have met on these journeys. Yet questions remain as to how accurate the accounts are and over what timeframes this would have developed. What happened beyond the territories described by the Arab travellers: how far do the connections extend north, west, or further east? There is no clear agreement on how inter-linked these worlds were. More than a century's worth of academic debate – sometimes hostile – has dwelled on whether the Vikings and Rus' really were one and the same. The separation between east and west is in part one of semantics: while, as some have said, the Rus' were not always Vikings, many Vikings were Rus'. The vital question here is one of identity. This was a melting pot of cultures (Scandinavian, Slav, Khazar, Byzantine and more) and it is plausible that the earliest Viking presence proved a catalyst for what the Rus' were to become. Yet this is contentious for deeply political reasons, made even more so by the oppressive hold the Soviet Union had on historians and archaeologists in this region for decades. As George Orwell famously said in his dystopian novel *1984*: 'Who controls the past controls the future. Who controls the present controls the past.' It has been said that in early medieval Europe 'to bear arms was to be a participant in politics' and for these eastern regions, studying the period in the present can be deeply political too.

Many of the controversies surrounding the Rus' and the Vikings boil down to a single historical source: the *Russian Primary Chronicle*. Apart from the accounts of the Arab travellers, which are skewed towards the Volga river region and the tenth century, there are few available historical documents that give more explicit details of when and by whom this region was settled. Much of what we think we know comes from the *Primary Chronicle*, which was compiled sometime between the mid eleventh and the early twelfth centuries. While it contains some reliable information, most of the contents must be taken with a pinch of salt: its writers, Christian monks based in Kyiv, seem to have taken quite a few liberties with historical accuracy, and the information contained in the *Chronicle* has provided an origin story for what is now Russia as well as for Ukraine.

The *Chronicle* is thought to have been written down by Nestor, a monk from the Monastery of the Caves in Kyiv, and is also known as the *Tale of Bygone Years*. The main story goes like this: in the early 860s the land of the Slavs was in turmoil. For a long time Slavonic tribes had been harassed by robbers from the north, groups of *Varangians* (another name often used as a synonym for the Rus', or the Vikings, later gaining a more specific use), who forced them to pay tribute. Eventually they revolted but this led to disaster. Internecine strife meant self-rule proved to be an unsuccessful venture; the Slavs were too busy fighting among themselves. To solve this problem, a request was made to another group of northerners, the Rus': 'Our land is great and rich,' the Slavs pleaded, 'but there is no order in it. Come to rule and reign over us.'

The call was answered by three brothers, who took with them their families and 'all the Rus'' to migrate. The three were Rurik, the eldest, who set himself up in Novgorod; Sineus, who settled in Beloozero on the southern bank of Lake Beloye; and Truvor, who took up residence in Izborsk, just east of the Russia–Estonia border. The land around Novgorod – the New City – became known as the land of the Rus' (and its people as the *Rus'ians*). The younger two brothers lasted only two years and afterwards Rurik took charge of the whole territory. And so, according to the *Chronicle*, the Rus' state was founded. In the years to follow, the nucleus of the Rus' was to move to Kyiv.

Two points in the story are crucial for understanding why this account became so problematic. First, that the protagonists came from the north and were most likely Swedish Vikings. Second, that the Slavonic tribes are described as incapable of keeping the Varangians at bay and of ruling themselves. It's easy to understand why such a version of events became controversial as an origin story. The debate has become a stand-off between *Normanists* and *anti-Normanists*, with the former arguing in favour of a heavy Scandinavian influence and the latter denying it almost entirely. The anti-Normanist viewpoint was particularly favoured under Soviet rule. Here the preferred narrative was that Scandinavians had no influence over early Russian politics, language or religion and the Rus' name referred to something else altogether: suggestions included anything from the river named Ros near Kyiv to the town of Rodez in France or the island of Rügen in the Baltic, or even, more creatively, that the name derived from the ancient Iranian tribe of Roxolani. Anything but Scandinavia.

At times the debates have been extreme, especially on the side of the Normanists, with Adolf Hitler infamously stating: 'Unless other peoples, beginning with the Vikings, had imported some rudiments of organisation into Russian humanity, the Russians would still be living like rabbits.' With statements like this, it's not difficult to understand the opposition to Viking connections and the dilemma for Slavic scholars forced to choose between a view crediting a superior, foreign people with creating their entire nation or an alternative story that is at odds with the written sources. As one nineteenth-century historian put it, the question was of 'whether or not we have created our own history'.

For a long time there seemed to be no middle ground and arguably this is one of the key reasons why the eastern sphere has often been excluded more generally from discussions of the Viking Age. The Iron Curtain that fell across Europe after the Second World War meant researchers into the northern past were at best discouraged and at worst silenced. It has even been suggested that research showing any form of outside influence – not just Scandinavians – having a positive impact on the Slavic people was unsafe.

A prime example of the effect of this kind of thinking is shown in another Slavonic location, where traditionally the Vikings are thought to have had little impact: Prague. In 1928 at Prague Castle, a Ukrainian archaeologist named Ivan Borkovsky excavated a grave dating to the tenth century: a time when Prague would have been an important, cosmopolitan centre. The male skeleton lay interred in a deteriorated wooden chamber and was accompanied by a familiar set of grave goods: a sword, axe, knives, a fire steel and a bucket by his feet. Many of these objects were of Scandinavian type, giving rise to one interpretation that this was the grave of a Viking, a proposal that was initially ignored. When Nazi Germany occupied Prague in 1939, the benefits of having a Viking burial at the castle were recognised: the presence of Germanic people in eastern Europe was expedient to Nazi ideology, as such a narrative could provide historical precedent for their occupation. Viking, Scandinavian and Germanic identities were quickly conflated, suggesting that the castle and by extension the whole territory were justifiably part of the Nazi birthright. Following the war, when Prague fell under the rule of the USSR, the alternative interpretation was emphasised: that this person was of Slavic origins. A team of researchers has tried to resolve the question using bioarchaeology but the results have, to date, been inconclusive: isotope analysis suggests that he wasn't local but came from somewhere in northern Europe, possibly around the fringes of the Baltic Sea – maybe somewhere like Denmark.[1] While that makes a Viking origin very feasible, we are well aware by now that geography does not equate to identity and the new scientific methods cannot ensure political neutrality.

This political minefield, then, serves as a backdrop for anyone trying to understand Vikings in the east. It's unlikely that the account in the *Primary Chronicle* is entirely true, not least because it was written down several hundred years later, and because the story has been formulated to present one particular lineage, that of Rurik and his descendants, as the only legitimate heirs to what became known as the Kyivan state, the political entity established by the Rus' in the late ninth and early tenth centuries. Nevertheless, many have tried to corroborate the story and to link the identity of Rurik to another known and very real Viking: Rörik, the nephew or brother of the Danish king Harald Klak, who died around 880. Rörik is mentioned in the *Royal Frankish Annals* and other continental sources, and the match makes sense in some ways as the two were certainly contemporary. However, there is nothing that links Rörik to Kyiv, so it's more likely to be a coincidence.

But what about archaeology and new evidence? In contrast to thirty years ago, the east is opening up for researchers and new lines of evidence are enabling us to find more ways to corroborate or contradict the historical texts. There are a number of archaeological sites in the upper Dnieper region, the most famous being Gnezdovo, near the city of Smolensk in western Russia, on the right-hand bank of the Dnieper. This may be the city originally called Smaleskia; at least, that is the name that appears in the Icelandic sagas. The site is rich in Scandinavian culture in both burial types and recovered artefacts. There's a reference in the

Primary Chronicle to Smolensk being captured by Oleg, the heir to Rurik, in the early 880s just before he kills Askold and Dir, two Rus' brothers who had arrived with the first migrants and established themselves as the rulers of Kyiv.

Here, at Gnezdovo, the importance of the rivers becomes crystal clear. Apart from the traffic south on the Dnieper, you'd have had access eastwards towards the Volga routes, as well as to the areas through Lake Ilmen and the Lovat river to the north. The burials are particularly wealthy and include chamber graves that closely parallel those at sites like Birka. The town has often been considered to be a *pogost*, a centre where tribute was collected and which would have been occupied by retainers of the later princes of Kyiv, the descendants of Rurik who came to rule the kingdom of the Kyivan Rus'. This may be a later attribution, but what's for certain is that Viking Age Gnezdovo had clear and significant links to Scandinavia while at the same time being a place of power in its own right. Now ancient DNA may have demonstrated this link for the first time, as one burial there has suggested a man had 'Danish-like' ancestry.

When you move further south towards the Dnieper, little is known from the written records and even accessing information from excavations can sometimes be difficult. However, in 2018, I was asked to lead a team of British students working with Ukrainian archaeologists to excavate a Rus' site north of Kyiv. The site in question is known as Vypovzyv, and lies around seventy-five kilometres north-east of Kyiv. To get there you drive across vast plains of sunflower fields, through remote villages filled with rusty tractors; here you pay for snacks in the village shop with hryvnia, the Ukrainian currency that originates from weight-based standardised metal bars with the same name, which literally means 'neck ring'. The monetary system in Ukraine dates back to currencies that were used more than a thousand years ago, having developed, slowly, from the wearable currency of the Rus'. The excavations were led by Ukrainian Vyacheslav Skorokhod, part of a new generation of archaeologists who were keen to engage with western researchers.

Vypovzyv was first spotted in aerial photographs taken by the Luftwaffe during the Second World War, and the Ukrainian team had worked at the site for ten years. When you see it from the air, the location makes sense: a long, thin peninsula juts onto a floodplain where the River Desna once flowed. Today the river is about three kilometres away but its scars and rapid movements are clearly evident in the landscape: satellite photographs show swirling, wavy patches of colour, where the grass and sand reveal the indelible marks left behind by its meandering path, the patterns testament to how powerful and fast-flowing it is. A smaller stream called the Krymka now flows slowly past the raised area of land and this tributary, or one just like it, would once have passed round the back of the site, a possible escape route from the busy Desna. Downstream, the main river flows into the Dnieper at Kyiv, while in the other direction you can travel north to the city of Chernihiv and, eventually, to the river's source near Smolensk over the border in Russia. Desna means 'right hand' in the old East Slavic language, perhaps because of its status as the largest tributary of the Dnieper. Between early December and April, the river is usually frozen.

At some point in the late ninth or early tenth century a hillfort sprang up on the prominent tip of the peninsula. Here the Ukrainian team found evidence of palisades and fortifications, making this a highly defended tower right on top of the hill: a place where you could easily have spotted enemies. At the same time the tower could not have been missed by anyone sailing up or down the Desna. Around the back, where the slower-flowing tributary circles the hillfort, there's evidence of a port zone, with traces of old channels, where boats could have been pulled up out of the water, and a pier. Among the sandy deposits lay rusty iron nails from ship repairs. On the main expanse of the plain, beyond the hillfort, the team found a large number of sunken buildings that had been part of a settlement. This appears to have been inhabited by local people, at least if the artefacts are telling the truth: objects are of typical Slavic forms that would have been common on any site in the area. There is evidence of craftwork everywhere, of small-scale cottage industries springing up in order to support the burgeoning settlement. But on the hillfort, the objects are different. They are of higher status and more of them come from elsewhere: things like silver dirhams and a minute fragment of chainmail – items that only an elite would have possessed. And it was here that a tiny orange object was uncovered during the excavation: a carnelian bead perfectly matching that found in Repton.

COMMODITIES

The primary role of sites like Gnezdovo and Vypovzyv would have been to control movement along the rivers and thereby to oversee and manage the expansion of the Kyivan state. These weren't so much permanent settlements or towns, more like staging grounds or transit hubs created to move and administer people. By doing so, they could control trade and taxation, which was a vital part of what happened here. When the Rus' newcomers arrived, the Slavs had already been paying tribute to the Khazars and the new overlords merely took over this profitable enterprise. In addition, they promised to protect those who paid their dues. In other words, this was a protection racket, not too different from what the Vikings did in the west.

Another profitable part of the operation was obtaining and

selling slaves. Here the success of the venture was so great that the very name of the people captured – the Slavs – has given rise to the word slave. Enslavement here was seasonal and certain times of year were used to go out to the hinterland and capture people who could be sold when moving along the Volga and Dnieper to markets in the south or north. This could mean that slaves would have to be held for weeks or even months at settlements like Vypovzyv, much as would surely have been the case in the western Viking camps. It may well be that having a number of slaves to hand made the movement of boats along the rivers and portages far more straightforward. Yet those slaves have again left no trace.

That slaves were an important part of these eastern societies is shown in numerous sources. In Ibn Fadlan's description of the Khazars, for instance, he explained that the king had sixty slave girls as concubines (in addition to his twenty-five wives) and each had a eunuch to protect her at all times. In Hungary, a twelfth-century account by the Andalusian traveller Abu Hamid Al-Gharnati explained that a beautiful slave girl was cheap: she could be bought for ten dinars most of the year, but during raiding season – when, presumably, the supply was high – a fine slave girl or a Greek boy may have set you back no more than three dinars. For comparison, he described that twenty sheep cost one dinar.

In the ninth century, there was such a high demand for slaves in the Islamic caliphate that a slave's price rose greatly, one source suggesting that prices reached as high as six hundred thousand dirhams. A century later, however, there appears to have been so much of a surplus that slaves would sell for no more than twenty or thirty dirhams each. Clearly, the ninth century was the heyday of the slave trader, and that is why it became such a popular business venture for the Vikings.

Slaves were, of course, just one of many commodities that these settlements and trading posts profited from: next on the list was the fur trade, a lucrative business the Vikings did well to get in on. Furs from the north were luxury items among the elite in Baghdad, just as beads and other exotic objects were luxuries in the north. While some furs would have come all the way from Scandinavia, many could be obtained throughout eastern Europe, which meant that those travelling the rivers could easily acquire them along the way. Different places offered their own specialities, such as the furs you could obtain from the Finns: stunning white and highly desirable winter coats of stoats, known as minivers. There were many different types used for different purposes, and some could be acquired only in certain regions and at certain times of the year. Take the ermine, or stoat, for example: it moults twice a year and in the winter grows a dense and silky coat that in northern latitudes is completely white. Such white furs have been popular throughout history and are often associated with high status even now. The traditional ceremonial robes of members of the UK House of Lords were trimmed with white ermine, as are the hood and trimmings on the cape of the University of Cambridge's vice-chancellor. The ermine is even the symbol of the flag of the Duchy of Brittany. That the fur was popular in the Viking Age is shown in a grave from Stavanger in western Norway: along with weapons, riding gear and other personal equipment, the man buried was found to have worn clothing with traces of ermine pelts. It is likely that this could have been one of the white furs referred to by the tenth-century Arab historian al-Masudi when he described the eastern fur trade in 956 as having red, white and black furs available of varying types, qualities and prices.

Al-Masudi also explained that the furs were traded from the Volga region, both southwards to the Islamic caliphate and north and west, even as far as Frankia and al-Andalus, i.e. Muslim Iberia. The rulers of non-Arab peoples, he wrote, delighted in wearing these furs and, in particular, the most prized and precious of them all, the black furs. They made them into garments like sleeveless tunics and bonnets: maybe this was a reference to the sort of hat worn by the Birka woman, Bj.581?

Just how prized such furs were is shown by al-Masudi's account of what the eighth-century caliph al-Mahdi did on a journey to Rayy, in modern-day Iran on the southern fringe of the Caspian Sea. These territories could grow bitterly cold during the winter and, far from being mere status symbols, black furs were clearly prized for their superior heat retention qualities, which the caliph tested with an experiment: during a particularly severe winter that brought intense cold and deep snow, he asked for several flagons of water to be brought to him. Every flagon was stoppered using a tuft of fur, each of a different kind. After leaving them overnight outside in the freezing cold, in the morning the Caliph asked to inspect each one. He found that all were frozen solid apart from one bottle, namely the one stoppered by the fur from a black fox – this, then, was the type of fur to provide him with the best heat and water protection. Al-Masudi explained just how well thought of these furs were: they kept you warm and dry, retaining more heat than that of any other animal, he said, while 'the humours it contains resemble those of fire'. Furthermore, he wrote, they were a perfect choice of garment for those of delicate health or the elderly.

Merchants and tradesmen also moved other commodities, like walrus tusks, from the far north, perhaps through this route. When Ohthere visited Alfred in England, he took with him 'walrus teeth' to give the king either as a gift or to sell, and it is possible that Ohthere himself had collected them: he stated, in fact, that he had killed sixty walruses or small whales on his journey around the North Cape in the far north of Norway. Clearly, it is possible that some of these commodities were not simply passed from person to person but actually travelled with the hunter, or maybe the organiser of the hunt, themselves.

At Vypovzyv, if you walk up the sandy path to the top of the hillfort and look out over the floodplain, you can understand how the plains, the rivers and the abundant resources available would have been desirable to an incoming group, especially one that could so easily place itself in a position of power to exploit the local communities. Yet there were likely benefits to those communities too, to those who were happy to trade and to take advantage of opportunities to develop their own entrepreneurship, supplying the demands that the incomers created. These settlements didn't grow in the way that towns often do, through increasing stability in response to a growing population, but rather from the specific need to establish trading posts and to control the most important routes of communication: the rivers. This also meant that while the towns didn't grow out of areas with hinterlands that could support them, they arose in areas that were strategically and topographically important, which may then have generated a rural economy. Maybe a similar situation can be seen in England, where, for example, the camp at Torksey acted as a catalyst for a pottery industry and subsequent settlement.

This also meant that locally procured commodities could sometimes become important, and a product that was essential to the maritime success of the Vikings has provided us with such an example: tar. It is clear that Viking ships needed extensive repair and maintenance, and the evidence for ironworking at the winter camps in the west demonstrates that they were places where this would happen outside the raiding season. But wood and iron weren't the only things needed to keep the fleets on the water: ships needed waterproofing too, which is precisely what tar would have been used for. It can be extracted relatively simply from most types of trees and used to treat and seal wood; on a sizable clinker-built ship, it has been estimated that around five hundred litres of tar would have been needed. It might also have been used for treating sails and ropes, to make them better able to withstand the difficult conditions at sea.

Something of a neglected commodity for a long time, it was only recently that a study showed precisely how large a part tar played in the Viking expansion. Research in Sweden has shown a large increase in tar production in the eighth century, through the use of special tar pits for extracting the resin. This coincided perfectly with the use of new shipbuilding techniques and with the intensification of maritime activities at the start of the Viking Age. Tar pits have also been found at Gnezdovo and evidence for tar or pitch* production was discovered at Vypovzyv too around the port zone, in the shape of pots with a small hole in the base, as well as ceramics showing traces of tar. In any case, the juxtaposition of craft, commerce, ports and fortification has strong parallels with sites like Birka (and maybe even with Great Army sites in England) and this is something that gives us vital clues to their functions.

WARRIOR STATES

One notable aspect of many of the important Rus' settlements is a very strong military component, which gives rise to an understanding of them as having been controlled by a *warrior* elite. Among the most commonly found artefact types in the east with clear Scandinavian origins or forms are weapons and military equipment. An obvious parallel to these is the military garrison at Birka, which emerged in its full form during the tenth century.

---

* Tar and pitch are often used interchangeably. Here pitch refers to the sticky resin obtained from trees and other organic sources.

There, a clearly separate part of the town was more heavily defended
with ramparts and palisades. The garrison contained buildings and
graves, both with extensive weaponry, including in a prominent
location, the grave of Bj.581. The stronghold had evidently been
home to a militarised unit, as a central hall had hundreds of knives
incorporated into its fabric and weapons stored in wooden chests
and hanging on the walls: spears, arrows and shields.

Intriguingly, there is also evidence at Birka of eastern fighters
among the graves, in particular the Magyars.[2] The most spectacular
indications of contact with these tribal nomads who established
themselves in the steppes of what is now Hungary have been found
in the graves that contain archery equipment: composite bows and
quivers filled with distinct arrows, as well as personal equipment
like belts and other insignia known to have been used by the
Magyars. This could mean two things: either that Birka was home
to migrant archers or that even deeper contacts existed between
the two regions, likely via the Rus'.

The implication of having what seems like a professional, organised military entity as part of the settlement is that they must have
been there to defend and support a ruler or ruling elite, to make
sure that order was maintained and that trade could carry on in
peace – in the way that the ruling group wanted to. These groups
may have included the druzhina, an elite retinue surrounding a
leader: in the *Russian Primary Chronicle*, the Rus'ian prince had
precisely such a military unit with him when out collecting tribute
or when he was at war. The high-status warrior graves found in the
Desna region are thought to have belonged to members of a druzhina
and this is often taken to mean one of the Kyivan princes, descendent
from Rurik. This may be stretching the evidence a little too far, as
it is likely that there were many more protagonists than we know
about from the records. Attachment to a ruler was important,
though, and this is why when the burial of the chieftain described

by Ibn Fadlan was complete, a marker post was inserted into the mound: this was inscribed with both the name of the deceased *and* the name of the king.

Military defences like those around Birka and sites like Vypovzyv were common across early medieval Europe and are well known from the Frankish and Ottoman empires too. They were particularly common in border zones where control of occupied territory had to be maintained. Conversely, they could be situated where forces threatening to occupy were kept out: the extensive building of *burhs* initiated by Alfred the Great in the ninth century to withstand the Vikings is a prime example. Another function of these sites, frequently found in western Europe among the Franks, was the collection of tribute. This provided a regular income for many economies, acting as a form of institutionalised plunder. Similar functions would clearly also have defined these eastern settlements and fortifications.

Frustratingly, we have very few written records of these groups to shed light on their political organisation in the early ninth century. Possible clues may be taken from events in the neighbouring Byzantine Empire, though. In 839, Emperor Theophilus established a brand-new province in Crimea known as the Climata (meaning 'the districts'), on a peninsula on the north coast of the Black Sea. This was clearly a strategic move because it was the part of Byzantine territory that lay closest to some of their key rivals, namely the Magyars (Hungarians) and the Khazars. The new province was obviously created for military reasons because it included a permanent garrison of considerable size, manned with a force of two thousand men. Theophilus must have felt under threat of losing Crimea, and it is possible that a new Rus' state was the reason: after all, the province was created in precisely the same year that the Rus' delegation was received by Louis the Pious in Frankia and we first hear of them by name.

In that very same year, the Khazars themselves were evidently feeling under threat, because they sent ambassadors to Theophilus asking for help to improve the fortifications of their base, the city of Sarkel on the River Don in what is now southern Russia. Theophilus promptly agreed to do so, sending an expedition including builders and architects. Upon returning to the Byzantine capital Constantinople, the leader of that mission declared that Byzantine territories in Crimea were indeed under threat, from the same people who were also causing the Khazars concern. Nobody really knows who this threat refers to and although some later sources suggest that it was the Magyars, it seems more likely that the defences were built to withstand the advances and threats of an emerging Rus' state.[3]

The reference in the *Annals of St Bertin* to the Rus' expedition to Frankia is also enlightening for what it tells us about political organisation. It's apparent from the account that the group had been sent there by a leader referred to in the letter as a *Khagan*, a word used by the Khazars for a ruler. Why the Rus' visited the Frankish kingdom is unclear, but it has been suggested that this diplomatic journey may have been made in order to announce the foundation of a new ruling power situated somewhere along the Dnieper.[4] In any case, it proves that a state of some sort, with a leader, *was* established in the 830s; one that was significant enough to be received by the leaders in both Constantinople and Frankia (regardless of what those leaders thought of them). At the same time, if Byzantium and the Khazars were both feeling threatened, perhaps there were a number of different groups and not just a single state. There's also the possibility of considerable internal conflict between different groups of Rus', which could, after all, explain why the settlement at Vypovzyv appears to have been extensively burned on more than one occasion. It has also been suggested that those who harried the Rus' delegation so much in

839 on their way to Frankia could have been not a foreign tribe but another group of Vikings that we know nothing about. Such different groups acting in the same region would be familiar across the Viking world. A similar point was raised by my collaborators at Vypovzyv one night, around the campfire: the possibility that at one time this territory had been ruled by an independent army, one we don't know about from the written sources; much like the Great Army in England, which the historical documents claim had a number of semi-independent leaders.

It's very likely that these eastern territories were ruled by chieftains and that the land of the Rus' was divided into different political units that waged war against one another on a regular basis. At both Vypovzyv and neighbouring settlements there appears to be evidence for this in layers of burning: charred wood remains are testament to fires having swept across the workshops and houses, cutting short lives and livelihoods and reducing them to blackened layers in the sandy deposits discovered a millennium later. These layers of burning are often related to the historically attested chiefs and conflicts, but it seems very possible that the protagonists may have slipped through unnoticed. One potential elaboration of this theory can be found in a series of treaties between Byzantium and the Rus' dating to the tenth century that deal with trading arrangements. In the treaties, numerous individuals described as envoys or their representatives are listed. There is no agreement on quite who those people were. Some believe they were members of the druzhina, the Kyivan prince's retinue. However, others have convincingly argued that these people – twenty-five in total – represented semi-independent rulers or landowners from across the Rus' territory. This may well be a very similar picture to the political situation in Scandinavia, where a series of local chieftains or 'petty kings' held sway.[5]

We should also bear in mind later saga sources set in the tenth century that describe attacks on eastern territories by Vikings from Scandinavia, such as Snorri described in *Heimskringla* for the year 997. This year, Snorri says, an earl called Eirik travelled to Sweden where he was given land and freedom by the Swedish king. Gathering up a number of men and ships, he travelled to Gotland where he spent a summer observing merchant vessels and occasionally ravaging coastal territories. The next spring he travelled across the Baltic to 'Valdemar's dominions', reaching and besieging Aldeigjuborg (Staraya Ladoga). Taking the castle, he killed a great many people before he 'carried destruction all around far and wide in Gardarike' for the next five years. Afterwards he travelled back to Scandinavia. Presumably, the purpose of the raid was one of obtaining loot rather than any form of settlement and there is no reason why similar raids – if real – wouldn't have taken place further south too.

The key is that these incoming groups were able to understand and take advantage of internecine politics, conflicts and dynamics. The Slavic tribes were farmers, not warriors; their societies were run on a small scale. They were already being exploited and controlled by the Khazars, so the Scandinavians were simply interlopers who offered a different form of oppression, likely a situation in which the locals had no choice but to submit. To be able to do so, the Vikings would have needed good local knowledge and information, excellent strategies and a reputation such that the threat of force may have been enough to convince the population to submit. Even in these distant territories, news would have travelled fast.

Another crucial point is that the Scandinavians in eastern Europe didn't have a single, coherent territory, but were spread across a very broad region, like little pockets among the varied groups and tribes. This pattern would have been mirrored in the west, in England, Ireland and Frankia. The Viking strength lay in their ability to adjust and to adapt, and to find (or rather, appropriate) their own niche. As such there are some consistent patterns of culture, identity and behaviour that are maintained both in the west and in the east over several hundred years. These could only have been so persistent with a constant flow of people between the different territories, going not just *out* of the homelands, but also back *in*.

While our overall understanding of these trading ports and their wider political organisation is increasing, there remains little evidence of the protagonists, and not least the roles of women. But one place might yield more answers. Not far from Vypovzyv lies another site, Shestovitsa – the better known of the two because it has been so extensively researched. Excavations were first carried out there in the 1920s. Shestovitsa is situated on the right bank of the Desna, about fourteen kilometres south-east of Chernihiv, and it contains two hillforts and a settlement, along with hundreds of graves. Today much of the site is covered by dense pine forest, planted in the 1950s to the detriment of much of what is buried underground; the tree roots poke through the sandy soils, moving and disrupting whatever lay silently underneath for a millennium.

Still, we have a good picture of what went on there. It was originally a Slavic village, and sometime before 900 there was an extensive fire. Afterwards the site was fortified with a hillfort built on a headland situated above the river: a clearly defensible location with views across the floodplain. The area is now dry, with the Desna flowing a short distance away and what was once the slower-flowing tributary river a field of sunflowers. The fort on the hilltop was soon joined by a settlement that grew up around it to the west, with extensive cemeteries of burial mounds to cater for the growing population. Evidence of iron and pitch production has been found within the buildings, hinting at craft production with a very specific purpose.

The choice of location is striking too. Both Vypovzyv and Shestovitsa are strategically placed at sites with a high point offering views over the surrounding landscape and near a tributary of the main river, which would have made it easier to unload ships and boats. What many of these sites have in common with settlements and emporia around the Baltic is that they are located where modes of transport could be changed, be that travelling from the sea to the river or perhaps from the river inland. In the twelfth century Vypovzyv was the place to change your horses when riding between larger cities, and it's very possible that some of these locations were also chosen to enable you to travel onwards on land in the wintertime.

This leaves us with an interesting thought about the ships. If you couldn't take the same vessel all the way on a long journey, you would be dependent on a safe harbour to leave it, potentially for quite some time, and on the availability of another mode of transport to take you onwards. In addition to the strategic use of waterways, the plains would have required horses and mounted warriors to control them; which is another similarity with the Mälaren region around Birka in Sweden, surrounded as it too was by an open landscape that needed monitoring.[6]

Yet it is the graves at Shestovitsa that are the most spectacular and that tell us most about who the inhabitants were. Just as elsewhere in the Viking world, some of the graves contained cremations and inhumations, many of them under mounds. Scandinavian artefacts appeared frequently: jewellery and weapons of distinctive types. Clearly, a number of those buried had Scandinavian affiliations of some kind, though there were also graves that revealed only local Slavic burial rites. The Scandinavian connections in Shestovitsa have been strongly disputed in the past, with the USSR sending the archaeologist Y.V. Stankevich there in 1946 to excavate in part to *prove* that there were no Scandinavian burials. However, the catalogue of finds from excavations over the years includes items from weapons to glass gaming pieces – both simple versions reminiscent of the lead pieces from England and several blue glass figures identical to Swedish versions. DNA evidence has now shown that two individuals from the same Shestovitsa burial mound most likely had 'Swedish-like' or 'Norwegian-like' ancestry: the two were brother and sister.

Remarkably there were also around thirty chamber graves at Shestovitsa that bear strong similarities to those found in Sweden – particularly at Birka. One, a subterranean, timber-lined chamber, contained a body along with a horse at its feet, kitted out with a stunning leather bridle decorated with gilded silver fittings, a saddle and stirrups with silver wire inlays. There was a lot more: an axe, a sword with a scabbard chape decorated in a Scandinavian-style twisted dragon design, a luxuriously decorated fighting knife, the remains of a cloak, and a Samanid dirham dating to the early tenth century. Most striking, however, was that the excavators found by the burial's head – the only remaining fragments of the deceased were a few pieces of skull bone – a mass of organic material representing a fur hat tipped with a beautifully ornate conical silver cap mount, almost identical to that worn in death by Bj.581, the warrior woman in Birka. There was jewellery too: a necklace of forty-one gilded glass beads in a bag and two silver rings. We don't know the sex of this person, as the skeletal markers were inconclusive. The parallels with Bj.581's grave, though, are irrefutable, making a strong connection between the two: the warriors of Birka belonged to the world of the Rus'. One way or another, women were part of this too.

THE WOMEN OF THE DNIEPER

There are other clues to women's roles in Shestovitsa. A number of women there were buried with the striking oval tortoise brooches that elsewhere are taken as proof of a Viking woman's presence. If we apply the same logic as for the female dress jewellery identified in England, that the artefacts accompanied migrant women, then the women here too may well have travelled from Scandinavia. The brooches are even mentioned by Ibn Fadlan, who, when describing the Rus' and their neck rings, also said that the women carried a 'box' on their chest. This could be the same as the common tortoise brooches or it could be a type of box brooch often found on Gotland. Who were these women, then: were they Scandinavian too?

I am reminded of the paragraph written by the monk Nestor on the brothers who first came to this region: in the *Russian Primary Chronicle* he stated that they brought all their kin and the rest of the Varangian Rus', who 'migrated'. In other words, if we believe what he says, this really *was* a family-based migration rather than an all-male expedition. This part of Nestor's account is rarely commented on, but we should have no reason to doubt that entire family groups travelled east. The archaeological evidence backs it up. At other sites too, like Gnezdovo, several graves clearly contain women, not only with Scandinavian affiliations, but also of high status.

Often, too, women are mentioned in descriptions of double graves in Ukraine, just like those that are familiar from other parts of the Viking world. Among these some seem particularly touching; they depict two skeletons side by side, a man and a woman, either holding hands or with the man's arm around the woman in what seems like a loving embrace. Each grave is carefully and deliberately arranged; a tableau frozen in time. There are two stories being told here. One is of the couple and what was presumably their relationship in life, as well as their aspirations to stick together in the afterlife. The other is of the mourners who placed them there and of the theatrical funeral performance that must have taken place. Such graves hammer home the point that a burial was for the benefit of the living as much as (or even more than) it was for the dead.

Yet there exists a more sinister side to this practice: the suggestion that in male–female double graves these were not accidental joint deaths, but rather a case of death and the sacrifice of a woman to follow her man into the afterworld. It's not clear when this interpretation arose, but it's one that has persisted. The record of Ibn Fadlan's funeral scene is partially to blame, but so is Norse mythology: for instance, when Baldur, one of Odin's sons, was about to be cremated, his wife Nanna was so overcome with grief that she died at once and was buried alongside her husband.

There *are* some graves where sacrifice seems to have been likely, such as a grisly example from Norway in which a burial is accompanied by other individuals whose hands and legs have been bound together: it suggests that those people were being forced to their deaths in some way. Yet this isn't the same as the care that was taken to show the couples at Shestovitsa as being *together*, both treated the same, with grave goods, jewellery and weapons. The common interpretation of a woman following a man into death is also clearly inspired by ethnographic comparisons to the practice of suttee in Hinduism, as practised in India until it was banned under British colonial rule. Here a mourning, bereaved wife would throw herself onto her deceased husband's funeral pyre to follow him into death. These women were associated with the goddess Sati, wife of Shiva, who flung herself into a fire to protest her father's lack of respect for her husband. The word *sati,* the name for those who sacrificed themselves in this way, comes from the

Sanskrit word meaning 'a good woman'. Intriguingly, the mid-tenth-century accounts of Al-Masudi make a direct link between the Rus' and Indian burial rites, describing that among the Rus' who lived in Itil, the capital city of the Khazars, a woman was 'incinerated while still alive' after her man died (but not the other way around). This was something she herself desired in order to enter Paradise in a custom, he says, that was similar to those found in India.

An account that might support this is that of the tenth-century Arabic author Ibn Rustah, who also described the funerary customs of the Rus': he said that if someone of importance died they were placed in the grave like 'a large house' (presumably, a chamber grave), along with precious items, food and offerings. He further explained that 'a woman he particularly favoured is buried alive with him, the grave is then shut and she dies there'. It's unclear how much attention we should give to his words, though, as he didn't make any of these observations in person, having been described more as an 'armchair geographer'. Presumably, the slave woman described by Ibn Fadlan was buried next to her master as if she were his wife, and it is unlikely that we would know anything about her former status from that type of burial. For here, she was essentially turned into his beloved partner in death and little would belie that appearance. The method by which she was killed by the 'Angel of Death' in the account would have left little trace on a skeleton, and certainly not after cremation.

An observation about Ibn Fadlan's report that is rarely made, though, is that in his account a slave was asked to volunteer to be sacrificed and this choice was offered up to both slave *boys and girls*, although according to the writer it was usually the girls who volunteered. This short note is important because it strongly suggests that it wasn't the slave's gender that was of significance, it was the need for *someone* to accompany the chieftain in death.

It might be difficult to reconcile this with the elaborate sexual exploitation that the 'volunteer' was subjected to before being murdered, but it could have made it less likely that the sacrifice of a *woman* specifically to follow 'her' man in death was the norm: there simply needed to be someone there alongside him. We should also remember that the Oseberg ship burial contained two women and not a husband and wife; there was clearly no need for the primary woman among the two to have a husband in the afterlife. Maybe gender wasn't such a big deal in death after all.

But all of this is problematic, because the assumptions about gender roles make it difficult to understand women's roles in these territories more broadly and to contextualise reports like the Greek historian Skylitze's remarks of women having fought in battle among the Rus'. With the presence of the eastern connections in Bj.581's grave and the evidence of trading women, we also have to make a place for a Rus'ian world where women could play a significant part. This may even be explicitly spelt out in the written sources. In the list of envoys witnessing the Byzantine treaties, the fact that many of them have Scandinavian names is often discussed but what is usually ignored is the fact that the list includes the names of several *women*. This must be seen as strong evidence that women could be in positions of power in tenth-century eastern territories, and some of those women may have been Scandinavian.

Within this environment, there is one very powerful woman with a particularly fierce reputation, namely Olga of Kyiv. Olga was the wife of Prince Igor, son of the legendary Rurik. The name Olga is derived from the Scandinavian name Helga, although many dispute her Scandinavian heritage. In the *Primary Chronicle*, she is depicted as being a particularly vicious and devious ruler, intent on avenging her husband's death in some rather creative, if gruesome ways. Igor had been murdered in 945 by the Drevlians (a tribe of eastern Slavs) when out collecting tribute. Olga took the throne in place of her son, Svyatoslav, who was too young to rule for himself. She took it upon herself to seek revenge by means described in graphic detail in the *Chronicle*, although it is fair to assume that much of the account is fictional.

Olga's payback was threefold and Machiavellian. First of all, when asked to marry Prince Mal, one of the Drevlians, she agreed. But when a delegation arrived in Kyiv by boat, she had all the men thrown into a deep pit and buried alive. She then sent a message requesting that the noblest of the Drevlians should accompany her as she travelled to her husband to be, as it wouldn't be fitting for her to journey on her own. When the aristocrats arrived in Kyiv ahead of the wedding, they were invited to wash in the bathhouse, at which point Olga locked them in and set fire to the building, killing them all.

If that wasn't enough, in a final step to finish off the remaining Drevlians, Olga travelled to their capital, Iskorosten, with a large army. Her unsuspecting future husband Prince Mal had not yet heard the fate of his men, so he had prepared a large feast for them in good faith. After eating, Olga and her army slaughtered as many of her foes as they could manage, but even this wasn't enough. Those who survived begged for mercy, offering to pay tribute. Olga agreed but said that she wanted only three sparrows from each household: after all, she could see how much they'd already suffered from her onslaught. The Drevlians willingly complied. When the birds arrived, Olga instructed her men to attach a piece of thread to each sparrow along with a piece of sulphur. In the evening, the birds were released, flying home to settle back in their nests in the rafters of the town's buildings. The sulphur made the roofs catch fire, burning the city to the ground.

The description of Olga's merciless killings of the Drevlians provides a chilling parallel to the fateful Salme ship, whose occupants had likely been part of a diplomatic mission: the Drevlians sent twenty of their 'best men' – who were killed in their boat – to try to convince Olga to accept Prince Mal's marriage proposal the first time around, then a group of chieftains the second time. It's also interesting that in both cases the Drevlians were clearly expecting to be welcomed and did not question Olga's demands nor her invitation to wash in her bathhouse before their meeting. It seems such arrangements were commonplace and part of diplomatic relationships, and that too fits well with the way the Salme men were buried.

Strangely, despite her sadistic legacy, today Olga is still venerated in both the Catholic Church and the Eastern Orthodox Church. This is because after her acts of vengeance, she converted to Christianity, the first ruler of the Kyivan Rus' to do so. She also worked hard to convert the rest of her people, although her son, Svyatoslav, remained a pagan. When she died Svyatoslav arranged for her Christian funeral, according to her wishes, despite his own feelings about the religion, and Olga became a revered saint. According to the *Chronicle*, it was the reigning Byzantine emperor Constantine VII Porphyrogenitus who managed to convert Olga, although, as he wanted to marry her, it seems that his intentions weren't entirely noble. Olga turned down his offer of marriage, but returned to Kyiv bearing gifts of gold, silver, silks and 'various vases'. When she arrived home, she received a letter in which the emperor reminded her of her promise to send back to him presents of slaves, wax and furs, as well as soldiers. Olga declined, saying that she would do so only if he were to spend as much time with her in her territory as she had spent on the Bosphorus.

If a woman could have this much power among the Rus' in the tenth century, while only a few decades earlier we have the actions of the militarily powerful Aethelflaed in Mercia, why would we question the possibility of someone like Bj.581 or indeed the Oseberg 'Queen' having a similar degree of military status and power? There seems to be no question mark in the written sources over Olga having commanded this position, or that any of the Rus' would have had problems taking orders from a woman. The *Chronicle* doesn't comment on or question her gender in any way. Obviously her rise to power was necessitated by the fact that her son was too young and no other leader could legitimately take his place in the meantime, but the fact that she was not only willing but also able to assume such a role – not to mention that she was supported in doing so – should tell us something about women's roles at this place and time.

MIXED IDENTITIES

Regardless of whether or not the stories of Olga's cruelty are true, the narratives about her and her son Svyatoslav are enlightening for a number of reasons. First, with regards to religion: while Olga became Christian, her son remained a pagan. The two still co-ruled without this causing any major difficulties. This suggests that the process of conversion in the early tenth century was not only gradual but also gentle. Second, their combined Slavic and Scandinavian identities. The *Russian Primary Chronicle* mentions a number of people around Svyatoslav who clearly had Scandinavian names: for example, his tutor Asmund and troop commander Sveinald. Still, it seems that at this point identities were beginning to mix, because Svyatoslav was the first ruler of the Kyivan state to carry a Slavic name.

While some of this may not be an accurate reflection of their tenth-century perspectives, but rather of the context in which it was written down by Nestor, it's important. The lasting legacy of the Rus' is evident in nearby Chernihiv, a city to the north of Shestovitsa. If you walk through its city park you will find it filled to the brim with small, undulating mounds, mostly covered by slender, leafy trees. Each and every one is a burial mound dating to the Viking Age; there are hundreds of them, right in the middle of the city, though we don't know whether their dead had Scandinavian origins.

Then, at the park's exit, on the high point of a steep cliff, are two enormous mounds, next to each other. These are two of three monumental mounds in Chernihiv, of which the third and most famous lies a little way away, currently squeezed in between buildings; known as the *Chernay Mogila* or 'Black Grave', it stands eleven metres tall. Legend has it that the mound was the resting place of the so-called Black Prince who some believe founded the city a millennium ago.

The Scandinavian affiliation of the mound's inhabitants (for there were two of them) is clear. Excavations in the 1870s revealed the two cremated bodies and a rich accompaniment of Viking Age objects: two helmets, chainmail, knives and weapons, two golden Byzantine coins, along with the remains of an elaborate funerary feast, as well as a small bronze figure depicting Thor. Allegedly, the grave also contained the bodies of slaves, but the literature on this is less reliable and it is possible that it is a creative interpretation. What is clear from all of the mounds, though, is that they represent an elite group, asserting both power and a very specific identity linked through burial to Scandinavian traditions.

It's difficult to work out how identities were formed here and to get an accurate understanding of the extent of Scandinavian influence. The reality is that we probably can't. We have the same problem in the west, where the Vikings are most commonly referred to as Danes (or simply pagans), when new evidence is showing that this is not an accurate reflection of their make-up from an ethnic or geographical perspective. The bioarchaeology makes that very obvious and, presumably, the same is the case in the east – we just don't have much evidence for it yet. So far, there are no isotopes, no DNA studies and, in many cases, we don't even have the burials to work with. What is clear is that this region, much like Birka, was a polyethnic melting pot of groups – Scandinavians, Slavs, Khazars and others, all fitting within the cultural context of the Rus'.

I'm especially interested in interrogating the idea that few apart from Swedish Vikings went in this direction, to the east. This has always been the prevailing narrative: the Danish and Norwegian Vikings headed west, the Swedes went east. For the most part, this was likely true, because much of the archaeological evidence supports it, as do many of the literary sources. But was the picture really that simple?

An important consideration is whether there was a much more direct connection between the east and the west than we have previously thought. The evidence that objects were coming to England in the 870s from the east has been growing significantly. But since the written sources are so silent, we have to look for other clues, and one particular type of objects is particularly interesting: falcon scabbard chapes. These small metal ornaments that fitted at the bottom of a sword's scabbard are very distinctive: a falcon in flight represented in bronze. They have a link to the east that is undeniable, as a survey has shown that with one exception they have not yet been found in the more westerly reaches of the Viking world.[7] The vast majority have been found in Sweden, around the Baltic, and down to eastern Europe; the furthest south is in Kyiv and four were found in burial mounds at Shestovitsa. The only one recorded to the west of Scandinavia was discovered in the enigmatic Viking ship burial at Île de Groix on the coast of Brittany.

Now there is another place to look: in the Portable Antiquities Scheme metal detectorists' database for England. And there, I found more. The database has shown another four chapes, with reference to at least two others not on the database, all found in recent years by detectorists. The matches are certain, and this is exciting news. The implication is that they have a direct link either to Sweden or to the east – or maybe to both. Whether they arrived through trade or came with people who had obtained them themselves is not clear, but it's tempting to see them as the belongings of those who held roles in a warrior retinue in the east, before travelling westward. This is evidence we didn't have before: any surveys in the literature show the distribution of these chapes to be entirely eastwards. It now seems that that might not entirely reflect the facts.

Returning to the Dnieper area, as we move into the tenth century, not only does the number of Rus' sites along these rivers increase, but it seems their organisation is also becoming more complex. In the first phase of their development, most travel took place between these sites and the north, back and forth towards Novgorod and beyond. In a later phase, this changed as the focus shifted to the south. Eyes were increasingly turned towards a megalopolis located a few weeks' sailing along the rivers and filled to the brim with riches and trading goods: the Byzantine capital, Constantinople.

9.

DRAGON'S HEAD:
TO MIKLAGARD AND BEYOND

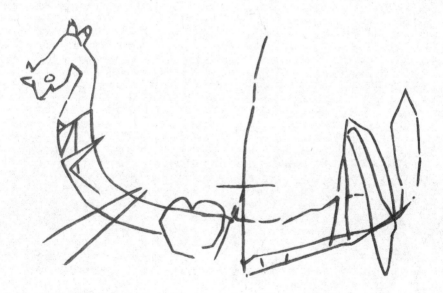

HAGIA SOPHIA, ISTANBUL, C.945

The interior of the building is cold but the throng of people pressing against you in all directions makes up for the chill in the air. It's starting to get dark outside, but there is still light gleaming in through the windows: flecks of dust dance in the bright beams that cast lines through the central dome, illuminating the impossibly bright golden scenes on the opposite wall. The figures look down at you serenely, seeming benevolent and kind, yet they mean little to you. Other people's gods. The sound of voices from the floor below is soothing, though you have no idea of the meaning of the words. You are tired, leaning against a column of smooth, even stone. As your hands run across it you feel the marks made on it by others: shapes, figures, writing. You feel for the knife hanging from your belt and test it against the stone. The material is surprisingly soft and all you need is a slight amount of pressure to make your own marks. You start at the top, cutting fine, curved lines. The person next to you notices and smiles, asking you what it is going to be, so you laugh, telling him to be patient. Soon the figure emerges, faintly: the curving head of a dragon facing west, with a large, benevolent eye looking towards you. You carve the beast's neck and it transforms into the hull of a ship with shields hung on it, ready for action at a moment's notice.

MIKLAGARD

The Dnieper snakes its way down to the north-western edge of the Black Sea, where it ends in the Dniprov'ska Gulf. Just beyond this is a tiny island by the name of Berezan; it's diminutive in size, only nine hundred metres long and just over three hundred metres wide. Today it's about a mile and a half from the coast but in the past it may well have been connected to land. Its location at the mouth of the Dnieper has turned it into something akin to a sentry, guarding access to the river system for those heading north or the access to the Black Sea for those heading south. There was a settlement here as early as the seventh century and it was even visited by the Greek historian Herodotus over a millennium before. On this small island, there is a trace of some of those who risked it all to make the treacherous journey, found on the southeasternmost runic inscription ever discovered.

In 1905, archaeologists excavated a burial mound on the island that had been reused over a long period of time, with new graves having been inserted into it seemingly at random. The excavators came across ten skeletons, one in a stone coffin with the skeleton's head and upper body resting on a flat stone. As one of the workmen lifted the stone to throw it on a spoil heap, the archaeologist in charge of the expedition noticed an inscription on its underside. The curved runes decorating the stone read: 'Grani made this vault in memory of Karl, his partner'. The Berezan stone is the only runestone that has ever been found in Ukraine or Russia. Yet the style the runes are carved in strongly suggests that the carver, and maybe Grani and Karl too, came from Gotland.[1]

Intriguingly, the word translated as 'partner' is the Old Norse term *felagi*, which describes a partnership either in raiding or in trading – possibly both. The term was also used for men who owned something together, perhaps a ship; maybe these two were business partners. It is impossible to date the stone, but we can guess what the men's final destination was – the place where many Vikings would likely have ended their journey: Miklagard, the 'Great City', from *mikill* ('big') and *gardr* ('wall' or 'stronghold'). Constantinople, or Istanbul as it is better known today, was the capital of the Byzantine Empire, the place where east met west. From Berezan, the route to Miklagard would have been straight-forward. Sail along the coast of the Black Sea, keeping south-west until you come to a strait some four kilometres across: the Bosphorus – the gateway to the west. The thirty-kilometre strait separates the Black Sea from the Sea of Marmara, which connects with the Mediterranean. At the western end of the strait lies the modern city of Istanbul, and it's easy to understand why the location was (and still is) of such strategic importance.

The first documented presence of the Rus' in Miklagard is one we have already encountered, if indirectly, and appears to have been relatively peaceful. The delegation that visited Louis the Pious in Ingelheim and stated that they belonged to the tribe of the Swedes came with a letter from Theophilus, the Byzantine emperor, suggesting that their journey must have started in Byzantium – and, in all likelihood, Constantinople. This places the Rus' in Constantinople as early as 839, several decades before the first documented raid on the city. Although we don't know if they used the Dnieper route to get there, their presence is important because it means Scandinavians had contact with Byzantium from the early ninth century. And not just any type of contact: to travel with a letter from the emperor himself, that vouched for them and asked for assistance on their behalf, must have meant that diplomatic relations were well established.

In fact, a coin of Theophilus has been found at Rurikovo Gorodische by Lake Ilmen, along with a Byzantine official seal dating to the first half of the ninth century, strongly suggesting that this would have been on the route taken. Similar seals have been found at Scandinavian trading sites like Hedeby, Ribe and Birka, which shows that movement and trade went in both directions. All of this suggests that Scandinavians may well have been present in Constantinople for quite some time before Theophilus' reign; these seals may not represent the first encounter.

It is also important to understand that those earliest contacts appear to have been peaceful. Yet for some reason, things seem to have changed fairly rapidly. The first recorded attack on Constantinople by the Rus' took place a few decades later, on 18 June 860. By the second half of the ninth century, then, the Rus' in this region were not only numerous enough to launch such a daring assault but they also had sufficient political organisation to be able to mount one that must have combined several groups of forces. They must also have been very familiar not only with the city itself and its defences, but with safe routes there and the logistics involved.

A contemporary account of the attack is given by Photios, the patriarch (archbishop) of Constantinople, whose words are evocative and scathing in their description of the attackers. According to Photios, they came from 'an obscure nation, a nation of no account, a nation ranked among slaves, unknown, but which has won a name from the expedition against us, insignificant, but now become famous, humble and destitute, but now risen to splendid height and immense wealth, a nation dwelling somewhere far from our country, barbarous, nomadic, armed with arrogance, unwatched, unchallenged, leaderless'. Photios makes it clear not just that these people came from the far north, as far north as you could possibly imagine, but also that they travelled by rivers and 'harbourless seas'. He went on to explain that the invaders had sailed past the walls and raised their weapons 'as if threatening the city with death by the sword'.

The attack is also mentioned in the *Russian Primary Chronicle*. Nestor's account is rather more fanciful and bears all the hallmarks of a literary tale (there's little to suggest that this version of events is any truer than Photios' version). Nestor claims that the attack was led by two Varangians named Askold and Dir, who had arrived in the east with Rurik and were later killed by Oleg, his heir.*

Regardless of the outcome of this first attack, afterwards things changed. From this point on the Rus' became a credible and significant entity that Constantinople had to deal with; a serious part of Byzantine foreign policy. A curious love-hate relationship ensued. Strangely, one of the best ways to handle this was through conversion to Christianity. Reportedly, the fortunes of the Rus' whose first attack was so successful quickly turned: on their way back home they were caught in a storm and perished. As a consequence, an envoy was sent to Constantinople from one of the Rus'ian leaders requesting baptism, which the Byzantines were only too happy to help with. There's a parallel here to what happened in England in 878, when Guthrum – one of the leaders of the Great Army that left Repton in 874 – agreed to be baptised along with several of his men, in order for the treaty with King Alfred to be agreed. Both in the east and the west, religion was obviously used as a political tool. Nevertheless, it doesn't seem that

---

* The *Chronicle* states that Askold and Dir stopped off in what was to become Kyiv, where they ruled the state of the Poliane. This was, apparently, a Slavic state in existence when the Rus' arrived, although no other evidence has corroborated this.

this newfound religion gained too much of a foothold among the Rus', as burials across the region continue to look distinctly pagan.

The *Primary Chronicle* describes a second Rus' raid in the year 904, led by Oleg. The attack was substantial, as he was apparently accompanied by two thousand vessels filled with 'pagans' from different tribes: Slavs, Varangians, Polyanians (from near Kyiv) and Croats among others. When they arrived in Constantinople, the emperor was ready for them. To deter the attackers, he had 'fortified the strait and closed the city'. Oleg, however, wasn't discouraged: he disembarked and ordered the ships to be beached, after which the attackers went on to inflict dreadful atrocities on the natives. Palaces were destroyed, churches were burned, and prisoners were taken, tortured and thrown into the sea.

Curiously, the *Chronicle* states that at one point Oleg commanded his warriors to attach wheels to their ships, then spread their sails and wait for a favourable wind, at which moment they 'set upon the city from the open country'. It was now that the defenders realised they were in trouble. Messengers were sent to Oleg begging him not to destroy the city and offering to pay tribute to stop the advance from going any further. Refusing their offers of food and wine to appease him (Oleg was no fool, realising this would surely be poisoned), he demanded tribute at a rate of twelve grivny, the local currency, per man. With an estimated forty men on each of his two thousand ships, this would have meant a total of 960,000 grivny, clearly a substantial amount.

Over the following years the relationship between Constantinople and the Rus' seems to have been a bewildering mix of attacks followed by diplomatic engagement, with both sides realising that peaceful associations were the most beneficial. The exact nature of the dynamics is unclear, which raises the question of whether we are dealing with one coherent group of people, or whether the term 'Rus' used in the written sources actually masks a range of different peoples. In any case, a section of the *Russian Primary Chronicle* gives us a glimpse into the lives of those involved. In what are likely the most reliable parts of this history, a series of treaties describe relations between traders and Byzantines. One, dated to 2 September 911, lays down rules for those who want to trade with Constantinople: fifteen individuals, most likely members of the Rus' ruling elite, are named as endorsing a bilateral treaty of peace and friendship with Emperor Leo VI. Five of them bear the unmistakably Old Norse names of Karl, Farulf, Vermund, Hrollaf and Steinvith.

The emperor evidently recognised just how dangerous the trading visits down the rivers were, making sure that if he were to encourage them to continue peacefully, some rewards would be necessary. Hence he awarded the Rus' a number of perks. First of all, those who made it to the big city would be exempt from customs payments and on arrival would be given not just free board and lodging but a monthly allowance, including bread, wine, meat, fish and fruit. This was tenable for up to six months. Free baths were, of course, also included in the deal. When you were ready to return up the rivers again, you would be given both sailcloth and anchors to aid your journey.

However, you couldn't just turn up in Constantinople without anything to trade, as the treaty specifically stated that 'Rus' coming here without goods shall receive no monthly allowances'. Gaining these trading rights was a strategic move on behalf of the Rus'. Access to Miklagard gave them resources and products that it would be difficult, if not impossible, to obtain elsewhere.

Yet despite this seemingly friendly cooperation, the Byzantines kept a watchful eye on their guests. Once in Constantinople, they were to reside only north of the Golden Horn, in the area of St Mamas's – outside the city walls – and when entering the city, they were allowed through one particular gate only. They weren't permitted to bear arms and a maximum of fifty could enter the gate at any one time, and only if they were accompanied by an imperial agent. The treaties also dictated a number of rules for how conflicts were to be resolved: a victim of theft, for example, had the right to slay a thief caught red-handed immediately.

It is easy to imagine Vikings there, in Miklagard, waiting for the right weather conditions before embarking on the long and hazardous journey home; killing time by wandering through the bazaars, bartering some silver for one of those translucent orange beads that had become so popular.

CONSTANTINOPLE

Constantinople had been founded in the fourth century by Emperor Constantine the Great as the 'Second Rome', the new capital of the Roman Empire. As a part of this move, a large-scale public works programme was started. In what is now the district of Sultanahmet – the main tourist strip in today's Istanbul – he built a new imperial residence, the Palatium Magnum or 'Great Palace'. This became not just the emperor's residence, but the seat of government, a function it retained throughout the Byzantine period.

While only some of the original palace remains have been excavated, much about it is known from the *Book of Ceremonies* that was commissioned by Emperor Constantine VII Porphyrogenitus in the tenth century. It was clearly a magnificent complex. The palace stretched between the hippodrome and the church of Hagia Sophia all the way down to the Bosphorus waterfront. The site incorporated churches and gardens, courtyards, throne rooms and baths, apparently built on six separate terraces to adapt to its height of thirty-two metres above sea level. Subsequent emperors had rebuilt and extended the palace grounds. A traveller from the north who was allowed into these hallowed surroundings would surely have been impressed by the fine mosaics adorning the palace floor, from detailed depictions of hunting scenes and exotic creatures to the humorous image of a donkey kicking its owner and the mythological eagle-headed griffin engaged in a bloody attack on a deer. And, surrounding it all, the almost impenetrable city walls.

The walls of Constantinople were infamous, and for good reason: their design and maintenance meant that they would be able to keep the city largely safe from attack for almost a millennium. Even today large sections of the walls remain, though it is hard to tell which of the brick and stone features are part of the structure that was created by the emperor Theodosius II in the fifth century, as subsequent rulers, including the Ottomans in the Middle Ages, continued to repair, extend and preserve the defences. At one point there were ninety-six towers protecting the walls and a number of heavily defended gates. The construction featured three levels, including a moat.

If this wasn't enough, the Byzantines had an infamous deadly weapon that successfully defeated and deterred many attackers: Greek fire. In an account of a later, tenth-century raid by the Rus' on the city, Liutprand of Cremona described it as follows: 'The Greeks began to fling their fire all around; and the Rus' seeing the flames threw themselves in haste from their ships, preferring to be drowned in the water rather than burned alive in the fire.' Greek fire appears to have been some sort of heated liquid, probably a form of crude oil mixed with resin, forced through a tube and fired at the enemy, with impressive results. This is what the Vikings would have been faced with when attempting to attack the city and it's not difficult to understand why they failed to besiege it successfully. Even if they had, the emperor himself would likely have remained safe, as the Great Palace's defences included underground corridors that connected it to the hippodrome and Hagia Sophia, along with hidden passageways down to the docks.

The visitor to the city could also visit the hippodrome, an immense horse-racing track that was the bustling social and ceremonial centre of Constantinople. It was a spectacular sight, with its obelisks and serpent-headed column in the middle. The importance of this space is manifested in one of those monuments, the obelisk of Theodosius: the magnificent stone had originally been carved by Thutmose III of Egypt in 1450 BC and was brought to the city by Constantine the Great, before finally being erected in the hippodrome by Theodosius I.

The drama of events at the hippodrome would have been intoxicating (disregarding any wine that you might have been able to obtain). There would have been chariots pulled by thundering horses, hurtling around the tight corners of the central *spina* dividing the track into two. Or perhaps you were there to watch a fight, or performances with acrobatics and exotic animals; you would have sat in the stepped wooden seats built up around the 429-metre-long arena. It's estimated that the hippodrome could hold thirty thousand spectators, or maybe even more, typically joined by the emperor who would be seated in a VIP box to one side that he could enter directly from the imperial palace. Such was the enthusiasm for the races that in the ninth century Emperor Theophilus himself took part after one of the teams, the blues, were instructed to let him win.

If we fast forward to the year 944, another treaty in the *Primary Chronicle* (probably made to re-establish diplomatic relations after new attacks by the Rus') fills in and repeats much of the information known previously and includes more on the type of goods that were traded. This and the earlier treaty detail what was to be done with stolen or escaped slaves. A runaway slave who was not found should, according to this treaty, be compensated for at the rate of two pieces of silk. However, if the Rus' were found to be trading in slaves originating from within Byzantine territories, those slaves could be freed by payment at different rates: young men and adult women were the most valuable and the ransom was placed at ten bezants (gold coins). For middle-aged slaves, the ransom was eight bezants and the least valuable were young children, who were worth only five.

We also hear more in the treaties about silk: specifically, that the Rus' were not allowed to buy silks that were worth more than fifty gold coins, known as solidi. Any silks purchased had to be shown to an imperial officer who would stamp them before they could be exported. This demonstrates clearly just how important silk was in Constantinople.

While it originated in China, the precious fabric had been coveted in the eastern Mediterranean possibly as far back as the Bronze Age and had been imported widely from the east for centuries. According to a medieval legend, two Christian monks had observed silk-making in China around the year 552 and smuggled silkworm eggs inside their hollow bamboo canes back to the Byzantine emperor Justinian. Under his supervision, the eggs kick-started a silk business that was to prosper enormously.

While the story is unlikely to be true, the emperor did successfully establish a silk industry in Constantinople, planting thousands of mulberry trees to sustain the silk moths. Soon Byzantine silk – often dyed a highly desirable purple hue – became an important commodity. As is seen in the tenth-century treaty, this trade was very heavily controlled even centuries later. There were also restrictions on foreign silks coming into Constantinople; in the tenth century Syrian merchants brought silk and clothing from Baghdad to the city but there were restrictions forbidding Bulghar merchants from buying Persian silks of higher value when they were in the city.

Silk was also one of the vital riches that made it all the way back to Scandinavia, as a symbol of wealth and access to the exotic. In the Norwegian Oseberg ship burial, over a hundred fragments of silk were found, belonging to many different garments, with at least fifteen different fabrics represented. Based on the method of weaving, it seems that the majority were made in central Asia, with two possibly from Byzantine workshops. At Birka, forty-nine graves contained silk and there too both Byzantine and central Asian types were found, but in one grave excavators found something unusual: a two-coloured silk damask with a pattern of stars and dots, likely to have been produced in China. Crucially, the date of 834 for the Oseberg burial means that such trading networks must have been open by this date, corroborating the early date of contact between east and west suggested by the Ingelheim story.

Silk fragments have even been found in England and Ireland: almost a hundred pieces at Viking Age sites in places like Dublin, Waterford, York and Lincoln. The latter of these was large, twenty centimetres wide and sixty centimetres long, and almost certainly would have been used as a headscarf, with a weave that matches Byzantine silks very closely. Even more remarkably, it is so similar to a piece found in Coppergate, York, that it's likely the two came from the same roll of cloth. This could be taken to suggest that the fabric was acquired through trade rather than being the personal possession of someone who had travelled, but we do have indications that some items were kept for the travellers themselves, too: in the *Laxdæla saga*, the flamboyant character Bolli Bollason (dubbed Bolli the Magnificent) returns home to Iceland from a stint in the Varangian Guard – the personal bodyguard to the Byzantine emperors – wearing nothing but the finest clothes made of scarlet and fur, clothes given to him by the emperor, and weapons and armoury decorated with gold.

GRAFFITI

The most spectacular sight for any foreign visitor to Constantinople may well have been the church of Hagia Sophia, commissioned by Emperor Justinian and consecrated in 537, one of the finest examples of Byzantine architecture. Those who came here from the north would never have seen a building on this scale before. Even today its immense exterior dominates Istanbul's skyscape. Stepping through the doors for the first time, the visitor from the north couldn't help but be awed both by the building's shape and its artwork (although the current peculiar mix of Islamic art and Christian architecture takes some getting used to – the church was converted into a mosque after the Ottoman conquest of Constantinople in 1453). And here we find the only certain example of something that Viking visitors left behind.

When you enter Hagia Sophia (or Ayasofya, to give it its Turkish name) today, you go in through a large marble entranceway with a deeply worn step known as the 'Emperor's doorway'. As its name suggests, this was the emperor's main entry through to the nave. Once inside, you see the vast dome with its decorations and arched windows around its lower edge bringing beams of light into the central space. If you didn't enter as part of the emperor's entourage, you would instead have used a side door, walking up a series of ramps. Here a gently sloping, paved floor of uneven-sized stones spirals upwards through a dark and narrow corridor, taking you to the upper galleries.

It is in these galleries, which give you a perfect view of the church below and all around, that there is a marble railing which bears a type of graffiti you'd be forgiven for thinking a fake: an inscription with the name 'Halfdan' and several more indecipherable runic characters, apparently the early medieval equivalent of incising 'Halfdan was here'. This runic inscription was discovered in the 1970s and not long after another, shorter inscription, possibly of the name 'Arni', was discovered too. Graffiti appears throughout the church: everything from Cyrillic to Greek, Armenian and Latin inscriptions can be found. Where dates can be estimated, most were made between the eleventh and fifteenth centuries and include names as well as pictures of animals, weapons and coats of arms. Halfdan was a common Scandinavian name and this runic script could date to anywhere between the ninth and eleventh centuries.

Excitingly, in 2009 a new discovery was made.[2] A team of Russian researchers were looking for more Cyrillic inscriptions, painstakingly taking photographs of every possible surface that could have been written on and scrutinising the pictures. Anything that looked like it could be runes was sent to a runologist, Elena Melnikova, and eventually she came up trumps: a third runic inscription that says 'Arinbarðr cut these runes' was found on a marble windowsill in the northern gallery. Looking at the specific ways in which the runes had been cut, Melnikova proposed that they dated to between the early eleventh and twelfth centuries, right at the end of the Viking Age.

That's not all, as yet another discovery has since been made in the church. Investigating more than thirty graffiti-figures of vessels, researcher Thomas Thomov determined that four were depictions of Viking ships.[3] The most convincing is found on a column at the corner of the same gallery as Halfdan's inscription, only ten metres or so away. You have to look carefully to find it, scratched into the stone, just below eye level. One part is unmistakable: the head of a dragon facing left, a single eye looking forwards. Its neck curves down and turns into the hull of a slender ship, with proportions that are instantly recognisable to anyone who has seen a Viking ship. Thomov also identified a mast and two circles along the side as shields attached to the side. This, then, is a dragon-headed warship. On the other side of the column, another sketch shows what may well be two more ship bows lying side by side in a harbour. These drawings are convincing and there is no reason to think they are fake; they were almost certainly made by someone familiar with Viking ships' shape and proportions.

Word of these splendid sites – the palaces and churches decorated with gold, glorious architecture separating the sacred from the profane – evidently reached home with those who travelled back to the north. In fact, it's very possible that these places directly inspired the way in which the homes of the Viking gods were described in later sources. The only accounts we have of Asgard, the world of the Norse gods, come from sources written down from the eleventh century onwards, most of them even later. This makes it unclear how much relates directly to belief structures dating to the Viking Age. Yet what *is* clear in these sources is that although the halls and buildings fit in with Scandinavian architecture on a general level, their descriptions must have been inspired by eastern splendour. Take, for instance, Glitnir, the hall of Forseti, the Norse god of law and justice, whose visitors would be dazzled by the sight of golden pillars and a roof set with silver. Could the inspiration behind this description have come from Byzantium?

There are other links to the east in northern origin myths too. Snorri, for example, explicitly spelt this out both in the thirteenth-century *Prose Edda* and the *Ynglinga saga*. The gods, he says, lived in the capital city east of the 'Fork of the Don', which presumably meant somewhere either near Volgograd in south-west Russia or even further east towards what is now Kazakhstan (although Snorri may not have meant it quite that literally). He states that there was a mountain range that separated Greater Svitjod from the rest of the world and to the south of these mountains, a short trip would take you to Tyrkland or the 'Land of the Turks'. There, apparently, 'Odin had large possessions'.

To cut a long story short, in his telling of the Norse creation story, the gods moved north from this homeland. Eventually, they arrived in Scandinavia, where Snorri lays out the history of their descendants who became the Scandinavian royal families. Similarly, the Danish historian Saxo Grammaticus stated that Odin originally lived in Byzantium, most likely Constantinople. While it is tempting to place such worldviews within a Viking Age framework, it is important to remember that these sources relate to medieval literary traditions, postdating the Vikings by several hundred years. For this reason, the links to the more easterly parts of Europe may reflect the significance placed on this region in a Christianised Europe for which pilgrimage to Jerusalem formed an important part of religious life.

By the end of the Viking Age, the journey to Miklagard had become so popular that special laws were imposed to govern what happened to your wealth back at home when you were abroad. The Norwegian Gulatingslov law code, for example, stated that your wealth could be managed for you for three years before it would go to your successors. But if you went to Byzantium, it would be given to them straight away.

Much of the fame of Miklagard that was transmitted back to the homelands related to a very particular segment of society: the Scandinavians became an even more crucial element in Byzantine affairs between the tenth and fourteenth centuries as they formed the majority of the Varangian Guard, a specialist mercenary unit founded in the latter part of the tenth century by Emperor Basil II to work as personal bodyguards to the Byzantine emperors. This had been instituted after a call for help by Basil to the ruler of Kyiv, Vladimir (grandson of Igor), in 987. Following a rebellion in Constantinople, a rival by the name of Bardas Phokas had claimed Basil's throne. Vladimir responded by sending a force of six thousand Rus' to help, in return for which he was offered the emperor's sister as his wife. The only caveat was that Vladimir had to convert to Christianity, something he agreed to do. With the help of the Rus', Basil succeeded in defeating the rebels and recaptured the throne.

However, it seems that Basil's request hadn't quite come out of the blue. In the *Primary Chronicle*, the treaty of 945 between the Rus' and Byzantium included the following statement: 'If our government shall desire of you military assistance for use against our adversaries, they shall communicate with your Great Prince, and he shall send us as many soldiers as we require.' If this part of the treaty is genuine, Basil was merely following up on an agreement made almost half a century earlier. The help from the north so impressed the Byzantines that it became a permanent fixture in the form of the elite guard. From then on, Varangians could be seen both in battle and at the Great Palace, working directly to protect the emperor and his family.

Had Halfdan and Arinbarðr been members of the Varangian Guard? Over the decades a stint working in Miklagard would become popular among Scandinavian men, not least because of the riches you could acquire. The most famous to do it was the Norwegian king Harald Hardrada, who worked for the Byzantine emperor for nearly a decade after fleeing Norway following his defeat at the Battle of Stiklestad in 1030, where his older brother Olaf was killed. Harald gained notoriety and respect in Constantinople for his military prowess (though also, briefly, imprisonment). He served Empress Zoe, whose golden image adorns the upper gallery of the Hagia Sophia, directly, before returning home and eventually attempting to win the English throne – unsuccessfully – at the Battle of Stamford Bridge in 1066.

While a majority of the Varangian Guard seem to have been Scandinavian, other nationalities could be part of it too. After Stamford Bridge, for instance, they included an increasing number of Anglo-Saxons fleeing England after the defeat by William the Conqueror (coincidentally also a descendant of Vikings).

THE CASPIAN SEA

From Constantinople, the trail further east becomes hazier. We have only a few hints of Rus' or Viking journeys in the Middle East, in descriptions of expeditions to the shores of the Caspian Sea and of later attacks on Persia. One such route started at the point where the Dnieper enters the Black Sea, near Berezan. If you travelled eastwards by boat, you could enter the Sea of Azov, from which you could follow the River Don to the town of Sarkel. This had been built by the Khazars in the 830s with the help of Theophilus, around the time the Rus' envoys travelled to Frankia. Continuing the journey, you could connect to the Volga or travel overland to Itil, the capital of the Khazars, on the shores of the Caspian. Alternatively, you could travel more directly overland by coming ashore in the eastern part of the Black Sea, in what is modern-day Georgia.

This latter route was chosen by one of the most infamous eastern travellers from Sweden, namely Ingvar the Far-Travelled. By his time in the eleventh century, the flow of silver to the north and west had begun to decline, with the result that fewer traders made their way to the east. Ingvar led an expedition that attempted to re-establish the trade routes, but the details are a little unclear. There is a highly imaginative saga account of his adventures, in which Ingvar, a warrior working for the Swedish king Olaf Skotkonung, travels east in search of his own kingdom. Along the way he encounters giants, dragons, witches and a queen who falls in love with him. Eventually he dies of illness.

Although most of this story involves creative licence on the saga writer's part, we do know that Ingvar was a real person: over twenty runestones in Sweden tell of his expedition and commemorate those who fell alongside him, strongly suggesting that the adventure ended in disaster. Ingvar was roughly contemporary with Harald Hardrada and according to the saga he, like Harald, spent some time in the retinue of the Kyivan ruler Yaroslav the Wise in Novgorod, before continuing his journey. According to the runestones, Ingvar and many of his men died in Serkland. Some of the stones are elaborate, with one from Gripsholm commemorating a brother (either real or metaphorical) of Ingvar with the following detail: 'They travelled in a drengr-like fashion, far for gold, and in the east gave (food) to the eagle, died in the south in Serkland.'[4]

No full explanation of where Serkland was has ever been found. Etymologically, the name could have a few different origins. One is that it means the 'Land of the Saracens' – i.e. Muslims, making its meaning something like the Islamic caliphate. Another popular interpretation is that the 'Serk' element comes from the Latin word *sericu*, meaning 'silk'. This would mean that the name referred to the territories where silk was made. An even more fanciful explanation is that there is a connection with the word *serkr*, meaning 'shirt' or 'gown' – so the 'Land of the Kaftan-wearers'. The geographical territory covered by the name Serkland changed over time, initially meaning the area to the south of the Caspian Sea but later on in the Viking Age coming to mean the whole of the Islamic world. A final possibility is that the name refers to the city of Sarkel itself, which was part of the territory of the Khazars.

The consensus seems to be that Ingvar's journey took him to Persia, possibly to what is now Georgia or somewhere else in the Caucasus region; certainly somewhere between the Black Sea and the Caspian – a stepping stone on a journey towards Baghdad. Ibn Khurradadhbih described the presence of Vikings in this region in the *Book of Roads and Kingdoms*; importantly, as this was written down in the 840s, it shows that even in the earliest years of the ninth century such contact had been established.* His account also

---

* It is perhaps significant to note that this region was also a source of carnelian, making it another possible origin for the beads that reached the north.

explained that these were trading expeditions, with men arriving by boat – some of whom chose to make an onward journey overland.

Those who arrived on the shores of the Caspian would have been entering prime Khazar territory, which meant that diplomatic relations had to be in order. The Arab historian Al-Masudi, writing in the early tenth century, stated that pagans (which included Rus') were living in Atil, the capital of the Khazarian kingdom in the north-western corner of the Caspian. They had a special area of the town to live in, which they shared with the Slavs – an important point because it makes a distinction between the two groups at that time. Crucially, Al-Masudi also wrote that both the Rus' and the Slavs served in the Khazarian ruler's army – much as in Constantinople.

While the earliest accounts of activity in this region suggest that relations were peaceful, it didn't take long before trade turned to raids. First to come under attack was the port town of Abaskun on the south-eastern shore of the Caspian Sea, though the attackers were all killed. In 909, sixteen ships launched another raid, but this too was quashed and, reportedly, in a reversal of the usual course of events, many of the Rus' raiders were taken away as slaves.

A few years later, Al-Masudi described a massive attack on multiple territories around the Caspian. Having been granted access by the Khazar Khaganate (using a typical tactic of promising a proportion of any future spoils), five hundred ships, each containing a hundred warriors, began raiding cities all around the southern shore of the Caspian. Attacks on modern-day Azerbaijan were described as follows: 'The Rus' spilled rivers of blood, seized women and children and property, raided and everywhere destroyed and burned. The people who lived on these shores were in turmoil, for they had never been attacked by an enemy from the sea, and their shores had only been visited by the ships of merchants and fishermen.' The parallel to Alcuin's account of the Lindisfarne attacks – that these were wholly unexpected – is striking.

Al-Masudi went on to explain that the raiders stayed in the Caspian for several months, living on islands a few miles from the coast, where none of the locals were able to reach them because they lacked ships of an appropriate type. Eventually, though, a fifteen-thousand-strong group of Muslims were able to defeat the Rus' as they returned to the Volga to head homewards: apparently, thirty thousand were killed in total. A couple of details are important here. First, the vast size of the Rus' fleet – fifty thousand men, if Al-Masudi is to be believed. The figure is almost certainly an exaggeration but even so, it is likely that this was a substantial force. Second, the account emphasises that it was the attackers' boats and maritime skills that led to their success.

Following this, an account of an attack in Azerbaijan in 943 is given by the philosopher and historian Ibn Miskawayh. With his book *Experiences of the Nations*, he was one of the first Muslim historians to write a chronicle using eyewitness accounts of contemporary events. The telling is detailed and vivid, not merely describing the Rus' and their equipment but also explaining, in a remarkably objective manner, the strategies they deployed as part of the attack. This particular raid, focused on the town of Bardha'a, was one of many such attacks on the Caspian Sea in the tenth century. Bardha'a was a flourishing town with a citadel, city walls and gates, as well as a weekly bazaar. It was surrounded by orchards and fields, and well known for its figs, fruit and hazelnuts as well as for its silk. Al-Masudi reports that the city was a market where furs from the north were sold, which is, presumably, how the Rus' got wind of its riches in the first place.

Bardha'a is located on a tributary of the Kura, a river that flows east from the Caucasus Mountains, draining into the Caspian Sea. According to Ibn Miskawayh, the Rus' had travelled across the

Caspian by ship, presumably from the Volga. When they arrived on the shore, the governor of Bardha'a was prepared, meeting them with a crew of six hundred, but he soon realised that this would not be enough. Needing reinforcements, he called upon five thousand volunteers to wage jihad, a holy war, against the unexpected invaders. Unfortunately, the defenders had not anticipated the strength and fighting abilities of the Rus'. Those who weren't killed immediately, turned and fled. The Rus' gave chase all the way to the town, which they entered and occupied at once.

What happened next is a little unexpected: according to Ibn Miskawayh, eyewitnesses reported that once inside Bardha'a, the Rus' hurried around trying to calm the citizens with the following words: 'There is no dispute between us on the matter of religion; we only want to rule. It is our obligation to treat you well and yours to be loyal to us.' The defending army didn't trust these words and resisted anyway, but they were swiftly defeated. The Rus' had ordered the rest of the citizens not to take part. Apparently, 'peace-loving men from the upper classes' followed this advice, but 'the common people and rabble' threw stones at them, angry and desperate to show their displeasure.

Eventually the Rus' tired of the squabbles and gave the town's inhabitants three days to leave. Many did, but those foolish enough to stay were either murdered or taken prisoner. According to the account, ten thousand men and boys, along with their wives and daughters, were locked up. The women and children were held in a fortress, and the men were imprisoned in the mosque. The plan was clearly to take advantage of the situation in typical Viking fashion, so the men were asked to ransom themselves and pay their way out of captivity.

At that point a Christian civil servant named Ibn Sam'un, who lived in the town, intervened to help negotiate between the two sides. After some deliberation, the Rus' agreed to a sum of twenty dirhams for each person's ransom. Ibn Miskawayh reported that the more intelligent among the Muslims agreed, while others refused on the basis that this would imply they were worth the same as Christians. Negotiations broke down and the invaders were unsure what to do. They desperately wanted even those small sums – cash in hand was always better than a room full of corpses – and held out hope for a little while longer. Finally, having realised the money would not be forthcoming, they resorted to a massacre. Nor did the women and boys get off lightly, being subjected to rape and enslavement. A few of the captives managed to escape or took up their own negotiations: bartering for their lives with whatever valuables they had on them, they fled with a stamped piece of clay to show that they had bought themselves the right to be left unscathed.

The most curious part of this account is what finally brought the Rus' down. News of the onslaught spread around the wider region and a joint expedition was organised to drive out the invaders. Yet despite a troop of thirty thousand men attacking the besieged town, morning and evening, day after day, they had no success. Then news broke that an epidemic had broken out among the Rus' who were dropping like flies, their number severely decreasing. It turned out that, according to Ibn Miskawayh, when they arrived in Bardha'a they had overindulged on fruit, something they were not accustomed to, coming as they did from 'a very cold country, where no trees grow'. The illness, combined with some clever tactics, meant that the defenders could gradually begin to wear out the Rus'.

The invaders retreated to their fort and eventually were exhausted. Finally one night they took their leave, carrying their loot on their backs, dragging women, boys and girls with them and leaving in their wake a slew of burning buildings. We hear that they had left their ships and their crews waiting in readiness by the river, along with three hundred of their men to protect them.

The account from Bardha'a is evocative, but it is also very

informative. The attack on the town was deliberate and not just a raid, for it seems that the Rus' planned to use Bardha'a as a raiding base or even to settle there permanently. Such an outpost on the shores of the Caspian Sea, with all its trade links with the Islamic world and onwards to other parts of the globe, would obviously have allowed for further trade and expansion. In the mid tenth century, the route here all the way from Scandinavia was active and thriving. A base here may even have disrupted access to goods for the Byzantines, at least without them having to go through the Rus' first.

On a more practical level, the narrative confirms the same use of negotiation, intermediaries and ransom that we see throughout the Viking world. The use of negotiators to handle the ransom was presumably commonplace. Finally, the account provides an observation of burial customs. Ibn Miskawayh states that when one of the men died, they were buried with their weapons, clothes and equipment. He also says that a man would be buried along with his wife or another of his women and possibly also his slave 'if he happened to be fond of him'. This seems to corroborate information from other sources, but it's unclear whether that means it was another eyewitness observation and that the wife and/or slave would in fact be sacrificed. It is even more important to note that after the Rus' left, the Muslims tended to dig up the graves, because in them they found swords which were in great demand thanks to their high quality. In other words, grave robbing appears to have been common, and this may explain why to date we haven't found any graves in this region that can be securely associated with Scandinavian cultural traits.

Towards the end of the tenth and early eleventh centuries, several further raids were carried out in this part of the world with varying degrees of success. Yet although these caused terror and devastation locally, the presence of Rus' and Scandinavians, wherever they originally came from, did not leave an enduring legacy. Nevertheless, it was not the end of the journey for everyone. Although we have not found any physical evidence, the Vikings did make it all the way to Baghdad with their trade of furs and swords. As far as we know, they never dared to attack the city. It is likely that those who made it that far would have been few in number and lacking logistical support and tactical advantage. Elsewhere, they could have relied not only on large numbers of troops but also the ability to escape by boat. But it's also possible that the Khazars were too successful in preventing them from moving further, as a letter written in 960 by the Khazar king Josef suggests. Josef wrote to the caliph of the Islamic caliphate of Cordoba, explaining that he lived by the mouth of the river and guarded it from enemies (including the Rus'), who came there to fight. He stated that 'If I would let them for an hour (to sail down to the Caspian Sea), they should raid the whole Arab country all the way down to Baghdad.'

Finally, then, some journeys may have gone overland to the splendour of Baghdad; the city of trade, knowledge and culture and a vital stepping stone on the Silk Roads. By the ninth century, the time when the carnelian bead found in Repton might have travelled through here, Baghdad had grown to vast proportions. The city was surrounded by fertile agricultural land and could therefore easily sustain a large urban population. In just over a century it had grown to become the world's largest city. It's not difficult to see why: its location, which had been strategically chosen by Caliph al-Mansur, placed it on the Tigris and at the closest point to the Euphrates, in the heart of what was once Mesopotamia (the land 'between two rivers'), ideally placed for trade, something that was crucial for its foundation right from the start.

Apparently, when al-Mansur had been searching for the best location for his new capital and asked around, he was told that this site was ideal as here, 'you receive supplies by ships from the west via the Euphrates and you receive goods of Egypt and Sham

[Syria]. You also receive supplies carried by ships from China, India and Wassi via Tigris.' This really was a nexus point for the Silk Roads. Sailing around five hundred kilometres downriver would take you directly to the Persian Gulf, from which you could connect through to the vastly significant Indian Ocean trading networks, and further onwards to India and China. Upstream, you could travel through a string of towns as far as what is now Turkey.

If your choice of transportation east was land-based, you could easily reach Baghdad by camel caravan. In the records of Ibn Khurradadhbih, he describes the routes through the Volga that end in Baghdad and states, crucially, that the Rus' were able to communicate with Slavic-speaking slaves who were already living there, and who had presumably learned Arabic. This is a vital piece of the puzzle. Those slaves, the hidden population that we can't quite uncover, evidently had another function, that of translating and interpreting. It is easy to imagine how you would have had no choice but to learn the language of your captors if you were to survive and maybe try to improve your life situation. Multilingualism would have been both a necessity and a clear advantage.

A traveller to the markets there would have wound their way through market stalls, with the scent of exotic spices and myriad sounds, from animals to diverse languages, assaulting the senses until they reached the river ports. There they would have seen a hundred ships of different types, loading and unloading precious cargoes. The range of goods you could find was mind-blowing: everything from silks from China, Japan and Korea to paper and silver from Samarkand, ebony and ivory from East Africa, copper and gold from Egypt, rugs and leathers from Bukhara, and saffron and horses from Azerbaijan, to mention just a few. And from India, spices, tigers, elephants, coconut and minerals – including gemstones like carnelian. While some goods would have been for internal consumption in Baghdad, a large proportion would have been exported.

For much of the Viking story, this is where it ends. Baghdad is the furthest south-east we have any evidence that anyone travelled, and it is most likely that this was the case. A few years ago there was a flurry of excitement when a researcher claimed that he had found evidence of Viking settlement on the Arabian Peninsula: rock art found in Qatar, he argued, that could only be depicting aerial views of Viking ships.[5] The shapes, he wrote, resembled the Skuldelev ships from Denmark with outstretched oars and were nothing like dhows, the ships you would find locally. However, the theory has since been disproven.[6]

Routes further east are described in Arabic records, like the adventures of Sallām, an interpreter who was sent by a caliph in Baghdad to inspect the so-called 'Alexander's wall', and whose accounts were later incorporated into Ibn Khurradadhbih's ninth-century *Book of Roads and Kingdoms*. It is clear that this wall was, in fact, the Great Wall of China, which demonstrates that overland routes to the far east were open and usable, something the trade in goods has also shown. These routes may have been used by intrepid travellers from the north, but such journeys would have been rare – it was the trade connections that were important. In the words of Danish archaeologist Søren Sindbæk: 'What caused the Viking Age in the North Atlantic and Baltic seas was, literally, global economic incentives.'[7]

THE UNEXPECTED EFFECTS
OF GLOBALISATION

Globalisation really is an appropriate term for what happened in this period, with spidery veins stretching out across the world, further than they had before. The increasing adoption of advanced maritime technologies in the north was coupled with a renewed hunger for prestigious and exotic commodities and a steady flow of silver from the Islamic caliphate. Tracing the objects and materials that went back and forth, the routes they travelled on, and the people who took part in the transactions, is a bit like watching a drop of water running down an uneven windowpane: flowing downwards with gravity, changing path and direction if it encounters a flaw in the glass, stopping when it reaches an insurmountable obstacle until its path is taken up again when joined by further drops that add the necessary momentum.

There is, however, one less desirable effect of this globalisation that we are only now beginning to shed light on. In the spring of 2020, when the world was in the midst of a global pandemic, a group of scientists published a research paper on the origins of the variola virus, better known as smallpox. The team had managed to extract the virus's DNA from ancient skeletons. This, they claimed, demonstrated that it was around possibly as early as AD 600. In a sample of 525 individuals from Eurasia and the Americas, they identified thirteen who had likely died with a smallpox infection. And it just so happens that this had everything to do with the Vikings and – I strongly believe – their connections to the Silk Roads.

The smallpox study showed that of the individuals identified with the virus, eleven dated to the Viking Age or up to two hundred years before, while the last two were modern. The samples came from Scandinavia, England and Russia. Radiocarbon dates from three of the samples suggested the virus had been prevalent *before* the Viking Age by almost two hundred years. But just as at Repton, the scientists had failed to take into account marine reservoir effects, despite at least two of the individuals sampled showing evidence of high marine diets. If you make the appropriate corrections, this pushes the dates forward, meaning that the virus was identified *only* in samples from the Viking Age, even though the researchers examined DNA spanning almost thirty-two thousand years of history. This is remarkable in itself, but digging deeper into the material reveals even more about the possible mechanisms. To understand what, we must look at a grave from Oxford.

In 2008, archaeologists were called in to excavate before the building of an extension to St John's College. They found something entirely unexpected: a mass grave containing thirty-five male skeletons, all seemingly having been thrown in a pit, with multiple injuries including blade wounds. The men had been robust and tall, most of them aged between sixteen and thirty-five. Some of the bodies showed evidence of charring, suggesting that they had been exposed to burning before they were buried. There were no grave goods. This, clearly, was the result of a massacre.

Radiocarbon dates placed the grave around AD 900–1000 and it was suggested that it could belong to victims of the so-called St Brice's Day massacre that took place in Oxford on 13 November 1002. On that day the English king Aethelred the Unready had ordered the killing of 'all the Danes who had sprung up in this island, sprouting like cockle amongst the wheat'. One of the eleven samples with the smallpox virus was from a man who was found in the middle of this mass grave. The man had several blade wounds to his upper body, including one to the back of his head and several to his ribs and shoulder blade. This was most likely what killed him, not the smallpox infection.

Prior to the discovery, there had been no evidence that smallpox was present in England at the time. So where had this man picked up the virus? It's unclear if the men in the grave were recent arrivals or residents, but their diets suggested the former. By comparing isotopes in their ribs and femurs, the team that analysed them could show that they had recently adopted more marine diets. This is because ribs 'turn over', forming new bone more quickly, so any change in diet shows up in the bone within two to five years. Femurs, on the other hand, are large and thick and reflect an individual's average diet over up to fifteen years. For this reason, the researchers concluded that the group as a whole had likely changed their eating patterns in very recent times. This could be consistent with having travelled, and that is exactly where we may, rather unexpectedly, find a clue to the source of the virus.

The geneticists who studied the Oxford grave were initially looking at ancestry across the entire Viking world, working on samples from across Europe. Surprisingly, they found a match between another man buried in the mass grave and someone much further afield. This second man's half-brother (or other second-degree relative like an uncle and nephew or grandfather and grandson) was discovered in a cemetery in Denmark at a site called Galgedil. And it just so happens that this half-brother in Denmark also carried the smallpox virus. What this could indicate is that the men in Oxford – likely part of a raiding party or military group – had lived in close proximity to each other and may recently have come over from somewhere like Galgedil. Just as with a modern pandemic that we are now all so familiar with, widespread travel and a high level of mobility – comparatively speaking – was likely a crucial factor explaining why smallpox seems to have appeared in north-western Europe during the Viking Age.

While there is no definite evidence of where this virus was picked up from in the first place, when we look at the samples of those who had it something is very clear. Many of the individuals came from locations that displayed a very high level of mobility and an influx of international traders; several were from the island of Öland near Gotland. One Swedish sample had strong connections with the Baltic, as strontium isotope data suggested that she had grown up on Gotland. Another individual buried in Sweden was a man who, the excavators stated, had been buried in Slavic fashion, suggesting he too was a migrant. The final two came from Gnezdovo, the Rus' site in the upper Dnieper region.

But that is not all. Digging through the archaeological reports of these eleven skeletons reveals that in the past, two of those with the virus were interpreted to have been slaves because of the way they were buried. While we should be careful about interpreting unusual burial rites as indicative of enslavement, if this really was the case, the two could plausibly have travelled from far further afield. They may also have been exposed to conditions that were very conducive to the spread of the disease. This isn't the first time a virus has been linked to Viking movements either. In 2017, the spread of a particular strain of leprosy was traced from Scandinavia to England through the discovery of *Mycobacterium leprae* in a female skeleton. The following year researchers discovered that leprosy in Ireland in the medieval period had also came from Scandinavia. Both these cases may have been linked to the trade in squirrel fur.

The links to the east or to Baltic trading posts are striking in the smallpox example. Perhaps that should not surprise us, because this is precisely where global connections to parts of the world that were previously inaccessible could now be found. Pathogens could, in particular, be transmitted through goods like furs, one of the key elements of the eastern trade. The riverine networks allowed for goods and people to flow from east to west, and from south to north, with unprecedented speed, meaning that stowaways like the variola virus could easily have moved along with them.

So much of the story appears to have been driven by a thirst for luxuries and for wealth: both the silver, silk, beads and jewellery that flowed north and the furs, amber and ivory that flowed south and east, not to mention those slaves that were so desperately needed to help the blossoming towns to maintain their high-status lifestyles. The Vikings blended in, and they became part of the fabric, part of a cultural mosaic in the west and in the east, as entrepreneurs and political players, or simply as ordinary settlers. Yet there was an enormous human cost: not just that of the oft-remembered, unsuspecting monks at Lindisfarne, but also those unknown slaves who left behind no trace but whose lives were traded for a shiny silver coin, or for a translucent orange bead.

The thirst for silver played a big part in this exchange, right to the end: by the beginning of the eleventh century, the supply of silver in the east had become so exhausted that Vikings had to look elsewhere. As a result, they started turning their backs on Islamic coins, now diluted by other metals, and looked instead to the west, where new silver resources were discovered in the Harz Mountains in Germany. This led to an increase in the minting of coins in Anglo-Saxon England and the kingdoms of continental Europe. It has even been suggested that the intensification of attacks on England in the 990s may have been a direct result.

Throughout the Viking Age and beyond, contact and movement continued north, south, west and east for hundreds of years, and over time cultural identities blended and evolved as migrants and locals interacted. But at the same time certain identities were maintained and perpetuated, such as that which we now call Viking, resulting in what's best described as a diaspora. We also need to remember how much events in one region would have affected those in another: ripples from the stone thrown into the water near Baghdad travelled all the way to Repton, albeit diffused, diminished and deconstructed. But they were still there. I believe that it is those earliest trade networks along the rivers, the vital arteries of Europe and central Asia, that are the evidence we need to investigate to truly understand Viking expansion in the west. But before the River Kings' journey can come to a close, there's one more destination to reach.

EPILOGUE

GUJARAT

I stand on a concrete rooftop in central Ahmedabad, India, on a sunny morning in January, eight years almost to the day since I first travelled to Oxford and started my Repton research. Up here, I get momentary relief from the madness that is the bustling twenty-first-century Indian city with its incessantly honking horns from cars, motorbikes and Uber-powered auto-rickshaws; all rather a lot to take in. Birds of prey circle overhead, and below monkeys play in a lush garden as I look out over yet another river. I am struck by the fact that there is not a single boat in sight and today this waterway serves no purpose in trade, commerce or the movement of people. I have come here because this is where my River Kings story ends, but also where it began.

I am a long way from home and this history is a long way from that of my Vikings. Yet to understand that carnelian bead's presence in England and what made it possible for this extensive trade in the exotic to flourish more than a millennium ago, I want to understand this part of it too. For the trade in these minerals represents a system of supply and demand that was so well established that it continued for almost five thousand years and is still alive today. The Vikings merely tapped into something that had been taking place for millennia on the routes along the Silk Roads, and it makes no sense to consider them in isolation; it's necessary also to reflect on the other end of the network.

It's unlikely that Vikings came this far, but many went from Sweden with Ingvar to the Caspian Sea; many thousands travelled to Miklagard and, probably, many too to Baghdad. Perhaps some did travel further east. Runestones tell of some who went both west *and* east, so it's not impossible that someone may have gone to Repton as well as to the Black Sea and beyond.

Clearly, in some spheres of the early medieval west there was a knowledge of these regions in the east – and of India, to be precise. In the year 965, while the Khazarian empire was being brought to its knees by the Kyivan Rus', the Jewish-Arab merchant Ibrahim al-Tartushi travelled to Magdeburg in Germany. There he was received at the court of Otto the Great, the Holy Roman Emperor. While on his travels, al-Tartushi also visited Mainz and made observations on what he saw in this very large city situated on the Rhine, in the land of the Franks. He noted with surprise that he could see dirhams in circulation that had been struck in Samarkand fifty years before, but there was something even more remarkable to him: 'It is extraordinary that one should be able to find, in such far western regions, aromatics and spices that only grow in the far east, like pepper, ginger, cloves, nard, costus and galingale. These plants are all imported from India, where they grow in abundance.'

Evidently, there were more things than carnelian that made it this far west, and the Vikings weren't the only ones to covet exotic objects and flavours. Other Arab travellers made journeys to the far east too: Al-Masudi – who wrote in the tenth century and who also described the Rus' attacking the Caspian Sea – travelled from India to Ceylon and then on to China, describing India in quite some detail based on both his own information and other compiled sources. If you reached Baghdad, there was a fair chance you could also find out about India.

But there is also evidence that India was well known in ninth-century England: a reference in the *Anglo-Saxon Chronicle* for the year 883 – ten years after the Repton winter camp – mentions an embassy sent to the shrine of St Thomas in 'India/Indea' by none other than Alfred the Great.[1] Having successfully fought off a Viking raid in London, Alfred vowed to send alms to both Rome and India, although many have argued that the latter was merely a mistranscription of Judea.

However, both St Thomas and St Bartholomew, who is also mentioned in the entry, appear to have been martyred in India according to other ninth-century sources. There are documented Christian communities in southern India from the fifth century onwards, so it certainly is not impossible. Spices like those described by al-Turtushi had been imported from both India and Sri Lanka since as early as the seventh century, according to charters and documentary evidence, which could well suggest that people travelled the whole way too. At the very least, India may have been on some people's radar – in the higher echelons of society.

The most exciting information about this possible journey for our purposes, though, comes from a later source. A twelfth-century document written by the chronicler William of Malmesbury claims to have identified the bishop who travelled on the mission to India ordered by Alfred, stating that he returned safely and brought with him 'exotic, precious stones'. These may well have been carnelian.

Trade across the Indian Ocean was nothing new. Transport and exchange from the Red Sea to India exploded in the decades that followed the Roman occupation of Egypt in 30 BC, with the Roman historian Strabo reporting that as many as 120 Roman boats made the journey each year. Gemstones and spices were just two of the commodities the Romans were looking for alongside other goods that could be found in the region. This trade evidently took place throughout the first millennium, but it is notable that during the eighth century the fringes of the Indian Ocean – specifically, East Africa – saw a spread and development of emporia, much like those found in the Baltic and North Sea region.

At the same time there is evidence of direct sea voyages between the Persian Gulf and China. Ibn Khurradadhbih described ninth-century trade routes from the Mediterranean to Egypt and the Red Sea. From there, you could travel to Medina and Mecca and eventually to India and China. During the Viking Age, the Golden Age of Islam expanded and extended the influence of the Middle Eastern regions and along with it strengthened the paths of the Silk Roads, paths that had been created millennia before. And the carnelian trade from India is a perfect example of this.

To the south-west of Ahmedabad is the archaeological site of Lothal. It is one of the most significant ancient cities of the Harappan or Indus Valley civilisation, and here archaeologists have found the earliest evidence for beautifully crafted carnelian beads dating back as far as 2700 BC. This, then, is the starting point for the trade that continued into the Viking Age and beyond: there's evidence that goods from here were traded across the Indian Ocean and to Mesopotamia, with artefacts having been discovered in ancient cities not far from what would later become Baghdad. The first step, of course, was by river from Lothal to the Gulf of Khambat.

In Lothal, I meet Anwar Husain Shaikh from Khambhat. He is an award-winning, fifth-generation bead-maker, and the only person in the world who makes carnelian beads in the Harappan style using traditional methods. The craft has been passed down in his family for well over a century. Anwar takes me to one of his workshops, a small house on a plot off the main road leading south to the coast. There's a clearing outside a brick-built, one-roomed house with a corrugated metal roof, and trees providing shade from the sun that will no doubt be scorching the sandy ground come summertime. He has brought the raw material he needs, several large lumps of carnelian and agate, which he expertly knaps into a rough shape by placing the stone against an iron rod pushed at an angle into the ground, hitting it with a soft wooden hammer. Chipping off pieces around the edges, he transforms the raw material into a shape that he will gradually manipulate into a long bead. Afterwards, when the bead has been polished smooth, the hole is drilled.

I get to try, my legs carefully positioned around a simple wooden prop, with water fed from a clay pot to keep the bead from over-heating. The drill is tipped with tiny diamonds from nearby Surat and moved by a bow pushed backwards and forwards. Holes are bored from each end until they meet in the middle. I have spent so long studying the Repton bead that I know this is exactly the way that was made too.

The next day Anwar takes me to the source of the minerals and on the way I wonder if I am the only Scandinavian to have made the full journey from Repton to Ratanpur, where the carnelian mines are to be found. But I am certainly not the first European to have gone hunting for these mines. In 1814, a certain John Copeland, Esq. described his trip there: 'We passed in our left the little village of Rutunpoor [...] And proceeded onward by a narrow footpath through a jungle, having rising ground almost the whole way to the mines. The diversity of scenery – hills and valleys, pebbly beds of rivers, precipitous rocks, and extensive plains covered with jungle – was sufficiently romantic. On account of the Tigers with which the country abounds, no human habitations were found nearer the mines than Rutunpoor, which is seven miles off.'

There are no tigers left by the time I get here, but I share Copeland's view of the scenery as romantic, although the jungle has largely gone too. Driving through the parched Gujarati land-scape, Anwar jumps out of the car at regular intervals, having spotted outcrops by the roadside: carnelian, jasper, bloodstone. When I see the rocks, the light, matte-surfaced pebbles seem unremarkable: light years away from the translucent reds and oranges that are in museum displays across the Viking world. But when Anwar starts picking them up and striking them, he shows me how the unremarkable turns remarkable – the variation in colour comes to light in the scar of their split and I begin to see what he sees.

While pebbles in many places abound on the surface, to get the quantities needed to fill today's ongoing thirst for the stones (a truck is filled every fifteen days) a more extensive approach is needed: deep pits are dug up to ten metres below ground, mirroring the account of Copeland: 'The mines are in the wildest part of the jungle, and are very numerous; they are shafts working perpendicularly downward about four feet wide; the deepest we saw was fifty feet: some, extend in an horizontal direction at the bottom.'

The earliest reference to these mines is in the sixteenth-century account of Ludovico de Varthema, an Italian traveller who visited Khambhat in 1504. This is thought to be around the same time that four Muslim brothers came from Africa and set up a new carnelian industry in the hills of Ratanpur: these hills are the final place that Anwar takes me and where he goes to pray. The mosque at the top of the hill is dedicated to Baba Ghor, the patron saint of bead-makers. While I wait for him, I climb the hill and the view is breathtaking. It is impossible not to feel moved by the thousands of years of history in these hills and plains; to consider the remarkable distances that those minerals have travelled. While there is no archaeological evidence here dating to the ninth century, to prove that the Repton bead travelled this way, we know Arab traders were settling around the Gulf of Khambat possibly as early as the seventh century. This means that trade with Baghdad would likely have flourished, including, I imagine, the trade in Ratanpur carnelian.

Al-Masudi travelled to Gujarat in 918 and stated that in Bharuch, on the Narmada river, there was a community of ten thousand Muslims: this is around thirty kilometres from Ratanpur. Yet after my visit to the mining areas, the lack of physical evidence doesn't surprise me. These were cottage industries that would have left behind little archaeological trace. There is, however, some hope in the future that we might get answers from the beads themselves: work is progressing on analysing the mineral directly, using both isotope analysis and trace element analysis. In principle, both can be applied to match chemical signatures in specific beads to possible sources from a geographic region. There are not yet enough reference materials available, but I am confident that it will happen soon.

Before I leave India, I travel to a beach on the Gulf of Khambat outside Surat (in Khambat, the original port, the harbour has silted up entirely and can no longer be used by boats). I want to see the sea, and looking out towards the west, I think of all the people whose lives have been affected by the global trade in precious stones. In the seventeenth and eighteenth centuries, carnelian beads were used to buy slaves in central Africa: a *girdle* of beads would have bought you one slave. On the coast of Africa, cargoes from past shipwrecks are often washed ashore, tiny beads found on the beach to remind us of this chilling trade; all part of the 'Sea Silk Route' as some have called it.

Going back to the Viking Age, the trade in beads like this died down too when the flow of eastern silver began to cease. The flood became a trickle until eventually it was barely present at all. Yet the changes it had brought with it over the years were immense. Whole new states had formed either directly or indirectly in response to the allure of the metal and to the adventure and entrepreneurship of those who had travelled vast distances on those eastern rivers.

Hundreds of years of goods, people and ideas travelled too, joining the camel caravans that moved to and from the inland deserts of the Middle East. Somewhere there, the River Kings were absorbed into the highways of the Silk Roads, as objects – including beads – moved along ancient routes to supply a newly created demand in the west, their stories interweaving into a ribbon stretching far beyond anyone's imagination.

KHAMBAT, GUJARAT, *C.*825

*I*n the stifling heat, a woman sits inside a hut on the outskirts of the bustling port of Khambat. The street outside is full of noise, animals and people vying for space. On the floor next to her stands a small basket of neatly cut stones; in front of her, the tools are lined up carefully. There is a small lathe beside her, and she gingerly removes the bead she has been working on, the final one left to cut, and holds it up to the light. There are some flaws in it, and the diamond shapes on either side are a little uneven, but it can't be helped. Nobody pays much attention to that level of detail. And the flaws prove it's genuine, that's what her father told her, the first time he let her come with him to collect the precious cargo up in the hills when she was a little girl. She likes to make up stories, in her mind, of who might end up wearing them, who might pick them up just like her and study the way the sun shines through the mineral's hazy surface. She has been told that some of them travel far across the sea, to lands where the sun stops shining at will and the rivers turn solid and cold in the winter. That these beads are prized and treasured; the best that can be found anywhere. She tries to imagine the bead strung in a chain around someone's neck, a beautiful woman with flowing long hair, just like her mother. But she will never know whose hands and lives this bead will touch.

ACKNOWLEDGEMENTS

River Kings is the culmination of almost a decade of research, and I feel immensely grateful to everyone who supported me along the way. I have my lovely agent Tessa David to thank for turning this from a list of vague ideas into a real book (and Laurie Robertson for picking up in her absence), along with the rest of the brilliant team at Peters, Fraser and Dunlop who look after me so well. I'm very grateful to my editor Arabella Pike for taking a chance on me in the first place and for all her insightful help, as well as everyone else at HarperCollins, especially Iain Hunt and Jo Thompson, for everything they've done to turn this into something far better than my initial drafts. A big thank you to Richard Osgood, who drew the gorgeous illustrations for each chapter!

For the research that led to this book, I have a huge number of people to thank for their help and support (with apologies to anyone inadvertently left out!):

Martin Biddle for giving me access to continue the work on the Repton material and for so generously sharing his research, time and knowledge. Sadly, I never got to meet Birthe Kjølbye-Biddle, but I have benefited enormously from all her hard work. My PhD supervisor and collaborator Mark Horton, for all his help, encouragement and brilliant discussions, as well as to Henry

Webber for all his work with us at Repton and Foremark. Martin Flowerdew, the vicar of Repton, for his help and friendship and for allowing us to repeatedly dig large holes in his lawn! All the local volunteers, especially Margaret and Andy Austen, and not least the several years' worth of volunteer diggers giving up their time so generously – too many to list – but you are all amazing! Rob Davis for sharing his finds at Foremark with us.

Tom Horne, for reading through drafts, sharing research and answering all sorts of questions, Marianne Moen for brilliant discussions on Viking women and for reading drafts, Jane Kershaw for advice and sharing her excellent research, Jess Treacher for comments on an early chapter draft. Numerous other colleagues have helped either directly or indirectly by answering questions, letting me pick their brains, or supporting my work over the years; especially Judith Jesch, Howard Williams, Neil Price, Lesley Abrams, Tamar Hodos, Clare Downham and Lars Fehren-Schmitz.

William Pidzamecky for inviting me to collaborate on the Vypovzyv excavations and for answering all manner of questions, and to our excellent teams of diggers in 2018 and 2019. A huge thank you also to a long list of new colleagues in Ukraine, who have been so incredibly welcoming in sharing their sites, research and friendship.

I am very grateful to Bernard Cornwell for his encouragement and advice, and for so generously helping me fulfil my dream of following the carnelian bead to its origin. In Istanbul, Safyie for expertly guiding me around the city walls. In India, Anwar Sheikh Hussain for all his time and hospitality and for sharing knowledge of his unparalleled skills with carnelian, alongside his lovely family, as well as Pratap Bahi and our fearless driver Raju, and to Professor Kuldeep Bhan for connecting me with Anwar at short notice.

Finally, the biggest thank you to my wonderful family for their constant support and endless patience.

NOTES

1 HAMMER OF THOR: BONES

1. A number of works have discussed the origins of the Viking Age in recent years; see for example J.H. Barrett (2008), 'What Caused the Viking Age?', *Antiquity*, 82 (317): 671–86, and D. Griffiths (2019), 'Rethinking the Early Viking Age in the West', *Antiquity*, 93 (368): 468–77.

2. For details of these excavations, see M. Biddle and B. Kjølbye-Biddle (1992), 'Repton and the Vikings', *Antiquity*, 66: 36–51. and M. Biddle and B. Kjølbye-Biddle (2001), 'Repton and the "Great Heathen Army", 873–4', in J. Graham-Campbell (ed.), *Vikings and the Danelaw: Select Papers from the Proceedings of the Thirteenth Viking Congress*, Nottingham and York, 21–30 August 1997. Oxford: Oxbow Books.

3. Whether such graves with weapons should be considered those of 'warriors' is widely debated in archaeology in general. See e.g. N. Price, C. Hedenstierna-Jonson, T. Zachrisson, A. Kjellström, J. Storå, M. Krzewińska, T. Günther, V. Sobrado, M. Jakobsson and A. Götherström (2019), 'Viking Warrior Women? Reassessing Birka Chamber Grave Bj.581', *Antiquity*, 93 (367): 181–98. doi:10.15184/aqy.2018.258 with sources cited.

4. For a thorough overview of the Ragnar Lothbrok legend, see Chapter 2 of Eleanor Parker (2018), *Dragon Lords: The History and Legends of Viking England*. London: Bloomsbury Publishing.

5. J. Kershaw and E.C. Røyrvik (2016), 'The "People of the British Isles" Project and Viking Settlement in England', *Antiquity*, 90 (354): 1670–80.

6. Anyone alive in the tenth century who passed on their genes has so many descendants today that this information is academically meaningless. For a thorough explanation, see Adam Rutherford (2016), *A Brief History of Everyone Who Ever Lived: The Stories in Our Genes*. London: Weidenfeld & Nicolson.

7. Catrine L. Jarman, Martin Biddle, Tom F.G. Higham and Christopher Bronk Ramsey (2018), 'The Viking Great Army in England: New Dates from the Repton Charnel', *Antiquity*, 92 (361): 183–99.

8. These may have been organised under the concept of the *lið*, warrior bands or retinues under a joint leader. See B. Raffield, C. Greenlow, N. Price and M. Collard (2016), 'Ingroup Identification, Identity Fusion and the Formation of Viking War Bands', *World Archaeology*, 48: 35–50.

9. T.D. Price, K.M. Frei, A. Siegried Dobat, N. Lynnerup and P. Bennike (2011), 'Who Was in Harold Bluetooth's Army? Strontium Isotope Investigation of the Cemetery at the Viking Age Fortress at Trelleborg, Denmark', *Antiquity*, 85: 476–89.

10. Viking raids certainly took place in both places, with new research suggesting Viking camps might also have been found on the Iberian Peninsula. See Irene García Losquiño (2019), 'Camps and Early Settlement in the Viking Diaspora: England, Ireland and the Case of Galicia', *Summa*, 13: 37–55. It is also possible for certain physiological reasons to cause elevated oxygen ratios.

11. A.B. Gotfredsen, C. Primeau, K.M. Frei and L. Jørgensen (2014), 'A Ritual Site with Sacrificial Wells from the Viking Age at Trelleborg, Denmark', *Danish Journal of Archaeology*, 3: 145–63.

2 DIRHAM: SILVER FOR A SLAVE

1. S. Goodacre, A. Helgason, J. Nicholson, L. Southam, L. Ferguson, E. Hickey, E. Vega, K. Stefansson, R. Ward and B. Sykes (2005), 'Genetic Evidence for a Family-based Scandinavian Settlement of Shetland and Orkney during the Viking Periods', *Heredity*, 95 (2): 129–35.

2. See http://vikingmetalwork.blogspot.com/

3. I am grateful to Jane Kershaw for facilitating this preliminary identification by Jani Oravisjärvi.

3 SHIP NAIL: RIVER KINGS

1. K. Hjardar and V. Vike (2016), *Vikings at War*. Oxford: Casemate Publishers, p. 139.
2. E. Andersson Strand (2016), 'Segel ock segelduksproduktion i arkeologisk kotext', in M. Ravn, L. Gebauer Thomsen, E. Andersson Strand and H. Lyngstrøm (eds.) *Vikingetidens sejl*. København: Saxo-Instituttet, Københavns Universitet, p. 22.
3. *The Younger Edda*. Chicago: Scott, Foresman and Company 1901), Kindle edition.
4. D.M. Hadley, J.D. Richards, H. Brown, E. Craig-Atkins, D. Mahoney Swales, G. Perry, S. Stein and A. Woods (2016), 'The Winter Camp of the Viking Great Army, AD 872–3, Torksey, Lincolnshire', *Antiquaries Journal*, 96: 23–67.
5. G. Williams (2013), 'Towns and Identities in Viking England', in L. Ten Harkel and D.M. Hadley (eds.), *Everyday Life in Viking-age Towns: Social Approaches to Towns in England and Ireland, c.800–1100*. Oxford: Oxbow Books, p. 13.
6. Cited in P. Holm (1986), 'The Slave Trade of Dublin, Ninth to Twelfth Centuries', *Peritia*, 5: 317–45, p. 325.
7. S. Mcleod (2006), 'Feeding the Micel Here in England c.865–878', *Journal of the Australian Early Medieval Association*, 2: 144.
8. A.M. Heen-Pettersen (2014), 'Insular Artefacts from Viking-Age Burials from Mid-Norway. A Review of Contact between Trøndelag and Britain and Ireland', *Internet Archaeology*, 38.
9. C. Downham (2017), 'The Earliest Viking Activity in England?' *English Historical Review*, 132: 1–12.
10. Cited in K. Wolf (2013), *Viking Age: Everyday Life During the Extraordinary Era of the Norsemen*. New York: Sterling, p. 119.
11. D. Száz, A. Farkas, A. Barta, B. Kretzer, M. Blahó, A. Egri, G. Szabó and G. Horváth (2017), 'Accuracy of the Hypothetical Sky-polarimetric Viking Navigation Versus Sky Conditions: Revealing Solar Elevations and Cloudinesses Favourable for this Navigation Method', *Proceedings of the Royal Society A: Mathematical, Physical and Engineering Sciences*, 473 (2205), 20170358.
12. Konungs-Skuggsja, from Angus Somerville and R. Andrew McDonald (eds.) (2019), *The Viking Age: A Reader*. Toronto: University of Toronto Press, p. 333.

4 BUDDHA: THE ALLURE OF THE EXOTIC

1. H. Haugen (2009), *Menn og deres perler: En studie av menns bruk av perler med hovedvekt på Midt-Norge i yngre jernalder*. Master's thesis, Norges teknisk-naturvitenskapelige universitet, Det humanistiske fakultet, Institutt for arkeologi og religionsvitenskap.

2. J. Bill and C.L. Rødsrud (2017), 'Heimdalsjordet: Trade, Production and Communication', in Z.T. Glørstad and K. Loftsgarden (eds.), *Viking-Age Transformations*. Oxon: Routledge, pp. 212–31.

3. C. Kilger (2008), 'Kaupang from Afar: Aspects of the Interpretation of Dirham Finds in Northern and Eastern Europe between the Late 8th and Early 10th Centuries', in D. Skre (ed.), *Means of Exchange: Dealing with Silver in the Viking Age*. Århus: Aarhus University Press Kaupang Excavation Project, pp. 199–252.

4. S. Stos-Gale (2004), 'Lead Isotope Analyses of the Lead Weights from Birka, Sweden', in I. Gustin, *Mellan gåva och marknad: handel, tillit och materiell kultur under vikingatid*. Lund: Lund Studies in Medieval Archaeology.

5. U. Pedersen, T. Andersen, S. Simonsen and M. Erambert (2016), 'Lead Isotope Analysis of Pewter Mounts from the Viking Ship Burial at Gokstad: On the Origin and Use of Raw Materials', *Archaeometry*, 58: 148–63.

6. S.K. Wärmländer, L. Wåhlander, R. Saage, K. Rezakhani, S.A. Hamid Hassan and M. Neiß (2015), 'Analysis and Interpretation of a Unique Arabic Finger Ring from the Viking Age Town of Birka, Sweden', *Scanning*, 37(2): 131–7.

7. This was proposed in 2017 by a Dutch linguist, Marijn van Putten. https://twitter.com/PhDniX/status/920584737168723968

8. T. Hodos (2018), 'Luxuries during the Mediterranean's Iron Age Period', in A. Fletcher (ed.), *An Age of Luxury: The Assyrians to Alexander*. Hong Kong: Hong Kong Museum of History, pp. 10–23.

9. http://vikingmetalwork.blogspot.com/2017/11/islamic-coins-as-jewellery-finds-from.html

10. E. Mikkelsen (1998), 'Islam and Scandinavia during the Viking Age', in E. Piltz (ed.), *Byzantium and Islam in Scandinavia. Acts of a Symposium at Uppsala University June 15–16 1996*. Åström, Gothenburg, pp. 39–51.

11. S. Oosthuizen (2019), *The Emergence of the English*. York: Arc Humanities Press.

12. A. Margaryan, D.J. Lawson, M. Sikora, F. Racimo, S. Rasmussen, I. Moltke, L.M. Cassidy, E. Jørsboe, A. Ingason, M.W. Pedersen, T. Korneliussen, H. Wilhelmson, M.M. Buś, P. de Barros Damgaard, R. Martiniano, G. Renaud, C. Bhérer, J.V. Moreno-Mayar, A.K. Fotakis, M. Allen, R. Allmäe, M. Molak, E. Cappellini, G. Scorrano, H. McColl, A. Buzhilova, A. Fox, A. Albrechtsen, B. Schütz, B. Skar, C. Arcini, C. Falys, C.H. Jonson, D. Błaszczyk, D. Pezhemsky, G. Turner-Walker, H. Gestsdóttir, I. Lundstrøm, I. Gustin, I. Mainland, I. Potekhina, I.M. Muntoni, J. Cheng, J. Stenderup, J. Ma, J. Gibson, J. Peets, J. Gustafsson, K.H. Iversen, L. Simpson, L. Strand, L. Loe, M. Sikora, M. Florek, M. Vretemark, M. Redknap, M. Bajka, T. Pushkina, M. Søvsø, N. Grigoreva, T. Christensen, O. Kastholm, O. Uldum, P. Favia, P. Holck, S. Sten, S.V. Arge, S. Ellingvåg, V. Moiseyev, W. Bogdanowicz, Y. Magnusson, L. Orlando, P. Pentz, M.D. Jessen, A. Pedersen, M. Collard, D.G. Bradley, M.L. Jørkov, J. Arneborg, N. Lynnerup, N. Price, M.T.P. Gilbert, M.E. Allentoft, J. Bill, S.M. Sindbæk, L. Hedeager, K. Kristiansen, R. Nielsen, T. Werge, E. Willerslev (2020), 'Population Genomics of the Viking World', *Nature*, 585, 390–6.
13. M. Krzewińska, A. Kjellström, T. Günther, C. Hedenstierna-Jonson, T. Zachrisson, A. Omrak, R. Yaka, G.M. Kılınç, M. Somel and V. Sobrado (2018), 'Genomic and Strontium Isotope Variation Reveal Immigration Patterns in a Viking Age Town', *Current Biology*, 28: 2730–8.
14. T.D. Price, C. Arcini, I. Gustin, L. Drenzel and S. Kalmring (2018), 'Isotopes and Human Burials at Viking Age Birka and the Mälaren Region, East Central Sweden', *Journal of Anthropological Archaeology*, 49: 19–38.
15. M. Krzewińska, G. Bjørnstad, P. Skoglund, P.I. Olason, J. Bill, A. Götherström and E. Hagelberg (2015), 'Mitochondrial DNA Variation in the Viking Age Population of Norway', *Philosophical Transactions of the Royal Society B: Biological Sciences*, 370: 20130384.
16. The results of this analysis were published in Per Holck (2006), 'The Oseberg Ship Burial, Norway: New Thoughts On the Skeletons From the Grave Mound', *European Journal of Archaeology*, 9 (2–3): 185–210. However, there has been uncertainty among researchers as to whether the results could have been contaminated and new analyses are planned for the future.

5 VALKYRIE: RIVER QUEENS

1. M. Krzewińska, G. Bjørnstad, P. Skoglund, P.L. Olason, J. Bill, A. Götherström and E. Hagelberg (2015), 'Mitochondrial DNA Variation in the Viking Age Population of Norway', *Philosophical Transactions of the Royal Society B: Biological Sciences*, 370: 20130384.

2. D.M. Hadley, J.D. Richards, H. Brown, E. Craig-Atkins, D. Mahoney Swales, G. Perry, S. Stein and A. Woods (2016), 'The Winter Camp of the Viking Great Army, AD 872–3, Torksey, Lincolnshire', *Antiquaries Journal*, 96: 23–67.

3. C. Hedenstierna-Jonson, A. Kjellström, T. Zachrisson, M. Krzewińska, V. Sobrado, N. Price, T. Günther, M. Jakobsson, A. Götherström and J. Storå (2017), 'A Female Viking Warrior Confirmed by Genomics', *American Journal of Physical Anthropology*, 164.4: 853–60.

4. An additional discussion has been focused around the possibility of non-binary gender roles for Bj.581, and the possibility that this was an individual whose gender identification in society was not what the genetics would suggest.

5. B. Tihanyi, Z. Bereczki, E. Molnár, W. Berthon, L. Révész, O. Dutour and G. Pálfi (2015), 'Investigation of Hungarian Conquest Period (10th c. AD) Archery on the Basis of Activity-induced Stress Markers on the Skeleton – Preliminary Results', *Acta Biologica Szegediensis*, 59: 65–77.

6. J. Olrik and H. Raeder (eds.), (1931), *Saxo Grammaticus: Gesta Danorum*. Copenhagen: Gutenberg online archive (https://www.gutenberg.org/files/1150/1150-h/1150-h.htm).

7. N. Price (2019), *The Viking Way: Magic and Mind in Late Iron Age Scandinavia*. Oxford: Oxbow Books, p. 274.

8. A.M. Heen-Pettersen (2014), 'Insular Artefacts from Viking-Age Burials from Mid-Norway. A Review of Contact between Trøndelag and Britain and Ireland', *Internet Archaeology*, 38.

9. J. Kershaw (2013), *Viking Identities: Scandinavian Jewellery in England*, Oxford: OUP.

10. L.H. Dommasnes (1987), 'Male/Female Roles and Ranks in Late Iron Age Norway', *AmS-Varia*, 17: 65–77.

11. J.H. Barrett (2008), 'What Caused the Viking Age?', *Antiquity*, 82: 671–86.

12. B. Raffield, N. Price and M. Collard (2017), 'Male-biased Operational Sex Ratios and the Viking Phenomenon: An Evolutionary Anthropological

Perspective on Late Iron Age Scandinavian Raiding', *Evolution and Human Behavior*, 38: 315–24.

13. M. Moen (2019), *Challenging Gender: A Reconsideration of Gender in the Viking Age Using the Mortuary Landscape*. Unpublished PhD thesis. Oslo: IAKH, University of Oslo.

14. A. Stalsberg (1991), 'Women as Actors in North European Viking Age Trade', in R. Samson (ed.), *Social Approaches to Viking Studies*. Glasgow: Cruithne.

15. Birka grave no. Bj.965.

6 KING PIECE: HEADING EAST

1. F. Androshchuk (2008), 'The Vikings in the East', in S. Brink and N.S. Price (eds.), *The Viking World*. London: Routledge.

2. E.M. Peschel, D. Carlsson, J. Bethard and M.C. Beaudry (2017), 'Who Resided in Ridanäs?: A Study of Mobility on a Viking Age Trading Port in Gotland, Sweden', *Journal of Archaeological Science: Reports*, 13: 175–84.

3. P. Frankopan (2015), *The Silk Roads: A New History of the World*. London: Bloomsbury Publishing.

4. P. Frankopan (2015), *The Silk Roads: A New History of the World*. London: Bloomsbury Publishing.

5. C. Kilger (2008), 'Kaupang from Afar: Aspects of the Interpretation of Dirham Finds in Northern and Eastern Europe between the Late 8th and Early 10th Centuries', in Dagfinn Skre (ed.), *Means of Exchange: Dealing with Silver in the Viking Age* Volume 2, Århus/Oslo: Aarhus University Press Kaupang Excavation Project, p. 211.

6. Maya Shatzmiller (2005), 'The Role of Money in the Economic Growth of the Early Islamic Period (650–1000)', *American Journal of Comparative Law*, 3 (4): 785–834.

7. Jüri Peets, Raili Allmäe, Liina Maldre, Ragnar Saage, Teresa Tomek and Lembi Lõugas (2012), *Research Results of the Salme Ship Burials in 2011–2012*. Archaeological fieldwork in Estonia.

8. T. Douglas Price, Jüri Peets, Raili Allmäe, Liina Maldre and Ester Oras (2016), 'Isotopic Provenancing of the Salme Ship Burials in Pre-Viking Age Estonia', *Antiquity*, 90 (352): 1022–37; and T. Douglas Price, Jüri Peets, Raili Allmäe, Liina Maldre and Neil Price (2020), 'Human

Remains, Context, and Place of Origin for the Salme, Estonia, Boat Burials', *Journal of Anthropological Archaeology*, 58: 101149.

9. Cited in Tatjana N. Jackson (2019), *Eastern Europe in Icelandic Sagas*. Leeds: Arc Humanities Press.

7 NECK RINGS: THE TALES OF THE RUS'

1. Cited in Wladyslaw Duczko (2004), *Viking Rus': Studies on the Presence of Scandinavians in Eastern Europe*. The Northern World Series. Leiden: Brill, p. 32.
2. Gy. Moravcsik and R.J.H. Jenkins (eds.) (1967), *Constantine Porphyrogenitus. De administrando imperio*. Washington: Center for Byzantine Studies.
3. Runestone G280, Scandinavian Runic-text Database, http://www.nordiska.uu.se/forskn/samnord.htm
4. Einar Østmo (2020), 'The History of the Norvegr 2000 BC–1000 AD', in Dagfinn Skre (ed.), *Rulership in 1st to 14th Century Scandinavia*. Berlin: De Gruyter, pp. 3–66.
5. See for example details in Anne Stalsberg (2001), 'Scandinavian Viking-Age Boat Graves in Old Rus'', *Russian History*, 28 (1/4): 359–401.
6. Søren M. Sindbæk (2003), 'Varægiske vinterruter: slædetransport i Rusland og spørgsmålet om den tidlige vikingetids orientalske import i Nordeuropa', *Fornvännen*, 98 (3): 179–93.
7. Judith Jesch (2001), *Ships and Men in the Late Viking Age: The Vocabulary of Runic Inscriptions and Skaldic Verse*. Woodbridge: Boydell & Brewer, p. 257.

8 BEAD: CROSSROADS

1. Nicholas J. Saunders, Jan Frolík and Volker Heyd (2019), 'Zeitgeist Archaeology: Conflict, Identity and Ideology at Prague Castle, 1918–2018', *Antiquity*, 93 (370): 1009–25.
2. For example graves Bj.1125b and Bj.996. Charlotte Hedenstierna-Jonson (2012), 'Traces of Contacts: Magyar Material Culture in the Swedish Viking Age Context of Birka', in Tobias Bendeguz (ed.), *Die Archäologie der Frühen Ungarn: Chronologie, Technologie und Methodik: internationaler*

Workshop des Archäologischen Instituts der Ungarischen Akademie der Wissenschaften und des Römisch-Germanischen Zentralmuseums Mainz in Budapest am 4. und 5. Dezember 2009. Mainz: Verlag des Römisch-Germanischen Zentralmuseums, pp. 29–46.

3. Warren Treadgold (1989), 'Three Byzantine Provinces and the First Byzantine Contacts with the Rus", Harvard Ukrainian Studies, 12–13: 132–44; Charlotte Hedenstierna-Jonson (2009),'Rus', Varangians and Birka Warriors', in Michael Olausson and Lena Holmquist (eds.), *The Martial Society: Aspects of Warriors, Fortifications and Social Change in Scandinavia.* Stockholm: Archaeological Research Laboratory, Stockholm University, pp. 159–78.

4. Wladyslaw Duczko (2004), *Viking Rus: Studies on the Presence of Scandinavians in Eastern Europe.* The Northern World Series. Leiden: Brill.

5. Petr S. Stefanovich (2016), 'The Political Organization of Rus' in the 10th Century', *Jahrbücher für Geschichte Osteuropas*, 64 (4): 529–44.

6. Charlotte Hedenstierna-Jonson (2012), 'Traces of Contacts: Magyar Material Culture in the Swedish Viking Age Context of Birka', in Tobias Bendeguz (ed.), *Die Archäologie der Frühen Ungarn: Chronologie, Technologie und Methodik: internationaler Workshop des Archäologischen Instituts der Ungarischen Akademie der Wissenschaften und des Römisch-Germanischen Zentralmuseums Mainz in Budapest am 4. Und 5. Dezember 2009.* Mainz: Verlag des Römisch-Germanischen Zentralmuseums, pp. 29–46.

7. Charlotte Hedenstierna-Jonson (2009), 'Rus', Varangians and Birka Warriors', in Michael Olausson and Lena Holmquist (eds.), *The Martial Society: Aspects of Warriors, Fortifications and Social Change in Scandinavia,* Stockholm: Archaeological Research Laboratory, Stockholm University, pp. 159–78.

9 DRAGON'S HEAD: TO MIKLAGARD AND BEYOND

1. Ture J. Arne and F. Braun (1914), 'Den svenska runstenen från ön Berezanj utanför Dnjeprmynningen: referat efter prof. F. Brauns redogörelse i Ryska arkeol. kommissionens meddelanden 1907', *Fornvännen*, 9: 44–8.

2. E.A. Melnikova (2017), 'A New Runic Inscription from Hagia Sophia Cathedral in Istanbul', *Futhark*: 101.

3. Thomas Thomov (2014), 'Four Scandinavian Ship Graffiti from Hagia Sophia', *Byzantine and Modern Greek Studies*, 38 (2): 168–84.

4. Judith Jesch (2001), *Ships and Men in the Late Viking Age: The Vocabulary of Runic Inscriptions and Skaldic Verse*. Woodbridge: Boydell & Brewer, p. 102. The meaning of giving food to the eagle is not entirely clear, but likely means they fought in battle. 'Drengr' here may mean warrior or someone who travelled in the service of a leader: see the text cited here for a discussion.

5. Guy F. Isitt (2007), 'Vikings in the Persian Gulf', *Journal of the Royal Asiatic Society*, 17 (4): 389–406.

6. James Edgar Taylor (2014), 'Vikings in the Gulf: Fact or Fancy?', *Proceedings of the Seminar for Arabian Studies*, 44: 325–36.

7. Søren Sindbæk (2017), 'Urbanism and Exchange in the North Atlantic/ Baltic, 600–1000CE', in Tamar Hodos (ed.), *The Routledge Handbook of Archaeology and Globalization*. New York: Routledge, pp. 553–65.

EPILOGUE: GUJARAT

1. https://www.caitlingreen.org/2019/04/king-alfred-and-india.html

INDEX